RALPH A. ROSSUM

The Supreme Court and Tribal Gaming

California v. Cabazon Band

of Mission Indians

UNIVERSITY PRESS OF KANSAS

Published by the University Press of Kansas (Lawrence, Kansas 66045), which was
organized by the Kansas Board of Regents and is operated and funded by Emporia
State University, Fort Hays State University, Kansas State University, Pittsburg State
University, the University of Kansas, and Wichita State University

Library of Congress Cataloging-in-Publication Data

Rossum, Ralph A., 1946–
The Supreme Court and tribal gaming : California v. Cabazon Band of
Mission Indians / Ralph A. Rossum.
p. cm.
Includes bibliographical references and index.
ISBN 978-0-7006-1777-7 (cloth : alk. paper)
ISBN 978-0-7006-1778-4 (pbk. : alk. paper)
1. Gambling on Indian reservations – Law and legislation – United States.
2. Indians of North America – Government relations. 3. United States.
Indian Gaming Regulatory Act. 4. California – Trials, litigation, etc.
5. Cabazon Band of Mission Indian – Trials, litigation, etc. I. Title.
KF8210.G35R67 2011
344.73'099--dc22
2011002772

British Library Cataloguing-in-Publication Data is available.

Printed in the United States of America

10 9 8 7 6 5 4 3 2 1

The paper used in this publication is recycled and contains 30 percent postconsumer
waste. It is acid free and meets the minimum requirements of the American National
Standard for Permanence of Paper for Printed Library Materials Z39.48-1992.

For G. David Huntoon,

my Rose Institute colleague at Claremont McKenna College,

who made this book possible

CONTENTS

EDITORS' PREFACE

One of the saddest and most ironic stories in American history is the near destruction of California's thriving and diverse native population by successive waves of European immigrants. The Spanish missionaries inadvertently brought diseases to which the Indians had no natural immunities. The Anglo settlers hunted the Indians the same way they hunted wolves and bears. But the Indians did not disappear and the legal triumph of the small Cabazon band of mission Indians chronicled in Ralph Rossum's superbly researched, deeply moving, and thoroughly persuasive account of the Cabazon band's fight to run their own casino is testimony to that fact.

American law and American politics were never kind to the first Americans. Rossum, an expert on Indian law, tracks the troubled course of this law through an almost impassable terrain of broken promises, abrogated treaties, unenforced Supreme Court decisions, confused congressional statutes, and harsh administrative rulings. Casino ownership came to be one way that Native peoples could reclaim their sovereignty and self-respect in the law, though the irony remained that the Casino was about as far from traditional Native ways as one could image. To achieve these victories, Native Americans had to overcome county and state opponents, gain the ear of the High Court, and in *California v. Cabazon Band of Mission Indians* (1987) regain "Indian country." The case would open the door to Indian casinos throughout the country and enable Indian bands to lift themselves from generations of impoverishment. But that was not the end of the story. Congress would once again intervene to broker state-Indian relations in the Indian Gaming Regulatory Act (IGRA) of 1988. Only this time, the result was not the forced migration of Indian peoples to lands far from their homes.

From the vantage point of *Cabazon*, Rossum surveys the entire landscape of Indian law. He takes us back to the first contact, carries the story through Chief Justice John Marshall's famous trilogy of Indian cases, and continues with the federal government's claim as trustee and administrator of Indian policy. Indians were to become assimilated, a stance that gave little credit to the diversity and richness of Indian belief systems and ways and would have crushed Indian identity. Rossum's is the first and will surely stand as the authoritative account of California's attempts to suppress Indian casinos, an attempt that began locally and ended in the Marble Palace. California's position was supported by twenty other states, the kind of odds that had throughout American history cost Indian lands and lives. But not this time. Even after the High Court, in *Seminole Tribe v. Florida* (1996) limited Indian rights to sue states, as permitted in the IGRA, tribes were able to use the revenue their casinos generated to gain concessions from otherwise recalcitrant state governments.

Rossum's account is detailed in the best way, explaining in terms we all can understand the intricacies of the law, the aims of the parties, the role of the various government agencies, and the path of the case through the courts. His closing comparison of the "straightforward and relatively uncomplicated" deployment of Foxwoods (Pequot) and Mohegan Sun in Connecticut with California's "protracted" struggle and the Seminole Tribe of Florida's caustic, politically-divisive twenty-five-year battle to fulfill the promise of the IGRA. The comparison is an apt and succinct lesson in how law can conciliate and facilitate win-win solutions or fall in the face of partisan and cultural animus. Such lessons go far beyond *Cabazon*, of course, making this story's moral one for every American to learn.

ACKNOWLEDGMENTS

This book had its origins with my appointment as director of the Rose Institute of State and Local Government at Claremont McKenna College in the summer of 2000. By the time of my appointment, the Rose Institute had already conducted several projects in Indian country, but over the course of the next decade under my direction, it has conducted forty more. These projects include over a dozen studies measuring the economic impact of tribal casinos on Southern California, a study of "best practices" for improving the relations between tribes and local governments, a history of the passage of the Indian Gaming Regulatory Act, a study of the financial supporters and opponents of ballot measures in California that gave the tribes a monopoly to engage in Las Vegas–style gaming in the state, and a series of Towns and Tribes conferences hosted by the Rose Institute that focused on public policy issues (e.g., education, economic development, and tourism) pertinent to both tribal and local governments.

These projects brought me into personal contact with tribal leaders across Southern California who introduced me to the fascinating issues of tribal sovereignty and federal Indian law. They stirred my curiosity and prompted me to explore a subject that few political scientists have researched. The result of that research is not only this book, but also a chapter in the first volume of *American Constitutional Law*, 8th Edition, entitled "The Constitution and Native American Tribes," that I coedited with G. Alan Tarr. It is the only casebook in the political science or law school market with such a chapter.

I wish to acknowledge my appreciation to Pamela Brooks Gann, president of Claremont McKenna College, for giving me the opportunity to serve as Rose Institute Director, and to Alan Heslop, founding director of the Rose Institute, who recommended me as the person to succeed him. Without their support, I would never have had the opportunity to gain the insights and make the connections necessary to write this book or to enhance so significantly the Rossum and Tarr casebook.

The sole reason that the Rose Institute has been able to do so many projects in Indian country is G. David Huntoon, a fellow at the Rose Institute. His personal connections with the tribal leaders of Southern California have been critical to what the Rose Institute has been able to accomplish and to the writing of this book. David introduced me to all the major players in the *Cabazon Band* case — the tribal leaders and their attorney, Glenn M. Feldman. The trust David had built up with tribal leaders over the years was indispensable in allowing me to obtain data and secure interviews. I am very much in his debt, and I have dedicated the book to him.

I also want to acknowledge my gratitude to Glenn M. Feldman, attorney to the Cabazon Band since 1979. He not only agreed to two interviews with me but also opened his extensive files on the *Cabazon Band* litigation to me — approximately 15,000 pages of court pleadings and motions. He was a joy to meet, and I very much appreciate his interest and assistance.

I wish to thank Ann Harvey, a Scripps College alumna, an undergraduate research assistant at the Rose Institute, current editor-in-chief of the *San Diego Law Review*, and soon-to-be associate with Jones Day (the second largest law firm in the country, and the same firm that hired Justice Scalia upon his graduation from Harvard Law School — *Antonin Scalia's Jurisprudence: Text and Tradition* [2006] was my first book with the University Press of Kansas), for her extensive assistance in researching the impact of the *Cabazon* decision on subsequent court decisions and in the law reviews. It was first-class research for which I am very grateful.

Professors Peter Charles Hoffer and N. E. H. Hull agreed to include this book in their series Landmark Law Cases and American Society, for which I am very much appreciative. Martha Whitt did a splendid job of copyediting the manuscript — her close attention to detail was remarkable; she has spared me many embarrassments. Finally, I would be remiss indeed if I did not thank Larisa Martin, production editor, and the Press's leadership team, Susan Schott, Michael Briggs, and Fred M. Woodward, for their superb efforts. They are the reason scholars want their works published by the University Press of Kansas.

Introduction

Today, Southern Californians take for granted the presence of pala-
tial tribal casinos along a 90-mile stretch of Interstate 10 (from 60
miles east of Los Angeles to 30 miles east Palm Springs). They have
all been built in the past ten years and rival the finest hotel-casinos of
Las Vegas or Atlantic City. Few Southern Californians know, however, that they exist because of the Supreme Court's critical decision
in *California v. Cabazon Band of Mission Indians*.

Located adjacent to Interstate 10 in Indio, California, and 30 miles
east of Palm Springs is Fantasy Springs Resort Casino. Owned and
operated by the Cabazon Band of Mission Indians on its reservation,
it has a 100,000-square-foot casino floor with 2,000 slot machines and
40 table games including Blackjack, California Craps, Pai Gow, and
more. It has an off-track betting facility and a bingo palace with 600
seats. Its 12-story hotel has 250 luxury rooms and suites, a 3,500 seat
Special Events Center that brings in first-class entertainment, top-
notch restaurants, conference facilities, and a 24-lane bowling alley.
It also has Eagle Falls Golf Course — an 18-hole, 6,715-yard, par 72
championship course designed by Clive Clark and voted one of the
"Best Courses You Can Play" by *Golfweek* magazine.

The Cabazon Band of Mission Indians is a small tribe of only
twenty-five members. Nonetheless, its tribal leaders are civically
involved and have hosted repeated Towns and Tribes conferences to
foster better understanding and cooperation between local and tribal
governments on topics ranging from education to the environment.
They have taken the lead in both Sacramento and Washington, D.C.,
to advocate for legislation on such matters as certifying tribal police
and fire departments by state and federal authorities and securing the
full authority of tribal governments to participate in the political
process. Their efforts, and the efforts of other tribes, have resulted in

their invitation, and the invitation of other tribes, to join as full members the Coachella Valley Council of Governments.

Also located adjacent to Interstate 10 in Cabazon, California, but this time 20 miles west of Palms Springs (and 90 miles east of Los Angeles) is Morongo Casino Resort & Spa. Owned by the 1,000 members of the Morongo Band of Mission Indians and located on its reservation, it is also a world-class facility. Its 27-story futuristic hotel rises from the desert floor with 310 luxury rooms and suites and 8 restaurants. Its 150,000-square-foot casino floor accommodates 2,400 slot machines and 100 table games along with a private 22-table poker room and a high-stakes room featuring high-limit blackjack and $100 slot machines. It has a bingo palace with 600 seats. Its Special Events Center attracts entertainers such as Michael Bolton, Bill Maher, Melissa Etheridge, and Engelbert Humperdinck. It has a 12,000-square-foot grand ballroom as well as smaller conference facilities and a 24-lane bowling alley.

Nearby in Southern California are even larger and equally lavish tribal casinos. The 400 members of the Agua Caliente Band of Cahuilla Indians have two casinos on their tribal lands. One is located 12 miles east of Palms Springs and adjacent to Interstate 10 in Rancho Mirage, California. Agua Caliente Casino, Resort, Spa has a luxury 16-story hotel with 338 rooms and suites; a 45,000-square-foot casino with 1,800 slot machines and 42 table games; a poker room with 11 tables, and a high-limits room with blackjack and Mini-Baccarat games to $5,000 and $100 slots. It has 6 restaurants, 13,000 square feet of conference space, and a 2,000-seat concert theater that books headliners like the Beach Boys, Sheryl Crow, Billy Idol, and Ted Nugent. The other casino is located in downtown Palm Springs; Spa Resort Casino has a 30,000-square-foot casino floor with 1,000 slots and 40 table games; an 11-table poker room; a high-stakes room; and 6 restaurants. Its hotel has 228 rooms and suites along with 7,000 square feet of conference space.

Located 60 miles east of Los Angeles and 60 miles west of Palm Springs adjacent to the 210 Freeway in Highland is the San Manuel Indian Bingo and Casino, owned and operated by the 175 members of the San Manuel Band of Serrano Mission Indians. Its casino floor of 120,000 square feet accommodates 3,000 slot machines and 130 table games. It draws to its Yuhaviatam Room entertainers such as Gloria

2   { *Introduction* }

Estefan, Rod Stewart, and Bill Cosby. And it has a 2,500-seat bingo hall.

Just outside of Temecula on Interstate 15 and 80 miles from Palm Springs, 60 miles from San Diego, and 90 miles from Los Angeles is the Pechanga Resort Casino, owned and operated by the 1,300 members of the Pechanga Band of Luiseño Indians. Larger than any other tribal casino west of the Mississippi and even larger than any Las Vegas casino, it has a 188,000-square-foot casino floor with 4,900 slot machines, 212 table games, a poker room of 54 tables, a high-rise hotel with 517 rooms and suites, a 53,000-square-foot conference center, 10 restaurants, a 1,200-seat theater attracting top entertainers, and a 7,200-foot, par 72 golf course designed by Arthur Hills. The tribe was invited and now is a member of the very influential Los Angeles Leadership Council, a business-led-and-sponsored public policy partnership for the Southern California region providing proactive leadership for a strong economy, a vital business environment, and a better quality of life for everyone living in California's Southland.

Thirty years ago, all of these tribes were utterly destitute; they occupied arid desert land with no natural resources and no prospects that their grim financial circumstances would ever change. Their members lived in abject poverty and faced a dismal future. But, one brave tribe challenged that future, and one Supreme Court case made today's reality for these tribes possible. The Web site of the Cabazon Band's casino captures it perfectly: "The Cabazon Band was the first Native America tribe in the United States to have gaming on its reservation. The Supreme Court 1987 *Cabazon* decision paved the way for other tribes to operate gaming centers."

Clearly not all tribes have benefitted from the *Cabazon* decision. The tribes mentioned above have been very fortunate to have decisive, courageous, and politically skilled leaders; but they have also benefitted enormously because their reservations all have in common the three most important attributes of real estate property: location, location, location. Their arid lands may be unsuited for agriculture and devoid of natural resources, but they are all conveniently located near one of the major metropolitan centers of the country — the one that includes Los Angeles, Orange, San Diego, Riverside, and San Bernardino Counties in Southern California. Their casinos are within easy driving range of tens of millions of customers, but, and this is equally important, they are not too close; their casinos, golf courses, and hotels make them attractive resort destinations, and they are so viewed by the public. However, they are not so close that those living in Southern California find the games they offer threatening to local community values or competing for entertainment dollars that would otherwise be spent locally. The Southern California public considers the tribes' casino resorts to be like Las Vegas – fun destinations to visit that are full of vitality, allure, excitement, and glamour – but they enjoy one distinct advantage over Las Vegas: they can easily be reached by car in an hour to an hour and a half, as opposed to the five hours it takes to drive from Los Angeles to Las Vegas. Their spectacular success has given encouragement – sometimes realistically, sometimes not – to other tribes in more remote and less densely populated areas of the country to attempt to follow their lead, often with mixed results.

This book explores how it is that Native American tribes across the country, and especially those near major metropolitan areas in Southern California, Florida, the Midwest, and the Northeast, have come to profit enormously from tribal gaming and, in the process, to reclaim their sovereign powers as tribal governments. It discusses in detail the Supreme Court's decision in *California v. Cabazon Band of Mission Indians* (1987) as well as Congress's actions following the *Cabazon* decision that resulted in the passage of the Indian Gaming Regulatory Act (IGRA).

On February 25, 1987, the Supreme Court held in *California v. Cabazon Band of Mission Indians* that states are barred from interfering with tribal gaming – i.e., tribally sponsored, high-stakes commercial gaming enterprises catering primarily to non-Indian participants and operating in Indian country. ("Indian country" is defined in 18 *United States Code* § 1151 as "all land within the limits of any Indian reservation under the jurisdiction of the United States Government.")

When the Cabazon Band and the neighboring Morongo Band of Mission Indians, agricultural tribes barely eking out a subsistence existence on the harsh desert lands of the remote Coachella Valley, opened high-stakes bingo facilities on their reservations to provide employment opportunities for their members and to raise revenues for tribal governmental services, their operations were raided and closed down by the State of California and the County of Riverside on the grounds that they violated California's gambling laws. The Tribes sought relief

4 { *Introduction* }

in federal court and secured a permanent injunction restraining the State and County from applying their gambling laws on the reservations. After the Ninth Circuit affirmed, California appealed to the Supreme Court, only to be told that states have no authority to enforce their gambling laws on the reservation of a federally recognized tribe.

The Supreme Court had held in earlier cases that state laws may be enforced on Indian reservations if Congress has expressly consented. In this case, however, it found that Congress had not consented to this assertion of state power either through Public Law 83-280 (1953), commonly and hereafter referred to as Public Law 280, which had delegated criminal/prohibitory but not civil/regulatory jurisdiction over Indian tribes to California and five other specified states, or the Organized Crime Control Act of 1970 (OCCA), which made specific violations of state and local gambling laws to be violations of federal law. It also found that under a federal common law balancing test, the states' interest in preventing the infiltration of tribal gaming by organized crime was insufficient to escape the preemptive force of federal and tribal interests.

Justice Byron White wrote for a six-member majority; his Opinion for the Court recognized the unique position Indian tribes occupy in the United States. While tribes are sovereign nations with inherent powers of self-government, their sovereignty is dependent on, and subordinate to, the federal government. In Chief Justice John Marshall's famous words from *Cherokee Nation v. Georgia* (1831), tribes are "domestic, dependent nations" whose "relation to the United States resembles that of a ward to his guardian."

White's reasoning reflected the principles of long-established federal Indian law: he accepted the traditional understanding of tribal sovereignty (i.e., the only government that can assert sovereign authority over the tribes is the federal government and not the states), and, in accordance with the standard canons of construction of federal Indian law flowing from that traditional understanding, he construed ambiguous language in Public Law 280 and OCCA in favor of the tribes. By contrast, Justice Stevens rejected these canons and embraced the opposite presumption; his dissent argued that a state's gambling laws apply on Indian reservations unless there is an express congressional statement to the contrary.

Cabazon is important for a number of reasons. To begin with, as a result of that Court decision, tribal gaming has swept the nation; in 2009, over $27 billion were wagered in 425 tribal casinos operated by 238 tribes in 29 states from Connecticut to California. Tribal gaming has become Indian country's most effective economic-development tool, and the slot machine has become for many gaming tribes their "new buffalo" — a single source capable of fulfilling all of their needs, including jobs, schools, social services, and infrastructure.

Cabazon is also important for having brought together in one case a debate over the meaning of tribal sovereignty, the relationship of tribes to the federal government and the states, and the appropriateness of having distinctive canons of construction for federal Indian law. It constitutes a fascinating introduction to the consideration of such questions as: what is tribal sovereignty? How has tribal sovereignty been understood over time, by both the Court and the popular branches? What is the source of Congress's power over the tribes? What powers, if any, do states have to enforce their laws in Indian country? And why are the canons of construction of federal Indian law different from those in other fields of law?

Cabazon is also important politically: it figured prominently in Congress's enactment one year later of the Indian Gaming Regulatory Act of 1988 (IGRA) and its requirement that tribes must enter into compacts with state governments before they engage in Class III gaming (i.e., Las Vegas–type gaming — slot machines, banked table games such as blackjack, craps, roulette, etc.). Tribal-state compacts vary widely from state to state — both in terms of the kinds of gaming a tribe is allowed to offer and the level of gaming revenues the tribe is obliged to share with the state. The need for the tribes to negotiate with state governments initial (and revised) compacts favorable to them has brought the tribes off their reservations and into the political process where they have often wielded the political clout their considerable gaming revenues provide them to their advantage. But these actions potentially threaten the continued willingness of the political branches to regard tribes as wards in need of the particular solicitude of the federal government and of the judiciary to construe federal Indian law based on its own unique canons of construction.

The chapters that follow develop these themes. Chapter One is an overview of the *Cabazon* case and the many interesting constitutional questions it raises.

6 { *Introduction* }

Chapter Two addresses the legal and constitutional foundations of tribal sovereignty and how Great Britain, the colonies, the United States under the Articles of Confederation, and the United States under the Constitution, regarded Indian tribes and interacted with them from the earliest British colonization until the 1830s. It focuses particularly on what has come to be known as the Marshall Trilogy — over a ten-year period, Chief Justice Marshall handed down three decisions that continue to define to this day the nature and extent of tribal sovereignty and the relation of the tribes to the federal government and the states.

Chapter Three explores two major consequences of the Marshall Trilogy, both of which invariably figured in the Court's decision in *Cabazon*. The first consequence, based on the tribes' status as "domestic dependent nations" and therefore on "the unique trust relationship between the United States and the Indians," has been the development of the canons of construction of federal Indian law. The second consequence has been well over a century of vacillating federal policy towards the tribes. As a trustee, the federal government is obliged to act in the best interests of the tribes. But, what does it mean to act in the best interests of the tribes? The federal government has vacillated between two opposite beliefs: during some periods of American history, it has believed it is in the best interests of the tribes that their members should be assimilated into American society, and during other periods — including the period from the late 1960s to the present — it has believed it is in the tribes' best interests that they be preserved and that the federal government promote tribal self-determination.

Chapter Four focuses on Public Law 280, the law California believed authorized it to enforce its gambling laws in Indian country. Public Law 280 was passed by Congress at the height of the last era of assimilationist thinking. But it was construed by the Court in *Cabazon* during the current era's embrace of tribal self-determination.

Chapter Five explores the appeal of *Cabazon* to the Supreme Court. It examines California's reasons for appeal in its Jurisdictional Statement, the Tribes' Motion to Dismiss, California's Reply to the Motion to Dismiss, and two amici curiae briefs filed by a total of twenty states in support of California's Jurisdictional Statement — all addressing the question of whether the Supreme Court should hear the case; and, once the Court agreed to do so, it takes up the arguments found in the brief of California, the brief of the Tribes, California's closing brief, three amici curiae briefs filed by a total of seven states in support of California, and eight amici curiae briefs filed by a total of seventy-one different tribes and tribal organizations in support of the Tribes.

Chapter Six then summarizes the oral argument before the Supreme Court and shows the contributions made by the briefs and oral argument to Justice White's majority opinion, affirming the judgment of the Court of Appeals and remanding the case for further proceedings consistent with his opinion, and Justice Stevens's dissent.

Chapter Seven begins by examining what happened in the lower courts on remand, by reviewing the initial press coverage of *Cabazon* and by exploring the scholarly reaction to *Cabazon* in the legal literature and the impact it has had on federal and state courts as a controlling precedent. It then proceeds to explore Congress's passage of IGRA—a measure whose passage was given urgency by the *Cabazon* decision but that was also what Robert N. Clinton has called a "simultaneous, somewhat independent, and coincident culmination" of previous federal court decisions and earlier but failed congressional responses to the development of a rapidly growing gaming industry in Indian country. It takes up in some detail IGRA's key provisions as well as the steps that culminated in its passage.

Chapter Eight concludes by considering tribal gaming after *Cabazon* and under IGRA. It does so by focusing on the widely differing compacting experiences of three states: Connecticut, California, and Florida.

CHAPTER I

Cabazon

The Legal and Constitutional Questions

The Cabazon Band and Morongo Band of Mission Indians are federally recognized Indian tribes residing on reservations held in trust by the United States in the desert region of Riverside County in southern California. The Cabazon reservation was authorized by presidential executive orders issued in 1876 and 1891, and the Morongo reservation was authorized by a presidential order issued in 1877. At the time the litigation surrounding *California v. Cabazon Band of Mission Indians* began, the Cabazon Band had 25 enrolled members and a 1,700-acre reservation; the Morongo Band had 730 enrolled members and a 32,200-acre reservation. Their lands are arid, and their climate is punishing. Their reservations have no natural resources to generate revenue to operate their tribal governments or to provide services or employment for their members; in fact, prior to commencing its tribal bingo operation, the unemployment rate of the 300 tribal members living on the Morongo reservation was in excess of 64 percent.

To fund its tribal government and to provide tribal services and programs for its members, the Cabazon Band General Council, at the recommendation of John Philip Nichols — their consultant — opened a smoke shop in May 1979, selling cigarettes and liquor that they believed were exempt from the State of California's excise and sales taxes. This venture proved lucrative but was short-lived. In June 1980, the Supreme Court held, 6-3, in *Washington v. Confederated Tribes of the Colville Indian Reservation*, that tribal sales of cigarettes on a reservation do not prohibit a state from exacting its sales and cigarette taxes from nontribal members purchasing cigarettes at tribal smoke shops. Justice Byron White held for the Court that the principles of federal Indian law, whether stated in terms of preemption or tribal self-government, did not authorize Indian tribes to market an exemption from state taxation to persons who would normally do their business elsewhere. And, even if the result of these taxes was to reduce or eliminate tribal sales to nonmembers, that market existed in the first place only because of a claimed exemption for these very taxes.

Anticipating that outcome and agreeing with tribal leader John James that a more profitable future could be secured through gaming, the Cabazon Band General Council enacted a tribal ordinance on February 9, 1980, authorizing and regulating bingo games on its reservation, and a tribal ordinance on May 24, 1980, authorizing a card club (and permitting and regulating the playing for money of draw poker, lowball draw poker, and panguingue—unbanked games allowed under the California penal code) on its reservation. The Cabazons authorized bingo first, but they opened their bingo palace two and a half years after their card club. They did so because the building in which they operated their smoke shop was large enough to be converted into a card club but was too small to be used for bingo.

The Cabazon Band opened its card club on October 15, 1980; three days later, on Saturday, October 18, it was raided and shut down by Police Chief Samuel Cross and fourteen police officers from the City of Indio who arrived in riot gear, thereby beginning a legal war over tribal gaming that would not be resolved until the *Cabazon* decision itself in 1987. John Paul Nichols, the card club manager, described the raid as follows in Ambrose Lane's book, *Return of the Buffalo*:

It was . . . Saturday night—103, 104 people came in the cardroom. It was the third night open and that's when they came in; I think there might have been 35 cops altogether. There were a lot of cops. It was way overdone with riot helmets—gear, visors—coming in every nook and cranny. . . . They seized the tables, arrested a few people, everybody else was cited. . . . One guy was arrested and that was the guy whose famous photo was on the front of the [Indio *Daily News* the next day]. . . . He was just a young kid who said, "I'm not going anywhere." Because he had handcuffs on, the photo made it look as if everything happened that way. Another girl was photographed being held in a stranglehold. They took all the chips, tables. Why they took those tables is beyond me. And that was it. The war started.

The City of Indio raided the Cabazon's card club and seized $81.25 in quarters, 7 poker tables, 544 decks of cards, and 117,000 chips. It did so because it claimed that the card club was located on a portion of the Tribe's reservation that the City claimed it had annexed in 1970 and because the playing of these card games for money was prohibited by the Indio City Code. The Cabazon Band insisted that the annexation effort was invalid, as applicable state law required an authorized municipality to annex federally owned territory only "if the Federal Government or agency thereof owning such territory consents to the annexation," and neither the Federal Government nor the Tribe had consented. They pointed to a September 7, 1973, letter from the Bureau of Indian Affairs advising the City of Indio that it was the opinion of the Department of the Interior that the attempted annexation of Cabazon Reservation land was void for failure to obtain the consent of both the United States and the Cabazon Band. Therefore, on October 22, the Tribe filed suit in U.S. District Court for the Central District of California seeking a temporary restraining order and a preliminary injunction.

The Cabazon Band's attorney was Glenn M. Feldman. Feldman had previously represented the Tribe in its smoke shop venture and would continue to be its attorney through the *Cabazon* decision and beyond. Feldman received his law degree from Georgetown University in 1973 and served as Counsel and Legislative Director to U.S. Senator James Abourezk when he was chairman of the Senate Select Committee on Indian Affairs. When Abourezk did not seek reelection in 1978, Feldman joined the senator's D.C. law firm of Abourezk, Shack & Mendenhall and was a member of that law firm when he began representing the Cabazon Band in 1979. He later moved to the Washington, D.C., firm of Ziontz, Pirtle, Morisset, Ernstoff & Chestnut, where he remained during most of the *Cabazon* litigation. In the summer of 1986 — as he was preparing to draft the Brief of the Appellees for the Supreme Court, Feldman moved to Phoenix, Arizona, and joined the law firm of O'Connor, Cavanagh, Anderson, Westover, Killingsworth & Beshears. In 1999, he moved to the law firm of Mariscal, Weeks, McIntyre & Friedlander, where he is a partner and remains the Cabazon Band's attorney.

Feldman's application for a temporary restraining order and a preliminary injunction was randomly assigned to U.S. District Court Judge Laughlin E. Waters. Waters had graduated from UCLA in 1939, interrupted his legal education to serve as a Captain in the Infantry in the U.S. Army during World War II, received his law degree from USC in 1947, served as a Republican member of the California Assembly from 1947 to 1953 and in that capacity chaired the legislative committee that reapportioned the California legislature in 1951, was appointed by President Dwight D. Eisenhower to serve as U.S. Attorney for the Southern District of California from 1953 to 1961, and was appointed to the federal bench by President Gerald Ford in 1976.

On November 10, Judge Waters denied Feldman's application for the restraining order but granted his motion for the injunction. The card club reopened on that same day. The Tribe and the City then filed cross motions for summary judgment. On May 18, 1981, Judge Waters granted the City's motion and dissolved the injunction. He did so because, while he acknowledged that "the City's failure to obtain the consent of the Cabazon Band pursuant to those sections [of the state law in question] rendered Indio's annexation of the Cabazon lands vulnerable to challenge," the statutory time allowed for the Tribe to initiate such a challenge had expired years ago and "thus the Cabazon Reservation lands in question are part of the City of Indio."

Feldman immediately filed a motion to vacate the summary judgment and, in the alternative, moved for a stay pending appeal on the ground that the revenue from the Tribe's card club was its sole source of income. He argued that without these funds, the Tribe would be immediately and irreparably harmed in that it would have no source of income to finance or operate its tribal government. On May 22, Judge Waters denied the motion for vacation of summary judgment but, in a highly unusual move, granted the motion to stay dissolving the injunction pending appeal. As Feldman would later recall:

> A stay pending appeal is a bizarre legal device where we asked the judge, who had just ruled against us and said we were not entitled to have the card club remain open, to give us a ruling which allowed it to remain open while that decision was appealed. It is very unusual and very rarely granted — you could ask 100 attorneys, and they would not be able to give you one successful example, but Judge Waters granted it. He allowed the Cabazon Card Club to

remain open while the case went up on appeal to the Ninth Circuit. (June 18, 2009, interview)

On expedited appeal, the Ninth Circuit received briefs from Indio and the Cabazon Band; both briefs focused exclusively on Public Law 280 and the question of whether the federal government had preempted California and its subdivisions from regulating gambling in Indian country. On December 14, 1982, the Ninth Circuit reversed the District Court and ruled on the Tribe's behalf in *Cabazon Band of Mission Indians v. City of Indio*. Judge Thomas Tang held for a unanimous three-judge panel that, since "Federal consent was . . . a condition precedent to the initiation of the city's annexation proceedings," its "failure to obtain such consent rendered Indio's annexation of the federally reserved land void ab initio." He rejected Indio's claim that "the running of the statute of limitations 'cured' its failure to comply with the procedural provisions of the annexation statute," by declaring that, since Indio's attempted annexation was void ab initio, "the Cabazon Band was not required to take action within any prescribed statutory time to establish invalidity." And, he continued, even if the annexation was not void ab initio, the state statute of limitations on which Indio was relying "may not bar the assertion of federal Indian rights." He observed that "it is well settled that statutes of limitation cannot bar suits brought to protect rights enjoyed by Indians and Indian Tribes" and quoted from the 1926 U.S. Supreme Court opinion in *United States v. Minnesota*: "And it also is settled that state statutes of limitation neither bind nor have any application to the United States, when suing to enforce a public right or to protect interests of its Indian wards."

It was a solid win for the Tribe, but winning this skirmish was not the same as winning the war, for just two months later, in the evening of Tuesday, February 15, 1983, sixteen officers of the Riverside County Sheriff's Department, under the direction of Sheriff Bernard J. Clark, raided the Cabazon Band card club. They issued misdemeanor citations to the thirty-one tribal members, employees, and patrons who were present, alleging they had violated Riverside County Ordinance No. 331 by engaging in, or permitting to be played, the games of draw poker, lowball draw poker, and panguingue. The officers also confiscated $3,000 in cash, files and records, and all of the cards and poker chips on the premises, and they stated their intention to continue to enforce Ordinance No. 331, by means of arrest, as long as the Cabazon card club continued to operate. As a result, the club immediately ceased operation.

On February 23, Glenn Feldman returned to the Central District Court of California seeking a preliminary injunction and temporary restraining order against the County's enforcement of Ordinance No. 331. The Tribe's motions were initially assigned to U.S. District Judge Cynthia H. Hall, but under the Central District Court of California's "Local Rules of Court," they were transferred to Judge Waters under what the Central District Court called the "Low Number Rule": a case could be transferred (with the consent of both judges) from one judge to another judge who had already heard a case that "appears to arise from the same or substantially identical transactions, happenings, or events," or that "involves the same or substantially the same parties or property." Feldman was very pleased with this transfer. Even though Judge Waters had ruled against the Cabazons in their litigation with the City of Indio, he sensed that Waters was a fast learner and was coming to appreciate the various dimensions of federal Indian law, including its canons of statutory construction. Before Judge Waters, Feldman made several arguments.

First, he argued that Riverside County misconstrued Public Law 280 when it concluded that it authorized the state and its subdivisions to enforce local ordinances on Indian reservations in California that would regulate, condition, interfere with, or prohibit conduct which is lawful under California state law and public policy and which is authorized and regulated by tribal ordinance.

Second, he noted that a private card club in Riverside County, located in the City of Lake Elsinore, offered the same card games as the Cabazon Band card club, and yet the County made no effort to enforce Ordinance No. 331 against persons engaging in, or permitting to be played, the same games at that facility. Feldman charged that the County had deprived the Cabazon Band of the equal protection of the laws in violation of the Constitution's Fourteenth Amendment.

Third, he pointed to *Barona Group of the Capitan Grande Band of Mission Indians v. Duffy*, decided December 21, 1981 (just a week after the Cabazon's victory in the City of Indio case), in which a three-judge panel of the Ninth Circuit Court of Appeals unanimously held that the Sheriff of San Diego County, John Duffy, could not enforce state and county bingo laws against tribally sponsored bingo games on a California Indian reservation. *Barona* followed and embraced what the Fifth Circuit had held just two and a half months earlier in *Seminole Tribe of Florida v. Butterworth* (1981): while Public Law 280 delegated to certain states the power to enforce their criminal/prohibitory laws in Indian country, it did not delegate the power to enforce their civil/regulatory laws, and since both Florida and California allowed charitable organizations to conduct bingo games under certain circumstances, bingo operations were not contrary to the public policy of the states and therefore tribal bingo operations were not subject to the states' criminal/prohibitory laws. Yet, despite the *Barona* decision, Riverside County officials had informed the Cabazon Band on February 22 that they intended to close down the 500-seat high-stakes bingo parlor (offering prizes in excess of $250 per game), which the Tribe was planning to open on March 1, just as they had closed down the Cabazon card club. The County's attempt to enforce its bingo regulations as spelled out in County Ordinance No. 558 would, Feldman argued, impermissibly infringe on tribal sovereignty and, by depriving the Tribe of needed revenues, violate its lawful right to self-determination, self-governance, and reservation economic development secured by federal law and public policy. He therefore requested that the County be restrained as well from enforcing Ordinance No. 558 on the Cabazon's reservation.

Fourth, Feldman argued that under the U.S. Constitution's Indian Commerce Clause of Article I, § 8 and its treaty language in Article II, § 2, the regulation of Indian affairs is entrusted to the federal government, to the exclusion of the states. Fifth, he argued that the County's actions violated the inherent sovereignty of Indian tribes recognized by the U.S. government as part of the federal common law. Sixth, he argued that various federal laws and policies promoting reservation economic development, including the California Mission Indians Relief Act of 1891, preempted Riverside County from enforcing its ordinances in Indian country. And seventh and finally, he argued Riverside County's actions violated 42 U.S.C. § 1983 by acting under color of law to deprive the rights, privileges, and immunities of the tribe secured by the Constitution, laws, and policies of the United States. Because of this § 1983 violation, he requested the Court to award the Cabazon Band damages in the amount of $12,500,000, along with costs and reasonable attorneys fees.

On February 24, the very next day, Judge Waters granted the Cabazon Band's request for a temporary restraining order prohibiting the Riverside County Sheriff's Department from enforcing Ordinance No. 331 (dealing with card clubs) and Ordinance No. 558 (dealing with bingo parlors) on its reservation. A temporary restraining order usually lasts while a motion for a preliminary injunction is being decided, and the court decides whether to drop the order or to issue a preliminary injunction. On May 6, 1983, Judge Waters issued a preliminary injunction against the County.

At the same time, the members of the Morongo Band were also moving toward opening their own bingo parlor, a much larger 28,700-square-foot complex accommodating 1,400 bingo players. The Riverside County Sheriff's Department had issued them a similar threat that they would be raided and shut down and any members, employees, or patrons on the premises cited if they opened their new facility. On May 16, just ten days after Judge Waters had issued his preliminary injunction against the County for the Cabazon Band, the Morongo Band, represented by Barbara E. Karshmer, entered Judge Waters's courtroom seeking a preliminary injunction against the County; she made many of the same claims Feldman had made on behalf of the Cabazon Band, including the County's violation of § 1983, and on that basis requested damages, court costs, and attorneys fees. (The amount of damages was unspecified, but in any case, on October 15, 1985, Judge Waters, on stipulation by the parties, dismissed Morongo's claim for money damages.) On May 20, 1983, Judge Waters granted the Morongo Band's motion and preliminarily enjoined the County from arresting, threatening to arrest, interfering with, or harassing any person on the Morongo reservation engaged in the playing of bingo. At an October 31, 1983, hearing, Judge Waters consolidated the Cabazon and Morongo cases and designated the Cabazon case, because it was filed first, as the lead case.

Because Judge Waters's preliminary injunction implicated California Penal Code § 326.5 and its regulation of bingo operations, the State of California, at that same October 31 hearing, filed a motion to intervene in the litigation, and on November 21, Judge Waters granted that motion. On June 26, 1984, the parties filed cross motions for summary judgment on the jurisdictional question whether state and county gambling laws applied on the Tribes' reservations. Accompanying these motions was a document entitled "Agreed upon Statement of Uncontroverted Facts between [the Parties] to be Used in Cross Motions for Summary Judgment." Among the uncontroverted facts was the following: the State of California and the County of Riverside "do not allege [that the gaming operations on the Cabazon and Morongo reservations] are associated with organized crime." Another was that neither the Cabazon Band nor the Morongo Band were "among the enumerated entities authorized to operate Bingo games" under California law.

On December 6, 1984, Judge Waters granted the Tribes' motion for summary judgment. He did so by simply accepting Feldman's Proposed Order and Proposed Judgment, which Feldman had submitted on December 4, crossing out the word "Proposed," and signing and dating them. Glenn Feldman had submitted these proposed documents containing the specific language Waters accepted based on his sense from the hearings Judge Waters had conducted of what the judge was likely to conclude. While Judge Waters did not issue a written opinion, findings of fact, or conclusions of law, he issued a permanent injunction restraining the State of California and the County of Riverside from applying their gambling laws on the Cabazon and Morongo reservations, awarded the Tribes court costs and attorneys fees, and retained jurisdiction to consider the Cabazon Band's damages issue. Less than two weeks later, on December 19, the State and County appealed to the Ninth Circuit.

The majority of the arguments found in the Brief of the Appellants and the Reply Brief, both filed by the State of California, and the Brief of the Appellees, filed by the Tribes, focused on Public Law 280 and the question of whether federal law preempted the State from enforcing its gambling laws on reservation land. California in its opening brief made the remarkable argument that the Ninth Circuit had to determine the effect of Public Law 280 "only if it rejects the argument that the federal common law authorizes the application of State and local laws here." It argued in its reply brief that both Public Law 280 and OCCA supported the enforcement of State and local laws in Indian country. The State of Washington filed an amicus brief in support of California, arguing that "if the State designs its criminal laws to prohibit high stakes commercial bingo and thereby prevent the intrusion by organized crime, while allowing other types of bingo, that criminal law is applicable to Indian reservations under Public Law 280." Washington also argued that the Supreme Court decision in *Rice v. Rehner* (described below) required a reexamination of the *Barona* decision. The Tribes responded in their brief, pointing out that California had gotten the issue "absolutely backwards." The federal common law argument on which California was relying applied only in the absence of an applicable federal statute, and Public Law 280 was that applicable statute, which, under the civil/regulatory–criminal/prohibitory dichotomy of *Barona* and *Seminole Tribe* flatly denied the State of California jurisdiction over the Tribes' games on their reservations.

On April 8, 1986, in *Cabazon Band of Mission Indians v. California*, the U.S. Court of Appeals for the Ninth Circuit unanimously affirmed Judge Waters's grant of summary judgment and his issuance of a permanent injunction in an opinion by Judge J. Blaine Anderson. Anderson systematically responded to the State's contention that state and local laws pertaining to gambling should apply on Indian reservations under (1) Public Law 280, (2) the Organized Crime Control Act (OCCA), and (3) federal common law.

Judge Anderson acknowledged that § 2 of Public Law 280 conferred on certain states, including California, full criminal jurisdiction over offenses committed by Indians on the reservation. He also acknowledged that § 4 of the act granted civil jurisdiction over Indian reservations in words that "on the surface seemed to make all state laws and regulations of general application effective." The relevant words in § 4 are as follows: Each mandated state, of which California was one, "shall have jurisdiction over civil causes of action between Indians or to which Indians are parties which arise in the areas of Indian country . . . to the same extent that such State has jurisdiction over other civil causes of action, and those civil laws of such State that are of general application to private persons or private property shall have the same force and effect within such Indian country as they have elsewhere within the State." But, Judge Anderson continued, the Supreme Court in *Bryan v. Itasca County* (1976) had denied that § 4 granted to the states general civil/regulatory power over Indian country, instead limiting it to giving states jurisdiction only over private civil litigation involving reservation Indians in state court.

Bryan addressed the question of whether the State of Minnesota had authority under § 4 of Public Law 280 to impose a personal property tax on the mobile home of an enrolled Chippewa Indian located on land held in trust for members of his tribe. Justice William Brennan wrote for a unanimous Court when he held that it did not. He noted that there was, in the legislative history of Public Law 280, a "total absence of mention or discussion regarding a congressional intent to confer upon the States an authority to tax Indians or Indian property on reservations." This omission had "significance in the application of the canons of construction applicable to statutes affecting Indian immunities, as some mention would normally be expected if such a sweeping change in the status of tribal government and reservation Indians had been contemplated by Congress." Brennan concluded: "The consistent and exclusive use of the terms 'civil causes of action,' '[arising] on,' 'civil laws . . . of general application to private persons or private property,' and '[adjudication],' in both the Act and its legislative history virtually compels our conclusion that the primary intent of § 4 was to grant jurisdiction over private civil litigation involving reservation Indians in state court."

Judge Anderson found that *Bryan* clearly prohibited California from employing its civil/regulatory power in Indian country. However, § 2 of Public Law 280 did confer on certain states, including California, full criminal jurisdiction over offenses committed by Indians on the reservation. So Public Law 280 authorized the State to apply its "criminal/prohibitory" laws on Indian reservations, but not its "civil/regulatory" laws. But, what distinguishes a law that is "criminal/prohibitory" from one that is "civil/regulatory"?

To answer that question, Judge Anderson turned to *Barona*, previously referenced by Feldman at the District Court level, in which the Ninth Circuit had held that a state law is criminal/prohibitive if the activity the statute addresses violates the "public policy" of the state and civil/regulatory if the activity does not.

The question then became whether the gaming activities conducted by the Tribes on their reservations violated the public policy of the State of California. Judge Anderson again turned to *Barona*, in which the Ninth Circuit had also concluded that California law contained no general prohibition against playing bingo but rather authorized "bingo operations by tax exempt organizations including, for example, fraternal societies, recreational clubs, senior citizen organizations, real estate boards and labor and agricultural groups." It regulated bingo as a money-making venture by limiting the size of prizes, requiring that all proceeds be applied to charitable purposes, and mandating that the games be operated by volunteers from the authorized organization. The *Barona* court concluded that "the fact that so many diverse organizations are allowed to conduct bingo operations, albeit under strict regulation, is contrary to a finding that such operations violate California's public policy"; so, too, was the fact that "the general public is allowed to play bingo at will in an authorized game. This cuts against a public policy prohibition."

Before Judge Anderson could conclude that the gaming operations on the Tribes' reservations were not contrary to the public policy of California, he was obliged to address the State's argument that the Supreme Court's decision in *Rice v. Rehner* (1983) compelled a reexamination of *Barona* and its civil/regulatory–criminal/prohibitory dichotomy. In *Rice*, the Court confronted the question of whether the State of California could require the Pala Band of Mission Indians (another California Tribe located in northern San Diego County), operating a general store on its reservation, to obtain a state liquor license in order to sell liquor for off-premises consumption. Justice Sandra Day O'Connor wrote for a six-member majority and said "yes." She argued that neither the text of the particular federal Indian statute in question (delegating to the states the power to enforce its liquor laws in Indian country) nor its legislative history revealed any intention by Congress to introduce the same criminal/prohibitory–civil/regulatory dichotomy as it held in *Bryan* that Congress had introduced in Public Law 280. Justice O'Connor went on to say that "in the absence of a context that might possibly require it, we are reluctant to make such a distinction."

Judge Anderson, however, was not persuaded by the State's argument. While admitting that "it can be said with equal force that neither the text nor the legislative history of Public Law 280 reveal any civil regulatory–criminal prohibitory distinction," he observed that the Supreme Court had held in *Bryan* that, in interpreting Public Law 280, "statutes passed for the benefit of dependent Indian tribes . . . are to be liberally construed, doubtful expressions being resolved in favor of the Indians." Thus, although California's bingo statute, with its strict provisions concerning the entities that can offer bingo (only nonprofits), the individuals who can operate the games (members of the nonprofits), and the limits on the prizes ($250), might arguably be interpreted as criminal/prohibitory, Judge Anderson applied the customary canons of construction of federal Indian law and insisted that "the resolution must be in favor of the Indian tribe." He concluded that the gambling activities of the Tribes on the Indian reservation did not violate California public policy and, under Public Law 280, California's bingo statute was therefore civil/regulatory in nature and did not apply on the Indian reservations.

Judge Anderson's consideration of the State's arguments based on OCCA was brief. For OCCA to apply, he observed that the activity, again, had to violate public policy. In *United States v. Farris* (1980), he noted that the Ninth Circuit held that whether a tribal activity is "a violation of the law of a state" within the meaning of the OCCA depends on "whether it is contrary to the 'public policy' of the state. Thus, *Farris* makes co-extensive the tests for application of state law to Indian reservations under [the OCCA] and for direct application of state law under Public Law 280. Because we have concluded that bingo games are not contrary to the public policy of California, the activity is not violative of the OCCA."

Finally, Judge Anderson also found the State's invocation of a federal common law balancing test to be unavailing. Quite irrespective of Public Law 280 and OCCA, California argued that the Supreme Court had through a series of cases adopted a federal common law to determine the applicability of state laws on Indian reservations, requiring what it described in *White Mountain Apache Tribe v. Bracker* (1980) as a "particularized inquiry" into "the nature of state, federal, and tribal interests at stake." Under this particularized inquiry test, state laws may be applied to Indian reservations unless such application, on balance, would either interfere with tribal self-government or impair a tribal right granted or reserved by federal law.

Turning to these "state, federal, and tribal interests," Judge Anderson noted that the State had a "significant" interest in prohibiting tribal bingo games in order to prevent the intrusion of organized crime in California. But, he continued, "there is no evidence whatsoever that organized crime exists on these Indian reservations," and therefore, "the State's interest, although commendable, is weak."

By contrast, he pointed out that "current federal policy is to encourage and foster tribal self-government and to promote reservation economic development." Quoting President Ronald Reagan's statement that "it is important to the concept of self-government that tribes reduce their dependence on federal funds by providing a greater percentage of the cost of their self-government," Judge Anderson found "the federal interest to be strong."

He then turned to the tribal interests. He observed that the Tribes had offered "a number of compelling interests in favor of their position." The bingo games operated on the reservations were "the Tribes' only source of income. The games are the major source of employment for the reservation Indians and the sole source of revenue for operating their tribal governments and for providing services to their members." California had insisted that these interests were weak, and for two reasons: (1) the Tribes were "marketing an exemption" from state laws to non-Indians who were going onto the reservation to engage in gaming prohibited by state law; and (2) the traditions of the Tribes did not encompass commercial gambling, particularly where predominantly non-Indian participants were involved. Judge Anderson took up each reason in turn.

California contended that the Tribes were "marketing an exemption" from California law and cited *Washington v. Confederated Tribes of the Colville Reservation Indians*. But Judge Anderson held that *Colville* did not support the State's contention. To begin with, the Supreme Court in *Colville* did not rule that a tribe's "marketing of a [tax] exemption" (untaxed cigarettes) enabled the state to prohibit the tribe from selling cigarettes, but that is exactly what the State was trying to accomplish in this case. And additionally, in *Colville*, the Court recognized that a tribe's interest in generating revenues for essential governmental programs "is strongest when the revenues are derived from value generated on the reservation by activities involving the Tribes." Instead of merely importing cigarettes to resell in a manner which deprived the State of Washington of revenues to be used to provide state services off the reservation, the Tribes in this case had built and were operating gambling facilities, were employing tribal members, were regulating and conducting these activities wholly within their reservation, and were utilizing the funds to provide necessary governmental services for their members. Judge Anderson found "the Tribes' interest to be strong."

California also contended the Tribes had not traditionally engaged in tribally sponsored, high-stakes commercial gambling operations catering primarily to non-Indian participants, and, since no such tradition existed, the Court should accord "less weight to the 'backdrop' of tribal sovereignty." Judge Anderson begged to differ: "The State's focus is too narrow." The focus in determining whether a tribal tradition exists should be, he insisted, on whether the tribe is engaged in a traditional governmental function, not whether it historically engaged in a particular activity. "The Tribes in this case are engaged in the traditional governmental function of raising revenue. They are thereby exercising their inherent sovereign governmental authority. . . . Having determined that a tradition exists which recognizes a sovereign immunity in favor of the Indians, we are reluctant to infer that the State should exercise authority in this case."

Weighing all the factors in the balance, Judge Anderson found that "the federal and tribal interests at stake here outweigh the State's interest. Therefore, under the federal common law's 'particularized inquiry' or balancing test, the State and County may not apply their gambling laws on the Indian reservations because application of these laws would interfere with reservation self-government." For the three-judge panel, he therefore affirmed Judge Waters's summary judgment and permanent injunction restraining the County and the State from applying their gambling laws on the reservations.

Just nine days later, on April 17, 1986, the State of California appealed to the U.S. Supreme Court; in its Jurisdictional Statement, it asked "whether state and local laws prohibiting commercial gambling apply to Indian gambling operations, conducted on Indian reservations, that are patronized primarily by non-Indians." Two amici curiae briefs were filed by a total of twenty states in support of California's appeal. On May 19, the Cabazon Band moved to dismiss the appeal, and on May 29, the State replied to the motion to dismiss. On June 9, 1986, the Supreme Court declared that further consideration of the question of whether it had jurisdiction to decide the issues involved would be postponed until the case was heard on the merits. With the Supreme Court having thereby noted probable jurisdiction,

California filed its opening brief on August 8, the Cabazon Band filed its brief on September 24, and the State filed its closing brief on October 20. The Court thereupon scheduled one hour of oral argument for Tuesday, December 9, at 2:00 p.m.

The arguments found in these briefs (and the eleven amicus curiae briefs filed by a total of seven states and seventy-one different tribes and tribal organizations) focused on the same issues that had been addressed at the court of appeals level: the meaning of tribal sovereignty; the canons of construction applicable to federal Indian law; the applicability of a federal common law balancing test, the construction of Public Law 280 and OCCA and whether those acts authorized the State to enforce its gaming laws in Indian country; and the relevance of various court precedents including *Bryan*, *Barona*, *Colville*, and *Rice*. However, before these issues can be fully appreciated, a number of key questions must first be answered. They include:

What is the nature of tribal sovereignty?

What is the constitutional and legal basis for the Court's recognition of tribal sovereignty?

How has tribal sovereignty been understood over time, by both the Court and the popular branches?

What are the sources of Congress's power over the tribes? What constitutional power authorizes Congress to pass, for example, Public Law 280 and OCCA?

What powers, if any, do states have to enforce their laws in Indian country, and under what circumstances?

Why are the canons of construction of federal Indian law different from those in other fields of law? Why, for example, did the courts introduce the criminal/prohibitory–civil/regulatory dichotomy, not present in the statutes themselves, into their interpretation of Public Law 280 and OCCA?

Chapters Two through Four provide answers to these questions so that the stage is fully set when Chapters Five and Six explore the *Cabazon* litigation before the Supreme Court.

Tribal Sovereignty
Origins and Development

As constitutionally and legally understood today by both the Congress and the Supreme Court, tribal sovereignty is the power of federally recognized tribes to govern on their reservations with full legislative, civil regulatory, civil adjudicatory, and criminal jurisdiction except where these powers have been expressly limited by Congress or expressly relinquished by the tribes. (There is one major exception — and derivative cases following from it — to this general characterization that must be mentioned: in *Oliphant v. Suquamish Indian Tribe* [1978], the Supreme Court held, 7-2, that Indian tribes do not have criminal jurisdiction on their reservations "over non-Indians absent affirmative delegation of such power by Congress.") It is this understanding of tribal sovereignty that will provide the backdrop for what follows, because it explains why the Congress and the Court have dealt with tribes as they have for the past 225 years; it makes the Court's decision in *Cabazon* and the Congress's enactment of Public Law 280 and IGRA understandable in political terms.

However, there is another understanding of tribal sovereignty held by many tribal leaders and members. It rejects the view expressed by the Court in *United States v. Wheeler* (1978) that tribal sovereignty "exists only at the sufferance of Congress and is subject to complete defeasance." It argues that tribal sovereignty is cultural sovereignty; as Wallace Coffey and Rebecca Tsosie argue in their important article entitled "Rethinking the Tribal Sovereignty Doctrine: Cultural Sovereignty and the Collective Future of Indians Nations," tribal sovereignty is "inherent" and is "*cultural sovereignty.*" It is "the effort of Indian nations and Indian people to exercise their own norms and values in structuring their collective futures. Inherent [tribal] sovereignty is not dependent upon any grant, gift, or acknowledgment by the federal government. It preexists the arrival of the European people and the formation of the United States. Cultural sovereignty is inherent in every sense of that word, and it is up to Indian people to define, assert, protect, and insist upon respect for that right." In the context of tribal gaming, this understanding of cultural sovereignty provides the tribes with the full authority "to exercise their own norms and values" and to structure "their collective futures" as they see fit and for them "to define, assert, protect, and insist upon respect" for their right to do so. This understanding of cultural sovereignty helps explains why the Cabazon Band was convinced that it was free, at its discretion, to open a smoke shop and later gaming facilities, and why so many tribal leaders were outraged when Congress passed IGRA, including its provisions requiring the tribes to enter into gaming compacts with the states.

What follows in this chapter is an exploration, not of the cultural sovereignty of the tribes, but rather the legal and constitutional foundations of tribal sovereignty and how England, the colonies, and the United States — first under the Articles of Confederation and then under the Constitution — regarded Indian tribes and interacted with them from the earliest British colonization until the 1830s.

During the colonization of America, England followed the lead of other European nations such as the Netherlands, Spain, and France and embraced three fundamental principles of how to deal with Native American tribes. These principles were first formulated by Francisco de Victoria, a Dominican theologian, in a series of lectures in 1532 entitled "On the Indians Lately Discovered" and were subsequently reflected in the seventeenth- and eighteenth-century treatises on international law of Hugo Grotius and Emmerich de Vattel. These principles held that (1) Indian tribes had both property rights and the power of a sovereign over their lands; (2) Indian lands could only be acquired with tribal consent or after a just war against them; and (3) acquisition of Indian lands was solely a governmental matter and not something to be left to individual colonists.

These principles were reflected in the earliest colonial laws. For example, in 1629, the Massachusetts Bay Colony proclaimed that colonists could acquire lands claimed by the Indians only by purchase, and five years later, it centralized these purchases by declaring that only it could grant the right to purchase land in the colony. The colonies of Virginia, Maryland, New York, Pennsylvania, Connecticut, Rhode Island, North Carolina, South Carolina, and Georgia subsequently enacted similar laws.

These principles were embraced, because it was not only just to do so but prudent as well. English colonists were outnumbered by tribal members for many decades, obliging them to acquire land by buying it from the Indians rather than by taking it by force.

Like the Dutch, Spanish, and French, the English colonists also recognized the sovereignty of the tribes by dealing with tribal governments through treaties. Perhaps the earliest example is Captain John Smith's exchange of gifts at the 1608 coronation of Chief Powhatan, head of the Virginia Tidewater confederacy. In 1621, New England colonists negotiated a treaty of friendship and alliance between King James I and Massasoit, the Chief Sachem of the Wampanoags, giving the English permission to acquire about 12,000 acres of land for the Plymouth Plantation. In 1666 the Maryland Colony and the Piscataway Chiefdom negotiated Articles of Peace and Amity that stated that "from this day forward there [shall] be an inviolable peace and amity between the Right honorable the Lord Proprietor of this Province and the Indians." Among other rights, the Articles ensured that the Piscataway would not have to give up their lands and promised that they could fish, hunt, and gather crabs without disturbance. In 1677, the English and a number of tribes in Virginia, including the Powhatan, signed the Treaty of Middle Plantation; it specified an agreement that the Indians would own their reservations and would be treated as Englishmen under the law, and that the English would not settle within three miles of an Indian reservation. It preserved the right of the tribes to hunt, fish, and gather natural resources in exchange for their agreement to pay a tribute of game to the Virginia governor every year. (At the time, these tributes helped feed the colonists.) These treaties often required lengthy and difficult negotiations; they were frequently complex — involving the exchange of lands — and their provisions had to be communicated in completely different languages. Differing cultural values made matters worse. For example, the tribal members believed that the earth was sacred and that land was there for the benefit of all; while tribes had certain territories that they occupied, individual members did not buy, sell, or hold title to plots of land.

While the colonies took the lead in negotiating treaties with the tribes, the ultimate authority over relations with the tribes continued to reside in the British Crown. When English relations with the tribes soured because of increasing resentment over English intrusions into their territory, and when French relations with the tribes improved because the French were more interested in establishing the fur trade than in acquiring land for agriculture, the British Crown stepped in. With the French and Indian War about to begin in 1754, it restricted the colonies' power to purchase Indian land in 1753. With the war under way, it prohibited colonial governors from issuing further grants of Indian lands and directed them to issue orders to all settlers on those lands to leave at once. It also centralized Indian affairs under two superintendents — one for the northern colonies and another for the southern — with responsibility to negotiate treaties and regulate trade with the tribes. With the end of the war, the British Crown issued the Royal Proclamation of 1763, declaring that "great Frauds and Abuses have been committed in purchasing Lands of the Indians, to the great Prejudice of our Interests and to the great Dissatisfaction of the said Indians." The proclamation also formally reserved all lands beyond the Appalachians for the tribes, prohibited British colonists from purchasing lands from the Indians unless authorized by the Crown, affirmed the sanctity of British treaties with the tribes, and proscribed British settlements in violation of those treaties. The colonists bitterly resented the royal proclamation and advanced the argument that the tribes should be able to sell their lands to whomever they chose, thus adding another timber to the fire that would grow into the conflagration known as the Revolutionary War.

Even prior to the onset of hostilities and throughout the struggle for independence, the colonies sought to address the causes of Indian resentment and to centralize Indian affairs. One of the first acts of the Second Continental Congress was a July 12, 1775, resolution that declared that "securing and preserving the friendship of the Indian Nations, appears to be a subject of the utmost moment to these colonies." It continued by asserting that "there is too much reason to apprehend that Administration will spare no pains to excite the several Nations of Indians to take up arms against these colonies; and that it becomes us to be very active and vigilant in exerting every prudent means to strengthen and confirm the friendly disposition towards

{ *Chapter 2* }

these colonies, which has long prevailed among the northern tribes, and which has been lately manifested by some of those to the southward." Noting that "as the Indians depend on the Colonists for arms, ammunition, and clothing, which are become necessary to their subsistence," the resolution provided "that Commissioners be appointed by this Congress, to superintend Indian affairs in behalf of their colonies" and established northern, middle, and southern departments of Indian affairs "to treat with the Indians in their respective departments, in the name, and on behalf of the united colonies, in order to preserve peace and friendship with the said Indians, and to prevent their taking any part in the present commotions." Evidence of how important these departments were is that prominent founders such as Benjamin Franklin and James Wilson of Pennsylvania were elected commissioners of the middle department.

To secure and preserve the friendship of the Indian nations, the Continental Congress entered into treaties with them. The initial treaties were not written but were rather formal diplomatic ceremonies involving the exchange of presents and solemn promises of friendship. The first written treaty between the United States and an Indian tribe was a 1778 treaty of alliance with the Delaware Indians, in which the parties agreed to an end of hostilities, pledged mutual assistance in just wars, and formalized certain trade protocols. In it, the United States guaranteed "to the aforesaid nation of Delawares, and their heirs, all their territorial rights, in the fullest and most ample manner, as it hath been bound by former treaties."

The committee of the Second Continental Congress that drafted the Articles of Confederation was also concerned with Indian affairs. It proposed in a July 12, 1776, draft that "the United States assembled" have "the sole and exclusive right of . . . Regulating the Indian trade, and managing all Affairs with the Indians." The July 26 debate on this proposal is worthy of attention.

John Rutledge and Thomas Lynch of South Carolina opposed giving the power of regulating the trade and managing all affairs of the Indians to the United States assembled, because "the trade is profitable." In response, James Wilson of Pennsylvania declared "We have no right over the Indians, whether within or without the real or pretended limits of any Colony. They will not allow themselves to be classed according to the bounds of Colonies. Grants made three thousand miles to the eastward, have no validity with the Indians." George Walton of Georgia joined the debate: "The Indian trade is of no essential service to any Colony. It must be a monopoly. If it is free, it produces jealousies and animosities and wars. [South] Carolina, very passionately, considers this trade as contributing to her grandeur and dignity. There is a great difference between South Carolina and Georgia. [South] Carolina is in no danger from the Indians at present. Georgia is a frontier and barrier to Carolina. Georgia must be overrun and extirpated before Carolina can be hurt. Georgia is not equal to the expense of giving the donations to the Indians, which will be necessary to keep them at peace. The emoluments of the trade are not a compensation for the expense of donations." Rutledge responded: "[South] Carolina has been run to an amazing expense to defend themselves against Indians. . . . We have now as many men on the frontiers, as in Charleston. We have forts in the Indian countries. We are connected with them by treaties." Lynch offered a compromise: "Congress may regulate the trade, if they will indemnify [South] Carolina against the expense of keeping peace with the Indians, or defending us against them." Wilson then reentered the debate: "No lasting peace will be [made] with the Indians, unless made by some one body. No power ought to treat with the Indians, but the United States. Indians know the striking benefits of confederation; they have an example of it in the union of the Six Nations. The idea of the union of the Colonies struck them forcibly last year. None should trade with Indians without a license from Congress."

These opposing views led to the final version of what became Article IX of the Articles which conferred to "the United States in Congress assembled the sole and exclusive right and power of . . . regulating the trade and managing all affairs with the Indians, not members of any of the States, provided that the legislative right of any State within its own limits be not infringed or violated." This language, of course, completely muddled the issue. While it seemed to reserve the power of the States over Indians who were "members of any of the States," it did not define who those "members" were. And, while it protected the States' "legislative rights within [their] own limits," it did not define the scope of those rights. As James Madison would observe in *Federalist* No. 42, this provision was "obscure and contradictory."

What description of Indians are to be deemed members of a State, is not yet settled, and has been a question of frequent perplexity and contention in the federal councils. And how the trade with Indians, though not members of a State, yet residing within its legislative jurisdiction, can be regulated by an external authority, without so far intruding on the internal rights of legislation, is absolutely incomprehensible. This is not the only case in which the articles of Confederation have inconsiderately endeavored to accomplish impossibilities; to reconcile a partial sovereignty in the Union, with complete sovereignty in the States; to subvert a mathematical axiom, by taking away a part, and letting the whole remain.

This confusion was not removed until 1789 when the U.S. Constitution, which eliminated all reference to state power with respect to Indian tribes, was ratified.

The Articles of Confederation were not implemented until March 1, 1781, when Maryland finally agreed to ratify them; the articles could not go into effect until ratified by all thirteen states, and Maryland refused to ratify until Virginia and New York agreed to cede their western lands to the United States. Once ratified and in effect, the United States began to enter into a series of nine treaties with Indian tribes. Among the first was the October 22, 1784, treaty with the hostile tribes of the Six Nations of the Iroquois—the Cayuga, Seneca, Mohawk, Oneida, Tuscarora, and Onondaga tribes. During the Revolutionary War, most Indian tribes allied with the English, believing the Royal Proclamation of 1763 would protect their lands from settlement by the colonists. This was true of the Six Nations. The Treaty of Paris of 1783 ending the war gave the United States control of over their lands. The Articles of Confederation authorized Congress to make treaties with Indian nations, and on October 22, 1784, U.S. commissioners concluded a treaty between the United States and the Six Nations that received these tribes "into their protection"—language that has been subsequently cited as a source of the U.S. government's obligation to treat Indian tribes as dependent nations.

On January 21, 1785, the United States concluded a treaty with the Wyandotte, Delaware, Chippewa, and Ottawa Nations that established the boundaries between the United States and these tribes, declared that the "said Indian nations do acknowledge themselves and all their tribes to be under the protection of the United States and of no other sovereign whatsoever," and provided that "if any citizen of the United States, or other person not being an Indian, shall attempt to settle on any of the lands allotted to the . . . nations in this treaty . . . , such person shall forfeit the protection of the United States, and the Indians may punish him as they please" — a provision repeated in many subsequent treaties.

And then in the Treaties at Hopewell, South Carolina, the United States agreed to bury the hatchet forever. The exact words of the concluding provisions of the Treaties with the Cherokees on November 28, 1785, the Choctaw Nation on January 3, 1786, and the Chickasaw Nation on January 10, 1786 — were: "The hatchet shall be forever buried, and the peace given by the United States, and friendship re-established between the said states on the one part, and the [three tribes] on the other, shall be universal; and the contracting parties shall use their utmost endeavors to maintain the peace given as aforesaid, and friendship re-established."

On August 7, 1786, the Congress of the Confederation adopted "An Ordinance for the Regulation of Indian Affairs." It divided the Indian department into two districts: a northern district covering the territory north of the Ohio River and west of the Hudson River, and a southern district covering all territory south of the Ohio River. Each district was to be headed by superintendents "who shall regularly correspond with the Secretary at War, through whom all communications respecting the Indian department, shall be made to Congress; and the superintendents are hereby directed to obey all instructions, which they shall, from time to time, receive from the said Secretary at War. And whenever they shall have reason to suspect any tribe or tribes of Indians, of hostile intentions, they shall communicate the same to the executive of the State or States, whose territories are subject to the effect of such hostilities." It also ordained that "none but citizens of the United States, shall be suffered to reside among the Indian nations, or be allowed to trade with any nation of Indians, within the territory of the United States. That no person, citizen or other, under the penalty of five hundred dollars, shall reside among or trade with any Indian or Indian nation, within the territory of the

United States, without a license for that purpose first obtained from the Superintendent of the district."

The above-mentioned treaties as well as others, along with Congress's Ordinance of August 7, 1786, outraged a number of the states. Pointing to the ambiguous language in Article IX of the Articles of Confederation, North Carolina, Georgia, and New York declared that what federal representatives were agreeing to and what Congress had adopted violated their state sovereignty. Nonetheless, while some states vehemently protested Congress's power to treat with tribes located completely within their boundaries, even they agreed concerning Congress's power to establish Indian policy in the territory of the United States. Perhaps the most noteworthy indication of their affirmation of Congress's power in this regard is found in the Northwest Ordinance, unanimously adopted by all the states on July 13, 1787, during the midst of the Constitutional Convention. It declared in the second sentence of § 14, Article 3 (immediately after these famous words, "Religion, morality, and knowledge, being necessary to good government and the happiness of mankind, schools and the means of education shall forever be encouraged."), the following:

> The utmost good faith shall always be observed towards the Indians; their lands and property shall never be taken from them without their consent; and, in their property, rights, and liberty, they shall never be invaded or disturbed, unless in just and lawful wars authorized by Congress; but laws founded in justice and humanity, shall from time to time be made for preventing wrongs being done to them, and for preserving peace and friendship with them.

The weakness and insufficiency of the Articles of Confederation to deal with matters domestic and diplomatic (and tribal matters partook of dimensions of both) had become sufficiently obvious to those in the Congress that on February 21, 1787, the delegates passed a resolution calling for a Convention that would meet in Philadelphia beginning on May 14 of that year to "revis[e] the Articles of Confederation and report to Congress and the several legislatures such alterations and provisions therein as shall when agreed to in Congress and confirmed by the states render the federal constitution adequate to the exigencies of Government and the preservation of the Union." A quorum of the states was not present until May 25, when the work of the Convention began in earnest. The delegates quickly concluded that the ends specified by the Confederation Congress (i.e., making the Articles of Confederation "adequate to the exigencies of Government and the preservation of the Union") could not be achieved by the means the Congress authorized (i.e., by revising the articles' provisions), and, so believing that the ends were more important than the means, they embarked on drafting an entirely new Constitution.

As they eventually worked out its many features, the framers designed a Constitution in which the people were proportionally represented in the House of Representatives and the states were equally represented in the Senate. In that regard, the first reference to Indians during the Convention came on the question of representation. It came on June 11 when James Wilson (who during the drafting of the Articles of Confederation had declared: "We have no right over the Indians.") proposed a scheme of proportional representation based on population that excluded "Indians not paying taxes, in each State." Wilson understood that there was a relationship between taxation and representation (remember the revolutionary slogan of "No taxation without representation"), and since many Indians were not taxed by the states, because they were living on Indian land (even though located entirely within a state), they were not to be represented by that state in the new House of Representatives. Wilson's proposal was accepted without debate and became part of Article I, § 2, cl. 3, which excluded from the basis of a state's representation in the House "Indians not taxed"; by accepting this language, his fellow delegates clearly recognized that even though they were within a state's borders, some Indians were not subject to that state's jurisdiction.

The framers also designed a Constitution that granted to Congress in Article I, § 8, cl. 3 the power "to regulate Commerce with foreign Nations, and among the several States, and with the Indian Tribes." The Virginia (or Large States) Plan that served as the first draft of the Constitution included no language for federal authority over Indian affairs. James Madison was the author of the Virginia Plan, and he eventually corrected his oversight on August 18, when he proposed language that would grant to the new federal government the power to "regulate affairs with the Indians as well within as without the United States." (On June 19, he had previously faulted the New Jersey [or Small States] Plan for its failure to "prevent encroachments on the federal authority . . . . By the federal articles, transactions with the Indians appertain to Congress. Yet in several instances, the States have entered into treaties and wars with them." He apparently was unaware that the same criticism could have been launched at the time against his own Virginia Plan.) His August 18 proposal was ultimately incorporated in the Constitution, if in different words. The contrast between the Constitution that was adopted and the Articles of Confederation could not have been clearer. Compared to the ambiguous language of Article IX of the Articles of Confederation, Article I, § 8 conferred an explicit, broad, and exclusive grant of power to the federal government to deal with Indian tribes. And, since its language appears to authorize Congress to regulate trade among various types of sovereigns, it makes clear that tribes possess sovereignty of a nature different than foreign sovereign nations or the states of the union.

The framers also designed a Constitution that in Article II, § 2 granted to the president the "Power, by and with the Advice and Consent of the Senate, to make Treaties, provided two thirds of the Senators present concur." No longer could commissioners of the federal government negotiate and conclude treaties with foreign powers or Indian tribes. The president, or individuals to whom he had delegated his power, had this authority, but subject to ratification by two-thirds of the Senate. The ambiguous role of the states with regard to Indian tribes under the Articles was clarified in the Constitution. Senators, elected by state legislatures and consequently the means by which the interests of the states as states would be represented in the new federal government, would have to ratify treaties with Indian tribes residing within state borders. The role of individual states regarding tribal affairs was no longer ambiguous as it had been under the Articles; rather, the role of states was now collective and critical, and it was spelled out in unambiguous terms.

Finally, the framers drafted a Constitution that in Article III created a Supreme Court and vested it (and such lower courts as the Congress was authorized to ordain and establish) with the judicial power of the United States. It also provided that this judicial power shall "extend to all Cases, in Law and Equity, arising under this Constitution, the Laws of the United States, and Treaties made, or which shall be made, under their authority." The framers, therefore, gave the federal courts jurisdiction over Indian matters that would arise under the laws of the new government as well as under existing and new treaties with the tribes.

With the ratification of the Constitution, the ability of the new federal government to establish Indian policy was clearly established and on immediate display. During the first five weeks of Congress's first session, it passed thirteen statutes, four of which dealt in whole or in part with Indian affairs. On August 7, 1789, it passed legislation establishing the Department of War and authorized the president to assign to it responsibility "relative to Indians affairs" (that responsibility was transferred to the Department of the Interior in 1849). On that same day, it reenacted the Northwest Ordinance of 1787. On August 20, it appropriated $20,000 to defray "the expense of negotiating and treating with the Indian tribes." And on September 11, it set the salary for "the superintendent of Indian affairs in the northern department." In passing these four statutes, Congress used its delegated powers to declare war, govern the territories, and spend money.

On July 22, 1790, Congress exercised for the first time its power to regulate commerce with the Indian tribes. It passed "An Act to regulate trade and intercourse with the Indian tribes." In § 1, it declared "that no person shall be permitted to carry on any trade or intercourse with the Indian tribes without a license for that purpose under the hand and seal of the superintendent of the department, or of such other person as the President of the United States shall appoint for that purpose"; in § 2 it provided for the recall of that license for the "transgress[ion of] any of the regulations or restrictions provided"; in § 3 it authorized the forfeiture of "all the merchandise" of those trading without that license; in § 4, it forbade the "sale of lands made by Indians, or any nation or tribe of Indians within the United States" to any person or state "unless the same shall be made and duly executed at some public treaty, held under the authority of the United States"; and in § 5, it provided for the punishment of non-Indians committing crimes and trespasses against the Indians. Section 5 clearly did not address an issue of commerce or trade, and it therefore deserves to be quoted at length:

If any citizen or inhabitant of the United States, or of either of the territorial districts of the United States, shall go into any town, settlement or territory belonging to any nation or tribe of Indians, and shall there commit any crime upon, or trespass against, the person or property of any peaceable and friendly Indian or Indians, which, if committed within the jurisdiction of any state, or within the jurisdiction of the said districts, against a citizen or white inhabitant thereof, would be punishable by the laws of such state or district, such offender or offenders shall be subject to the same punishment.

The First Congress's belief that the Indian Commerce Clause delegated to it the power to pass such legislation is significant, for it set in motion the first of many federal laws predicated on the assumption that the federal government has plenary power over Indian tribes. This deserves additional comment: the Congress from the outset and the Court from the time of the Marshall Trilogy have both understood the Indian Commerce Clause as granting to the federal government a plenary power in Indian country that they have never understood the Interstate Commerce Clause as having granted to the federal government over commerce "among the several states."

This first Indian Trade and Intercourse Act was subsequently expanded by additional Trade and Intercourse Acts in 1793, 1796, and 1799. All of these acts were temporary and contained language indicating how long they would remain in force. On March 30, 1802, the Seventh Congress enacted the first permanent Trade and Intercourse Act, which declared in § 22 that it "shall be in force" thereafter. It carried forward the policies previously adopted while adding three new ones of interest. Section 6 provided that "if any such citizen, or other person, shall go into any town, settlement or territory belonging to any nation or tribe of Indians, and shall there commit murder, by killing any Indian or Indians, belonging to any nation or tribe of Indians, in amity with the United States, such offender, on being thereof convicted, shall suffer death" — clearly another example of how broadly Congress construed the Indian Commerce Clause. Section 13 provided that "in order to promote civilization among the friendly Indian tribes, and to secure the continuance of their friendship, it shall be lawful for the President of the United States to cause them to be furnished with useful domestic animals, and implements of husbandry, and with goods or money, as he shall judge proper" (up to $15,000 annually). Section 21 authorized the president "to take such measures, from time to time, as to him may appear expedient to prevent or restrain the vending or distributing of spirituous liquors among all or any of the said Indian tribes" — a measure that addressed the shameful way in which alcohol was used as a means of defrauding Indians and of fomenting violence between Indians and whites.

With the ratification of the Constitution, the United States also began entering into and ratifying treaties with the Indian tribes. The first treaty ratified by the Senate was, however, actually negotiated by a commissioner under the Articles of Confederation and before the inauguration of George Washington as the first president on March 4, 1789. Two treaties were negotiated at Fort Harmar by Commissioner Arthur St. Clair and signed on January 9, 1789; one was with the Wyandotte, Delaware, Chippewa, Ottawa, Potawatomi, and Sac Nations, the other was with the Six Nations of the Iroquois. Even though these treaties had not been made by the president, on May 25, 1789, Washington sent them to the Senate, asking the Senate to "concur in their approbation of the said treaties" and suggesting that "it might be proper that the same should be ratified and published." On September 8, the *Senate Executive Journal* reports that the Senate passed a resolution that "the President of the United States be advised to execute and enjoin an observance" of the treaty with the Wyandotte and associated tribes; by contrast, it was altogether silent on the treaty with the Six Nations.

On September 17, President Washington sent a message to the Senate, in which he asked the Senate formally to ratify these treaties:

> It is said to be the general understanding and practice of nations . . . not to consider any treaty negotiated and signed by such officers as final and conclusive until ratified by the sovereign or government from whom they derive their powers. This practice has been adopted by the United States respecting their treaties with European nations, and I am inclined to think it would be advisable to observe it in the conduct of our treaties with the Indians. . . . It strikes me that this point should be well considered and settled, so that our national proceedings, in this respect, may become uniform, and be directed by fixed and stable principles.

Washington also noted that "it would be proper for me to be informed of your sentiments relative to the treaty with the Six Nations . . . and I therefore recommend it to your early consideration." On September 22, the Senate passed a resolution advising and consenting to the treaty with the Wyandotte, etc.; however, it postponed ratification of the treaty with the Six Nations because it "may be construed to prejudice the claims of the States of Massachusetts and New York." That treaty was never ratified, and the Senate's role in protecting the interests of the states as states when it came to Indian affairs was on full display from the very beginning.

The first treaty negotiated under the new Constitution was entitled "A Treaty of Peace and Friendship made and concluded between the President of the United States of America, on the Part and Behalf of the said States, and the undersigned Kings, Chiefs, and Warriors of the Creek Nation of Indians, on the Part and Behalf of the said Nation." It announced a "perpetual peace and friendship between all the citizens of the United States of America, and all the individuals, towns and tribes of the Upper, Middle and Lower Creeks and Seminoles composing the Creek nation of Indians." It declared "the Creek nation to be under the protection of the United States of America, and of no other sovereign whosoever" and stipulated that "the said Creek nation will not hold any treaty with an individual State, or with individuals of any State." It provided for an exchange of prisoners, set and guaranteed the boundaries of the Creek nation, and stated that "if any citizen of the United States, or other person not being an Indian, shall attempt to settle on any of the Creeks lands, such person shall forfeit the protection of the United States, and the Creeks may punish him or not, as they please." It provided for federal punishment of those whites committing crimes against Indians and Indians committing crimes against whites. In an effort to lead the Creek nation "to a greater degree of civilization, and to become herdsmen and cultivators, instead of remaining in a state of hunters," it proclaimed that "the United States will from time to time furnish gratuitously the said nation with useful domestic animals and implements of husbandry." Finally, it proclaimed that "all animosities for past grievances shall henceforth cease; and the contracting parties will carry the foregoing treaty into full execution, with all good faith and sincerity." This treaty was signed on August 7, 1790, ratified by the Senate on August 12 by a vote of 15-4, and proclaimed the next day.

After the ratification of the Creek treaty, the new federal government successfully negotiated a treaty with the Cherokee Nation. Its provisions, similar in many respects to the Creek treaty, were approved on July 2, 1791, and ratified by the Senate on February 7, 1792. In *Worcester v. Georgia* (1832), one of the three cases referred to in the Introduction as part of the Marshall Trilogy and which will be discussed shortly, Chief Justice John Marshall referred to this treaty as "explicitly recognizing the national character of the Cherokees, and their right of self-government; guarantying their lands; assuming the duty of protection, and of course pledging the faith of the United States for that protection."

The U.S. Senate subsequently ratified 374 additional treaties with Indian tribes. Most of these treaties were for land cessions. The United States was required by its own laws to purchase land from the Indians, and they did so using treaties. Treaties were, therefore, used to purchase tribal lands by the federal government in exchange for trade items such as fur, cotton, wheat, and agricultural produce; in some cases, the lands were acquired by offering the Indian tribes other lands located to the west of the borders of the United States. An additional 150 treaties were negotiated that were never ratified. States and citizens also worked out treaty-like agreements with several tribes. (Even the Confederate States of America entered into 12 treaties with Indian nations during the Civil War.) By the early 1870s federally appointed intermediaries had negotiated well over 100 intertribal treaties. Even after Congress officially ended the policy of making treaties with Indian tribes, the federal government negotiated 75 additional agreements that are often called "treaty substitutes" (bilateral agreements negotiated with the tribes in the manner of treaties but then ratified or confirmed by both houses of Congress), the last in 1914.

The official end of treaty making occurred when Congress passed the Appropriations Act of March 3, 1871; in fact, the last treaty with an Indian tribe was concluded with the Nez Percé tribe of Indians in the Territory of Washington on August 13, 1868, ratified by the Senate on February 16, 1869, and proclaimed on February 24 of the same year.

The Appropriations Act contained the following language: "Hereafter no Indian nation or tribe within the territory of the United States shall be acknowledged or recognized as an independent nation, tribe, or power with whom the United States may contract by treaty." (It also declared that "nothing herein contained shall be construed to invalidate or impair the obligation of any treaty heretofore lawfully made and ratified with any such Indian nation or tribe.") This act was passed as a result of the growing resentment by the members of the House of Representatives of the power that the Senate wielded over Indian relations because of its constitutional power to ratify treaties. Most treaties with Indian tribes carried with them financial obligations for which the House of Representatives, obligated by Article I, § 7 of the Constitution to initiate all money bills, was forced to pay. The House wanted to participate in Indian affairs as an equal partner, not as a subordinate supplier of funds. After years of pressure by the House, the Senate capitulated.

However, the end of treaty making has had little legal effect, as the federal government has continued to deal with tribes in much the same manner but now through executive agreements enacted by Congress into statutes. Justice William Brennan made this very clear for a seven-member majority of the Supreme Court in *Antoine v. Washington* (1975). The end of treaty making, he declared,

> meant no more . . . than that after 1871 relations with Indians would be governed by Acts of Congress and not by treaty. The change in no way affected Congress' plenary powers to *legislate* on problems of Indians, including legislating the ratification of contracts of the Executive Branch with Indian tribes. . . . Once ratified by Act of Congress, the provisions of the agreements become law, and like treaties, the supreme law of the land.

Consistent with the constitutional design, the legislative and executive branches were principally responsible for the shaping of U.S. policy toward the Indian tribes. But the Supreme Court also played a role, and in fact a pivotal one. In the late 1820s and early 1830s, Chief Justice John Marshall handed down on behalf of the Supreme Court three decisions that have come to be known as the Marshall Trilogy—

three decisions that continue to define the nature and extent of tribal sovereignty and the relation of the tribes to the federal government and the states. They were *Johnson v. McIntosh* (1823), *Cherokee Nation v. Georgia* (1831), and *Worcester v. Georgia* (1832).

In *Johnson v. McIntosh*, the Court addressed the question of which of two competing parties held valid title to a parcel of land in the Northwest Territory. As a result of a land sale on July 5, 1773, from the Illinois Indians and a land sale on October 18, 1775, from the Piankeshaw Indians, Thomas Johnson (who was the first governor of the State of Maryland and served briefly on the U.S. Supreme Court from 1791 to 1792) acquired title to land in what would later become the state of Illinois. Upon his death in 1819, the property, of which he had never taken physical possession, was inherited by his son Joshua and grandson Thomas Graham.

In 1776, the colony of Virginia, which under the terms of its royal charter of 1609 was given dominion over the lands in question by King James I, declared its independence from Great Britain. In 1783, Virginia completed the transfer of ownership of these lands to the United States — the condition of Maryland had imposed before it would agree to make unanimous the states' ratification of the Articles of Confederation. In 1818, the United States sold these lands to William McIntosh, who took immediate possession of them.

McIntosh was a Scottish immigrant who fought for the British during the Revolutionary War and who, once the war was over, operated in the Illinois country as a fur trader for a concern based in Detroit; financially ambitious, he amassed a fortune speculating in land. He fought politically the future president of the United States, William Henry Harrison, who was at the time the governor of the territory, because of Harrison's impositions of higher taxes on real estate; for his efforts, McIntosh was denounced by Harrison's chief adjutant, Benjamin Parke, later to become Indiana's first federal judge, as "an arrant knave, a profligate villain, a dastardly cheat, a perfidious rascal, an impertinent puppy, an absolute liar and a mean cowardly person."

Upon inheriting these lands, Johnson's heirs also sought to take possession of them, only to find them occupied by McIntosh, whereupon the Johnson heirs brought an action of ejectment (i.e., an action for the recovery of the possession of land) in the federal district court for Illinois. The district court ruled for McIntosh, based on his purchase of the land from the United States. The case reached the U.S. Supreme Court on a writ of error.

In his opinion for a unanimous Court, Chief Justice Marshall also held for McIntosh. He held that, because of the principles of discovery and conquest, Indian tribes had no power to grant lands to anyone other than the federal government.

He began by noting that when North America was discovered, European powers competed for acquisition of its lands, and to "avoid conflicting settlements, and consequent war with each other," they established a "principle, which all should acknowledge as the law by which the right of acquisition, which they all asserted, should be regulated as between themselves." That principle was discovery; discovery, he argued, "gave title to the government by whose subjects, or by whose authority, it was made," and it conferred on that government "the sole right of acquiring the soil from the natives, and establishing settlements upon it."

While the principle of discovery helped to prevent "consequent wars" among the nations of Europe, it did not address the relation of the discoverer to the original inhabitants of North America. Those relations, Marshall insisted, were determined by the discoverer. And, in the establishment of these relations, the discoverer "necessarily" and "to a considerable extent" impaired "the rights of the original inhabitants." While the tribes remained "the rightful occupants of the soil, with a legal as well as just claim to retain possession of it, and to use it according to their own discretion," their rights to "complete sovereignty, as independent nations, were necessarily diminished, and their power to dispose of the soil at their own will, to whomsoever they pleased, was denied by the original fundamental principle, that discovery gave exclusive title to those who made it."

The United States, Marshall continued, had "unequivocally acceded to that great and broad rule." It had maintained, as all other nations had maintained, "that discovery gave an exclusive right to extinguish the Indian title of occupancy, either by purchase or by conquest; and gave also a right to such a degree of sovereignty, as the circumstances of the people would allow them to exercise."

Marshall refused to debate the justice of this principle. "Whether agriculturists, merchants, and manufacturers, have a right, on abstract principles, to expel hunters from the territory they possess, or to contract their limits" were questions he would not address. "Conquest gives a title which the Courts of the conqueror cannot deny, whatever the private and speculative opinions of individuals may be, respecting the original justice of the claim which has been successfully asserted."

Marshall noted that the British government had asserted a title to all the lands occupied by tribes within the British colonies, "limited sovereignty" over them, and the "exclusive right of extinguishing the title which occupancy gave to them." These rights had been "maintained and established as far west as the river Mississippi, by the sword." As a result of independence, these rights had "passed to the United States," and, he insisted, "it is not for the Courts of this country to question the validity of this title, or to sustain one which is incompatible with it."

Marshall conceded that "the pretension of converting the discovery of an inhabited country into conquest" was "extravagant." But, he insisted, "if the principle has been asserted in the first instance, and afterwards sustained; if a country has been acquired and held under it; if the property of the great mass of the community originates in it, it becomes the law of the land, and cannot be questioned." And, Marshall continued, neither could its "concomitant principle" that the tribal members are "merely" occupants of the land who are "incapable of transferring the absolute title to others." (As Professor David Wilkins points out in *American Indian Sovereignty and the U.S. Supreme Court*, because the tribes in question were not parties to the suit, they were unable to establish that they had in fact received valid title to these lands from the British Government prior to independence or that other pre-revolutionary land transactions between tribes and white settlers had been recognized as valid by the federal government.)

Marshall was clearly uncomfortable with the implications of his argument, appreciating that this restriction of the tribes "may be opposed to natural right, and to the usages of civilized nations." Yet, because this restriction appeared to have been "indispensable to that system under which the country has been settled," the Court could not "reject" it.

Johnson v. McIntosh was a serious assault on tribal sovereignty by limiting the ability of tribes to dispose of their lands (although prominent scholars argue that its pernicious effects were limited by the Supreme Court's 1835 decision in *Mitchel v. United States*—see the Bibliographic Essay in the book's back matter), but Marshall's opinions in the two *Cherokee Nation* cases acknowledged the sovereign status of the tribes. In *Cherokee Nation v. Georgia* (1831), the Cherokee Nation of Indians, claiming the status of a foreign state, brought suit in the U.S. Supreme Court, under the Court's original jurisdiction, against the State of Georgia. It did so under those provisions of Article III, § 2 of the Constitution giving the Court jurisdiction in cases and controversies in which a state of the United States or the citizens thereof, and a foreign state, citizens, or subjects thereof, are parties and original jurisdiction in all cases in which a state shall be a party. The Cherokee Nation sought an injunction to prevent the execution of various Georgia laws that sought to assert control over Cherokee lands within the state that were protected by the 1790 U.S. treaty with the Cherokees discussed above. The issue for the Court was whether the Cherokee Nation was a foreign state in the sense in which that term was used in the Constitution (and, therefore, whether the Court had jurisdiction to hear the case). Marshall concluded that it was not.

He noted that the relation of the Indians to the United States "is perhaps unlike that of any other two people in existence" and "is marked by peculiar and cardinal distinctions which exist nowhere else." Foreign nations, he observed, do not owe a "common allegiance to each other." But, he continued, consider the tribes. Their territory is "part of the United States," and "in any attempt at intercourse between Indians and foreign nations, they are considered as within the jurisdictional limits of the United States." Tribes "acknowledge themselves in their treaties to be under the protection of the United States," and the "right to the lands they occupy" can be "extinguished by a voluntary cession to our government." They could not, therefore, be "denominated foreign nations." Rather, he insisted, they were "more correctly . . . denominated domestic dependent nations." They occupied land to which the United States asserts "a title independent of their will." They are, he declared, in "a state of pupilage. Their relation to the United States resembles that of a ward to his guardian."

After all, he continued, the tribes look to the United States "for protection; rely upon its kindness and its power; appeal to it for relief to their wants; and address the president as their great father." And, foreign nations consider the tribes as "so completely under the sovereignty and dominion of the United States" that any attempt by them to acquire tribal lands, or to form a political alliances with them would be regarded as an "invasion" of U.S. territory and a clear "act of hostility."

Marshall found that his conclusion that tribes are not foreign nations – and therefore not authorized to pursue "an action in the courts of the United States" – was strengthened by the text of Article I, § 8 of the Constitution, which granted to Congress the power to "regulate commerce with foreign nations, and among the several states, and with the Indian tribes." The Commerce Clause "clearly contradistinguished" the tribes from both foreign nations and the several states composing the union. They were "designated by a distinct appellation." The Constitutional Convention, he concluded, "considered them as entirely distinct."

In *Worcester v. Georgia* (1832), however, Marshall made it clear that, while the Tribe's sovereignty was inevitably limited by its "domestic dependent" status, it was certainly not effaced. Samuel A. Worcester was a citizen of Vermont and a Congregationalist missionary to the Cherokee Nation. He was convicted in Gwinnett County (Georgia) Superior Court and sentenced to four years of hard labor for violating an 1830 Georgia statute that prohibited "white persons" from "residing within the limits of the Cherokee nation without a license" and "without having taken the oath to support and defend the constitution and laws of the state of Georgia." The court rejected Worcester's argument that the Georgia statute was unconstitutional and void because the Constitution gave the power to establish and regulate trade and intercourse with the Indians tribes exclusively to the government of the United States and because this power had been exercised by treaties and by acts of Congress that were directly applicable to the Cherokees. His case was then brought before the U.S. Supreme Court on a writ of error. For a unanimous Court, Marshall found Georgia's statute to be void "as being repugnant to the Constitution, treaties, and laws of the United States" and ordered that Worcester's conviction "to be reversed and annulled."

Marshall described Georgia's statute as seizing the whole of Cherokee country, parceling it out among the neighboring counties of the state, extending its criminal code over the Cherokees' land, abolishing its institutions and its laws, and therefore annihilating its political existence. This, he argued, was contrary to congressional policy, and therefore to the Constitution. Congress had passed numerous acts to regulate trade and intercourse with the tribes (they were discussed above), treated with them as nations (also discussed above), respected their rights, and manifested a firm purpose to afford the protection that the treaties stipulated. For Marshall, all of these acts "manifestly consider[ed] the several Indian nations as distinct political communities, having territorial boundaries, within which their authority is exclusive, and having a right to all the lands within those boundaries, which is not only acknowledged, but guaranteed by the United States." The laws and treaties of the United States, therefore, contemplated that Indian territory was "completely separated from that of the states" and provided that "all intercourse with them shall be carried on exclusively by the government of the union."

Marshall argued that "a weaker power," according to the "settled doctrine of the law of nations," does not "surrender its independence — its right to self-government, by associating with a stronger, and taking its protection." In order "to provide for its safety," it "may place itself under the protection of one more powerful, without stripping itself of the right of government, and ceasing to be a state." This was a critical point in his argument: Marshall denied that tribal sovereignty was diminished when tribes put themselves under the protection of the United States — the treaty language in question imposed a duty on the federal government, not a limitation of the power of the tribes.

With all of that said, Marshall then powerfully asserted that the Cherokee Nation was "a distinct community occupying its own territory, with boundaries accurately described, in which the laws of Georgia can have no force, and which the citizens of Georgia have no right to enter, but with the assent of the Cherokees themselves, or in conformity with treaties, and with the acts of Congress." He concluded with equal power and clarity: "The whole intercourse between the United States and this nation, is, by our Constitution and laws, vested in the government of the United States."

Equally important, in the long run, was a statement in a concurring opinion by Justice John McLean. He wrote that "the language used in treaties with the Indians should never be construed to their prejudice" and emphasized that "how the words of the treaty were understood by this unlettered people, rather than their critical meaning, should form the rule of construction." McLean made much more explicit what Marshall had hinted at in his majority opinion when he wrote: "There is the more reason for supposing that the Cherokee chiefs were not very critical judges of the language, from the fact that every one makes his mark; no chief was capable of signing his name. It is probable the treaty was interpreted to them."

In brief, the Marshall Trilogy established the position that tribes are nations whose independence is limited in only three essentials: the ability to convey land (although, see *Mitchel v. United States*, mentioned above), deal with foreign powers, and engage in external commerce apart from that authorized by Congress. For all internal purposes, however, the tribes are sovereign and free from state intrusion on that sovereignty—unless Congress explicitly acts to grant the states this power. The consequences of these three decisions on the future shaping of federal Indian law and policy are explored in the next chapter.

CHAPTER 3

What the Marshall Trilogy
Has Wrought
Unique Canons of Construction and
a National Debate over Tribal
Assimilation v. Self-Determination

This chapter explores the two major consequences of the Marshall Trilogy, both of which invariably figured in the Court's decision in *Cabazon*. The first consequence, based on the tribes' status as "domestic dependent nations" and therefore on what the Supreme Court in *County of Oneida v. Oneida Indian Nation* (1985) called "the unique trust relationship between the United States and the Indians," is the development of a distinctive set of canons of construction for federal Indian law.

The second consequence was well over a century of vacillating federal policy towards the tribes. As a trustee, the federal government is obliged to act in the best interests of the tribes. But, what does it mean to act in their best interests? From the early 1850s to the late 1960s, the branches of the federal government have vibrated between two polar opposites: during some periods of American history, they have acted in the belief that it is in the best interests of the tribes that their members should be assimilated into American society and that they should be subject to the same laws as all other citizens, and during other periods — including the current period that began in the late 1960s, they have acted in the belief that it is in the best interests of the tribes and their members that they be preserved and that the federal government promote tribal self-determination and self-government.

The development of a distinctive set of canons of construction for federal Indian law is a clear result of the Marshall Trilogy. The federal courts in general and the U.S. Supreme Court in particular have developed over time canons of construction to help them ascertain what the drafters of a statute — the Congress or a state legislature — or the signatories to a treaty—the United States and a foreign nation or an Indian tribe—meant by ambiguous language they may have used in the statute or treaty. The canons apply only when language is ambiguous, i.e., when reasonably well-informed persons could understand the language in either of two or more senses; under the plain-meaning rule, if there is no question as to the meaning of the language in question, there is no need to apply the canons.

If language in a statute or treaty is found to be ambiguous, courts then apply a variety of canons or rules to help determine the meaning of the language in question. When, for example, the language of a statute is ambiguous, one canon would require courts to ascertain what was the intent of the legislature when it enacted the statute by exploring the legislative history of prior enactments on a similar subject, the proceedings surrounding the passage of the statute (including floor debates and committee reports), and interpretations of the law by administrative agencies.

There are other canons as well that aid in the interpretation of an ambiguous statute that are unrelated to the activities preceding its passage. They help courts to analyze the internal structure of the text and the conventional meanings of the terms used in the statute. Many of these are expressed in well-known Latin phrases or maxims. One is *ejusdem generis* (of the same kind, class, or nature); the phrase means that when general words follow specific words in a statute in which several items have been enumerated, the general words are construed to embrace only objects similar in nature to the objects enumerated by the preceding specific words of the statute. Thus, if a statute authorized a governmental agency to sell "gravel, sand, earth or other material," "other material" would include materials of the same general type and not include, for example, commercial timber. Another canon of statutory construction is *expressio unius est exclusio alterius*, a phrase that means that whatever is omitted is understood to be excluded. For example, if a statute provides for a specific sanction for noncompliance with its provisions, other sanctions are excluded and cannot be applied. This canon has wide application and has been used by courts to interpret constitutions, treaties, wills, and contracts as well as statutes. Still another canon is *noscitur a sociis*, a phrase that means that a word is known by the company it keeps. The Supreme Court employed this canon in *District of Columbia v. Heller* (2008) when it concluded that the "right of the people to keep and bear arms" in the Second Amendment is an individual right, just as are "the right of the people . . . to petition the Government for a redress of grievances" in the First Amendment and "the right of the people to be secure . . . against unreasonable searches and seizures" in the Fourth Amendment.

While these canons generally apply to other fields of law, the Supreme Court has often declared, as in *Montana v. Blackfeet Tribe* (1985), that "they do not have their usual force in cases involving Indian law." The canons of construction that have developed for federal Indian law require that treaties, treaty substitutes, statutes, and executive orders are to be liberally construed in favor of the Indians, that all ambiguities are to be resolved in their favor, and that tribal property rights and sovereignty are to be preserved unless Congress's intent to the contrary is clear and unambiguous. In addition, treaties and treaty substitutes are to be construed as the Indians would have understood them.

These canons were first developed in the context of treaty interpretation. Beginning with the treaties that formed the foundation of the two *Cherokee Nation* cases, the Supreme Court read them broadly in favor of the tribes; resolved ambiguous expressions in favor of the tribes; interpreted treaties as the Indians would have understood the treaty and the negotiations; and considered the history and circumstances behind the treaty in question. The canons were developed because the tribes were regarded, if not actually at least metaphorically, thanks to Chief Justice Marshall's language in *Cherokee Nation v. Georgia*, as wards of the federal government, their guardian; as the third branch of that federal government, the Court had to act in the tribes' best interests. Additionally, the Court recognized the manner in which treaties were negotiated with tribes — they were initiated by the United States and drafted by the United States, not the tribes, and they were written and explained in English, a language very few Indians spoke and none could read, meaning that the tribes had to rely on the representations and promises of the federal representatives. The canons of construction thus arose from the disadvantaged bargaining position that Indians often occupied during treaty negotiations. As a result, as the Supreme Court declared in *United States v. Winans* (1905), "We have said we will construe a treaty with the Indians as 'that unlettered people' understood it, and 'as justice and reason demand, in all cases where power is exerted by the strong over those to whom they owe care and protection.' "

Over time, the Supreme Court in a series of cases consistently extended these canons beyond treaties to treaty substitutes, e.g., *Winters v. United States* (1908); statutes, e.g., *County of Yakima v. Confederated Tribes and Bands of the Yakima Indian Nation* (1992); and executive orders, e.g., *Arizona v. California* (1963). It has determined that federal legislation, orders, and regulations relating to Indians are to be given a liberal construction, and doubtful expressions are to be resolved in favor of the interests of the tribes whose members resemble wards of the nation who are dependent wholly on its protection and good faith. Courts as well as all federal agencies are to follow the general rule that federal statutes passed for the benefit of Indians are to be liberally construed.

While the Supreme Court will typically employ these canons of construction, there are several qualifications that need to be noted. To begin with, as the Court made clear in *Northern Cheyenne Tribe v. Hollowbreast* (1976), it will not apply these canons if the contesting parties are an Indian tribe and a class of individuals consisting primarily of tribal members. Additionally, the Court has announced in a series of opinions that there are three categories of federal law where the canons do not presumptively apply; these include unexpressed exceptions from federal taxation, *Chickasaw Nation v. United States* (2001); most federal criminal laws, *United States v. Dion* (1986); and the reach of the Federal Power Act, *Federal Power Commission v. Tuscarora Indian Nation* (1960). Finally, these canons are essentially rules of interpretation that the Court is free to apply or ignore – they have been described by Professor Philip P. Frickey in his famous article in the *Harvard Law Review*, "Marshalling Past and Present: Colonialism, Constitutionalism, and Interpretation in Federal Indian Law," as nothing more than "quasi-constitutional" rules that the Court can recognize or reject at its discretion. While the Supreme Court faithfully employed these canons in the *Cabazon Band* case, it has not always done so. A recent example is *Carcieri v. Salazar* (2009), in which the Supreme Court, without explanation, departed from the canons. At issue in this case was the language in the Indian Reorganization Act (IRA), enacted in 1934, authorizing the Secretary of Interior to acquire land and hold it in trust "for the purpose of providing land for Indians," and defining "Indians" to "include all persons of Indian descent who are members of any recognized tribe now under Federal jurisdiction." In a 6-3 decision, the Court defined the ambiguous word "now" narrowly and held it applied only to tribes that were under federal jurisdiction in 1934; it refused to define "now" liberally and in the best interests of the tribe in question by holding that it also meant tribes currently under federal jurisdiction. This prompted Justice Stevens to complain in his dissent that the majority had engaged in "a cramped reading of the statute" and had ignored the "principle deeply rooted in [our] Indian jurisprudence" that " 'statutes are to be construed liberally in favor of the Indians.' "

The first consequence of the Marshall Trilogy has been, therefore, the distinctive canons of construction of federal Indian law. A second consequence, equally profound, has been a continually vacillating federal policy toward the tribes. Marshall declared for the Court that the tribes were "domestic dependent nations" whose relationship to the federal government resembled that of a ward to its guardian. Marshall, therefore, held the federal government, as a guardian (and hence a trustee) of the tribes, to a very high standard: it was to exercise its powers in the best interests of the tribes. While Marshall had spelled out the federal government's duties toward the tribes, he did not specify (and as a member of the Supreme Court, he should not have specified) what those duties entailed, i.e., what was in fact in the tribes' best interests. That determination was left to the popular branches — to the president and Senate during the period when the federal government was still treating with the tribes and to the president and the Congress after 1871. Through the years, the popular branches have been of two minds on the question of what is in the best interests of the tribes and their members: Both public opinion and legislative action have swung back and forth between termination of the tribes and the assimilation of their members into American society on the one hand and tribal self-governance and self-determination on the other.

Marshall's insistence that, as a trustee, the federal government is obliged to act in the best interests of the tribes was not a notion that was immediately embraced. It slowly took root but only after the Jackson Administration's policy of "Indian removal" and the extreme hardships experienced by the Five Civilized Tribes – the Cherokees, Choctaws, Creeks, Chickasaws, and Seminoles – as they were forced to travel the Trail of Tears from the Southeast to what is now Oklahoma. However, by about the middle of the nineteenth century, attitudes were starting to change. One bit of evidence: in 1849, the Bureau of Indian Affairs was moved from the War Department – where tribal matters had been addressed since 1789 – to the Department of the Interior.

The period from roughly 1850 to the early 1880s marked the end of the era of "Indian removal" and the creation of the reservation system. The policy of "Indian removal" was causing a problem on the frontier. White settlers were moving westward and occupying the lands to which the tribes had been removed. Commissioner of Indian Affairs George M. Manypenny, one of the architects of the removal program, therefore recommended a policy of restricting tribes to specified reservations. As he declared in his annual report of the Commissioner of Indian Affairs to the Senate in 1854, the federal government must pursue a policy that "restrict[s] the limits of all the Indian tribes upon our frontiers, and cause[s] them to be settled in fixed and permanent localities, thereafter not to be disturbed." This policy was embraced by the federal government and was pursued through treaties in which tribes, in return for subsistence, livestock, and schooling in the mechanical and agricultural arts, ceded much of the land they occupied, often based on earlier treaties, to the United States while reserving for themselves a much smaller portion (hence the term "reservation").

Reservations were originally intended by the federal government to protect the tribes from being engulfed by the stream of white settlers and to keep the peace between Indians and non-Indians. They were the federal government's idea of what was in the best interests of its wards. They represented a move toward tribal self-determination. So, too, was the Supreme Court's decision in *The Kansas Indians* (1866), which powerfully affirmed the canons of construction of federal Indian law and Chief Justice Marshall's opinion in *Worcester v. Georgia*. The question in this case was whether the State of Kansas had the power to tax the lands held severally by individual Indians of the Shawnee, Wea, and Miami tribes and to seize the lands for nonpayment of those taxes. The Court unequivocally said "no." Justice David Davis for a unanimous Court declared that if the tribal governments of the tribes remained intact and were recognized by the federal government, "then they are 'a people distinct from others,' and to be governed exclusively by the government of the Union." The following passage captures the logic of Justice Davis's opinion.

> While the general government has a superintending care over their interests, and continues to treat with them as a nation, the State of Kansas is stopped from denying their title to [the lands in question]. She accepted this status when she accepted the act admitting her into the Union. Conferring rights and privileges on these Indians cannot affect their situation, which can only be changed by treaty stipulation, or a voluntary abandonment of their tribal organization. As long as the United States recognizes their national character they are under the protection of treaties and the laws of Congress, and their property is withdrawn from the operation of state laws.

In truth, however, during the period that the reservation system was being created, the federal government's commitment to tribal self-determination was considerably attenuated. To begin with, in keeping with the idea of acting in the tribes' best interests, the federal government also came to view reservations as a means of "civilizing" the Indians. By 1858, it was adopting policies that encouraged tribal members on reservations to become Christians, educated in western ways, and agriculturalists — in short, to become assimilated into American life.

During this same thirty-year period, other forces kept the federal government's commitment to tribal self-determination in check. One was the Civil War. Armies of both the Union and the Confederacy claimed Indian lands of strategic military importance, paying little heed to past treaty language. The southern states had generally opposed easy settlement of the West because they feared that as those territories grew in population, they would eventually enter the Union as free states; however, when they attempted to secede and no longer sent representatives to Congress, the northern states were able in 1862 to pass the Homestead Act, opening vast areas in the West to white settlement. Finally, the Confederacy, eager for recognition and alliances, entered into treaties with the Five Civilized Nations, promising to protect their lands and granting them political and financial concessions they had been unable to secure from the United States. This in turn prompted the Congress in July 1862 to authorize President Lincoln to abrogate all treaties with tribes in actual hostility with the United States. When the Confederacy surrendered, the Five Civilized Tribes paid a high price: in treaties negotiated in 1866, they surrendered vast portions of their territories, opened their land to railroad access, and granted the federal government considerable control over their tribal governments.

Finally, it is also during this period that the process of formally entering into treaties with tribes was ended. Congress passed language in an 1871 appropriations act that provided that no tribe thereafter was acknowledged or recognized as an independent nation with which the United States could make treaties. As a result, federal Indian law thereafter has depended entirely on what the Congress has passed, the president has signed, and the courts have construed; it does not depend at all on what tribes have agreed to as a result of formal treaty negotiations. (It must be noted, however, that the same appropriations act also stated that the federal government's obligations to the tribes as specified in all Indian treaties then in effect remained valid and unimpaired.) Among the major consequences of the appropriations act was that reservations established after 1871 were created either by statute or, as was the case with the Cabazon and Morongo Bands, by executive order, until Congress ended the practice in 1914.

This first post–"Indian removal" period was followed by a second. From the early 1880s until the early 1930s, the federal government was definitely of the view that what was best for the tribes was allotment of their reservation lands to individual Indians and assimilation.

Assimilation of tribal members into American life did not begin during this second period; it was clearly foreshadowed by federal actions in the previous period undertaken to see to it that the Indians were "civilized," Christianized, provided schooling, and made farmers instead of hunters/warriors. After 1880, however, the pressures to assimilate the Indians greatly intensified. The completion of the transcontinental railroad, marked by the driving of a golden stake at Promontory Summit, Utah, on May 10, 1869; the continued development of steam power; the invention of the steel plow by John Deere and the mechanical harvester by Cyrus McCormick and their subsequent widespread use that made possible and profitable the farming of the great plains; the explosive potential of the Second Industrial Revolution and the development of the oil industry; and the waves of European immigrants seeking a better life in America were but a few of the powerful social forces that led to westward expansion into Indian country. As *Cohen's Handbook of Federal Indian Law* puts it so well: "Landless Americans from older sections, as well as newer [im]migrants temporarily settled, demanded that seemingly vacant Indian lands be put to work. There was no place left to remove the Indian, and there was little sympathy for the preservation of a way of life that left farmlands unturned, coal unmined, and timber uncut." Add to that the reaction of the public to the various Indian wars, including the Battle of Little Bighorn in June 1876 (during the first period), the Apache Wars from 1862 up to 1886, and the Wounded Knee (South Dakota) massacre in late December 1890, and the pressure on federal authorities to terminate the tribes and assimilate their members into American society grew even stronger. Public opinion demanded, and soon thereafter an accommodating Congress agreed, that old hunter/warrior ways could no longer coexist with a new and continental industrial era.

The pressure to have tribal members assimilate into American life had many dimensions. One was the growing belief that the same criminal laws should apply in Indian country as in the rest of the federal territory; this issue first surfaced dramatically as a result of the Supreme Court's decision in *Ex parte Crow Dog* (1883). Crow Dog murdered Spotted Tail on the Sioux Reservation located in the Dakota Territory. After the Brule Sioux band of the Sioux Nation of Indians applied to him its own criminal sanctions, he was prosecuted, convicted, and sentenced to death in the federal district court of the territory. Crow Dog petitioned the Supreme Court for a writ of habeas corpus, arguing that the federal district court had no jurisdiction to try him. He cited Title XXVIII of the Revised Statutes, which was adopted by Congress in 1854 and related to "Indians and the Government of Indian Country." While § 2145 declared that "the general laws of the United States as to the punishment of crimes committed in any place within the sole and exclusive jurisdiction of the United States, except the District of Columbia, shall extend to the Indian country," Section 2146 offered an important qualification: "The preceding section shall not be construed to extend to crimes committed by one

Indian against the person or property of another Indian, nor to any Indian committing any offence in the Indian country who has been punished by the local law of the tribe."

The federal prosecutor countered by arguing that § 2146 had been repealed by the operation and legal effect of an April 29, 1868, treaty with the Sioux Nation. The first article of that treaty stated that "if bad men among the Indians shall commit a wrong or depredation upon the person or property of any one, white, black, or Indian, subject to the authority of the United States and at peace therewith, the Indians herein named solemnly agree that they will, upon proof made to their agent and notice by him, deliver up the wrong-doer to the United States, to be tried and punished according to its laws." And the second article declared that "Congress shall, by appropriate legislation, secure to them [the Sioux Nation] an orderly government; they shall be subject to the laws of the United States, and each individual shall be protected in his rights of property, person, and life."

In a unanimous decision for the Court, Justice Stanley Matthews rejected the prosecutor's argument and issued the writ of habeas corpus. His opinion fully embraced the canons of construction of federal Indian law and the idea of tribal self-determination and self-governance. To begin with, he argued that the first article's mention of "bad men among the Indians" could be equally construed to mean bad men who were in Indian country as opposed to bad Indians. And additionally, he argued that the second article's language that the federal government would secure to the Sioux Nation "an orderly government" and that its members "shall be subject to the laws of the United States . . . could have no such effect as that claimed for them."

Concerning the words, "an orderly government," Matthews concluded that "the pledge to secure to these people, with whom the United States was contracting as a distinct political body, an orderly government . . . necessarily implies . . . self-government, the regulation by themselves of their own domestic affairs, the maintenance of order and peace among their own members by the administration of their own laws and customs." In short, the tribe is to punish crimes by Indians against Indians. And he continued, while the treaty declared the Sioux were to be "subject to the laws of the United States," they were not subject

in the sense of citizens, but, as they had always been, as wards subject to a guardian; not as individual, constituted members of the
political community of the United States, with a voice in the selection of representatives and the framing of the laws, but as a dependent community who were in a state of pupilage, advancing from
[that] condition . . . to that of a people who, through the disci-
pline of labor and by education, it was hoped might become a
self-supporting and self-governed society.

He therefore concluded: "To give to the clauses in the treaty of 1868
. . . effect, so as to uphold the jurisdiction exercised in this case, would
be to reverse in this instance the general policy of the government
towards the Indians, as declared in many statutes and treaties, and recognized in many decisions of this court, from the beginning to the
present time." Applying the canons, he insisted that "to justify such a
departure . . . requires a clear expression of the intention of Congress,
and that we have not been able to find."

Ex parte Crow Dog affirmed the principles of the Marshall Trilogy
and embraced the thinking of the first period, during which tribes on
reservations were encouraged to emerge from a "state of pupilage" and
become "self-supporting and self-governed" societies. But, public
opinion and congressional attitudes had changed. Congress was outraged by the Supreme Court's decision in *Ex parte Crow Dog* and
responded by passing § 9 of the Indian Appropriations Act of 1885 —
otherwise known as the Major Crimes Act of 1885. Among its various
provisions, it gave jurisdiction to the courts of the United States for
seven crimes (murder, manslaughter, rape, assault with intent to kill,
arson, burglary, and larceny) committed on an Indian reservation
within a state of the Union. In particular, it provided that all

Indians committing any of the above crimes against the person or
property of another Indian or other person, within the boundaries
of any State of the United States, and within the limits of any
Indian reservation, shall be subject to the same laws, tried in the
same courts and in the same manner, and subject to the same penal-
ties, as are all other persons committing any of the above crimes
within the exclusive jurisdiction of the United States.

That same year, the secretary of the interior also initiated the creation of the Courts of Indian Offenses under the Bureau of Indian Affairs, which were designed to replace traditional Indian courts hearing lesser offenses.

With the passage of the Major Crimes Act, Congress explicitly held that the serious crimes by Indians against Indians were to be tried exclusively in federal court. The next year, in *United States v. Kagama* (1886), the Court confronted the question of whether Congress had the authority to pass this act. When Kagama of the Hoopa Indian Tribe was indicted for murder on the Hoopa Valley Reservation in Humboldt County, California, a division of opinion between the judges on the Circuit Court for the District of California as to whether the Major Crimes Act was "a constitutional and valid law" sent the case to the U.S. Supreme Court. Justice Samuel Miller held for a unanimous Court that it was. His opinion explaining why was most interesting.

The federal government had defended the constitutionality of the act by arguing that it was based on the Commerce Clause and that it was "a regulation of commerce with the Indian tribes." (This was clearly the basis on which the First Congress had passed the 1790 Indian Trade and Intercourse Act, discussed in Chapter Two.) However, Miller rejected this; he found it "a very strained construction of this clause, that a system of criminal laws for Indians living peaceably in their reservations, which left out the entire code of trade and intercourse laws justly enacted under that provision . . . was authorized by the grant of power to regulate commerce with the Indian tribes." So, what made the act constitutional? It was, he concluded, the tribes' "dependent" status. "These Indian tribes are the wards of the nation. They are communities dependent on the United States. Dependent largely for their daily food. Dependent for their political rights." Miller noted that the tribes owed no allegiance to the States and received from them no protection. In fact, "because of the local ill feeling, the people of the States where they are found are often their deadliest enemies." The tribes, he continued, were "weak" and "helpless." They were "remnants of a race once powerful, now weak and diminished in numbers" due largely "to the course of dealing of the Federal Government with them." As a consequence, "there arises the duty of protection, and with it the power." Miller invoked the language of the Marshall Trilogy just as Matthews had previously in *Ex parte Crow Dog*, but now for a very different purpose. Instead of invoking it to advance tribal self-government, Miller invoked it to declare for the first time that Congress's power over the tribes was based not on the text of the Constitution but on the "duty of protection" and that this power was plenary. He was clearly signaling that the Court would not interfere with the assimilationist policies that Congress was soon to adopt.

While one pressure to have tribal members assimilate into American life was the belief that the same criminal laws should apply alike to Indians and non-Indians, another was increasing dissatisfaction by those in the federal government with the reservation system. Those who sought what was in the best interests of the tribes recognized that individual Indians were living in grinding poverty with few prospects for improving their situation. Others resented that large tracts of land were unavailable to white settlement. As Ninth Circuit Court of Appeal Judge William C. Canby, Jr., has put it, "The combination of these two sentiments produced the most important, and to the tribes, the most disastrous piece of Indian legislation in United States history," namely, the General Allotment Act of 1887, commonly referred to as the Dawes Act because of its principal sponsor, Henry L. Dawes, Republican Senator from Massachusetts.

Dawes and other congressional and governmental leaders supporting the act's passage were sympathetic to the Indians. They earnestly believed that if tribal members were given plots of land to cultivate that they would individually own in fee simple, they would prosper and become assimilated into American life as middle-class farmers and full participants in the American system. Their goal was concisely stated by T. J. Morgan, in his annual report to the Congress in 1890 as Commissioner of Indian Affairs: "It has become the settled policy of the Government to break up reservations, destroy tribal relations, settle Indians upon their own homesteads, incorporate them into the national life, and deal with them not as nations or tribes or bands, but as individual citizens. The American Indian is to become the Indian American." The tribes, they believed, were impediments to the economic development of Indians, and the more quickly they withered away, the better. Of course, this belief also served the interests of land speculators and frontier settlers who wanted to break up the reservations for more productive use and ultimate transfer the title of the land to non-Indian owners.

The Dawes Act authorized the president to allot portions of the reservation land of most tribes to individual Indians. Although Senator Dawes had originally favored a voluntary program, the act as passed made no provision for the consent of the tribes or individual Indians. It provided for allotments of 160 acres for each head of a family and 80 acres to others, and it doubled the allotments for land suitable only for grazing. To protect the Indian allottees from immediate state taxation until they had time to learn the agricultural arts and to acquire the necessary capacity to manage their individual affairs, the act specified that the title to the allocated land would remain in the United States in trust for twenty-five years, after which it would be conveyed to the allottees in fee simple free from all encumbrances. It also provided that upon receiving allotments in fee simple, the Indian allottees were to become U.S. citizens and, as a consequence of the language of § 1 of the Fourteenth Amendment, were also to become state citizens and therefore subject to state criminal and civil law. Finally and of great significance for those eager to have legal access to Indian lands, § 5 of the act provided that "at any time after lands have been allotted to all the Indians of any tribe as herein provided . . . , it shall be lawful for the Secretary of the Interior to negotiate with such Indian tribe for the purchase and release by said tribe . . . of such portions of its reservation not allotted as such tribe shall, from time to time, consent to sell."

In 1887, the year the Dawes Act passed, the total amount of Indian-held land was 138 million acres. In 1934, the year the allotment policy was abandoned, only 48 million acres were left in Indian hands, and 20 million of those acres were desert or semi-desert. Most of the 90 million acres were lost when tribes sold excess lands remaining after their members had received their allotments. The rest of these acres were lost when, for three major reasons, they passed out of the hands of the allottees.

The first reason was allottees' failure to pay state property tax. After twenty-five years, allottees received title to their lands and owned them in fee simple; however, at that point, they were also subject to state property taxation. Many Indians lost their allotted lands as a result of forced sales because of their nonpayment of these taxes.

The second reason was the impact of "competency commissions," established under a 1906 amendment of the Dawes Act. These commissions were empowered to ascertain whether allottees were "competent and capable" to become citizens and receive their lands in fee simple before the twenty-five-year time period had expired. These commissions were free to act on their own volition and did not always inform the tribal members of their actions. As a result, in a number of cases, the Indians who were deemed competent were not informed of the commissions' decisions or that their allotments were now fee patents, as opposed to trust land, and were being taxed. After a period of unpaid taxes, their land was sold without their consent to pay past taxes. This process was known as the "forced fee patent process."

The third reason was allottees' decisions to sell their lands. Once their lands were no longer held in trust, they were free to sell their property, and many did so. However, many were poor negotiators who ended up selling their allotted lands to non-Indians on terms unfavorable to themselves. The Dawes Act created problems even for those Indians who retained their lands; the passage of allotted lands out of Indian hands created a large "checkerboard" pattern of Indian and non-Indian lands, a largely unfixable problem that made sizable farming and grazing projects impractical.

Even when allotted lands were not lost for nonpayment of taxes or by sale to non-Indians, the Dawes Act failed to achieve its sponsors' objectives. Leasing of allotted lands to non-Indians — land held either in trust or in fee simple — became common, thereby defeating the sponsors' intentions of turning Indians into farmers. Additionally, the act subjected allotted land, whether or not it was held in trust, to state inheritance laws. At their deaths, the allottees' land was divided among their heirs; the result was fractionated heirships and multiple owners, often rendering the land unusable. Yet, despite these and other problems, the federal government expanded the allotment program in 1891, 1900, and again in 1906. Eventually, these problems, along with questions such as what limitations should apply to allotments to intermarried white males and how to resolve disputes concerning the quality of the land that was allotted and the evenhandedness of its distribution, finally prompted Congress to pass a major revision of the Dawes Act in 1910.

The federal government's unilateral allotment of reservation lands was in clear violation of treaties it had made with many tribes. In *Lone Wolf v. Hitchcock* (1903), the Kiowas and Comanches challenged Congress's power to abrogate tribal treaties. Their efforts, however, were unavailing.

In 1867, the Kiowas and Comanches signed the Treaty of Medicine Lodge which, among other things, stipulated in § 12 that no part of the Kiowa-Comanche reservation could be ceded without the consent of a three-fourths majority of the tribes' adult males. However, by an act of June 6, 1900, Congress abrogated this treaty and provided that heads of families could select tracts of land within the reservation, not exceeding 320 acres, that would thereafter cease to be held by the tribes in common, and that these tracts would be for the exclusive possession of the person making the selection, so long as he or his family continued to cultivate the land. Kiowa leader Lone Wolf, on behalf of himself as well as all other members of the confederated tribes residing in the Territory of Oklahoma, brought suit in federal court against the secretary of the interior, challenging the constitutionality of the act and asserting that by altering the allotment of certain lands to the Indians and by ceding to the United States 2 million acres of these lands, which would then be open to settlement by white men, the act violated the property rights of individual Indians who had acquired land under the language of the treaties.

The Supreme Court proved to be of as little help in protecting tribal interests in *Lone Wolf* as it had been in *Kagama*. Justice Edward White held for a unanimous Court that Congress had the power unilaterally to abrogate tribal treaties. He found no limits to Congress's power over the tribes, calling it plenary. He noted that it was true that in previous decisions, the Court has stated that "the Indian right of occupancy of tribal lands, whether declared in a treaty or otherwise created . . . [was] sacred." But, he continued, none of those cases involved a controversy between Indians and the power of Congress to administer the property of the Indians. Rather, they all "concerned the character and extent of such rights as respected States or individuals." He continued that "plenary authority over the tribal relations of the Indians has been exercised by Congress from the beginning," and that power, including the power to abrogate tribal treaties, "has always been deemed a political one, not subject to be controlled by the judicial department of the government." He went on to presume that "such power will be exercised only when circumstances arise which will not only justify the government in disregarding the stipulations of the treaty, but may demand, in the interest of the country and the Indians themselves, that it should do so." He reminded the tribes that they were "wards of the government," and he insisted that the Court "must presume that Congress acted in perfect good faith in the dealings with the Indians" and that it "exercised its best judgment in the premises." In any event, he concluded that "as Congress possessed full power in the matter, the judiciary cannot question or inquire into the motives which prompted the enactment of this legislation. If injury was occasioned, which we do not wish to be understood as implying, by the use made by Congress of its power, relief must be sought by an appeal to that body for redress and not to the courts."

Allotment was one means by which Congress sought to promote the assimilation of tribal members into American life. Another was conferral of citizenship. The Citizenship Act of 1924 made American citizens of "all non-citizen Indians born within the territorial limits of the United States." This act completed a process that had begun years before when a few Indian treaties provided citizenship for the tribal members of the signatories, that had continued with the Dawes Act providing citizenship to those Indians who received allotments, and that was further expanded with the Citizenship Act for World War I Veterans of 1919, conferring U.S. citizenship on Indians who served in the military. (In 1916, the Supreme Court had held in *United States v. Nice* that being a U.S. citizen was not incompatible with tribal membership and did not impair any interest in tribal property.)

Just four years after the assimilationist Citizenship Act, however, public opinion and federal policy started to shift once again toward self-determination. On February 21, 1928, Lewis Meriam, a technical director for the Institute of Governmental Studies at the Brookings Institution, delivered to Secretary of the Interior Hubert Work a report of a two-year survey of conditions on Indian reservations in twenty-six states that he had prepared at Work's request. Financed by the Rockefeller Foundation, it was formally entitled *The Problem of Indian Administration* but was popularly known as the Meriam Report. The survey team consisted of ten experts in various fields, including sociology, family life and women's activities, education, history, law, agriculture, health, and research methods. The Meriam Report's pages were filled with evidence of the failure of the federal government's allotment and assimilationist strategy of the past half-century; while it did not call for a change in policy direction, it helped to spur a shift toward tribal preservation and self-government that began in earnest during the Herbert Hoover Administration with its reorganization of the Bureau of Indian Affairs and a doubling of its budget and with the passage of the Leavitt Act of 1932, which released all reservation lands from past and future assessments for construction of costly irrigation projects not required or beneficial to Indian tribes. However, momentum picked up considerable speed after the election of Franklin Delano Roosevelt.

Roosevelt named John Collier as his Commissioner of Indian Affairs in 1933; Collier was an Indian activist and editor of the magazine *American Indian Life* from 1926 until 1933. His scathing criticisms of the Bureau of Indian Affairs were partially responsible for Secretary Work's request for what became the Meriam Report. Soon after his confirmation by the Senate, Collier spelled out his plans for reform in an address to the National Conference of Social Workers in June 1933. "The next session of Congress will be for the Indians and the Indian service a fateful time. The allotment law must be radically amended. Tribal status and the machinery for Indian organization must be defined. . . . Legislation protecting and fostering the Indians' arts and crafts must be advanced. A system of financial credit for Indians must be established. Tribal funds must be protected." He worked feverishly on behalf of a "New Deal for Indians." He worked with the Congress to pass the Johnson-O'Malley Act of 1934, which subsidized education, medical attention, and other services provided by the states for Indians living within their borders; the act helped to offset costs of tax-exempt Indians making use of state-owned and funded schools, hospitals, and other services. His crowning achievement, however, was the passage of the Indian Reorganization Act of 1934 (also known as the Wheeler-Howard Act), which officially ended the practice of allotments, extended indefinitely the trust period for existing allotments still in trust, restored tribal ownership of any surplus land acquired from the tribes under the Dawes Act, authorized the acquisition of land and water rights for the tribes and the creation of new reservations, and encouraged the tribes to set up business corporations and legal structures for self-government.

In keeping with its commitment to tribal self-government, the IRA also had language that its provisions would not apply to any tribe that voted against its application at a special election that would be called by the secretary of the interior within a year of the act's passage. As a result of these elections, a total of 181 tribes, representing 129,750 Indians, voted to accept the IRA and to set up tribal governments under it — although not all the tribes that voted for it actually formed constitutions or established legal charters. Another 77 tribes, representing 86,365 Indians, rejected it.

Less than twenty years later, public opinion and federal policy in support of tribal preservation and self-determination shifted yet again toward tribal termination and assimilation. On August 1, 1953, Congress adopted House Concurrent Resolution 108 declaring it the policy of the Congress "as rapidly as possible to make the Indian subject to the same laws and entitled to the same privileges and responsibilities as are applicable to other citizens and to end their status as wards," and two weeks later, on August 15, it passed Public Law 280. Pursuing an assimilationist agenda, Congress between 1954 and 1964 enacted fourteen statutes terminating tribal status for over 109 Indian tribes and bands occupying over 1,365,801 acres of land. As a result of termination, the tribes' special relationship with the federal government was ended, their members were subjected to the full panoply of state criminal and civil law, and their lands were converted to the private ownership of their members or were sold. While these acts were for the most part repealed, about forty-four tribes remain permanently terminated. What accounts for this rapid and profound change of direction? There are many factors, but the overwhelming explanation is the impact of World War II. Thomas D. Morgan in "Native Americans in World War II" perfectly described that impact: "No group that participated in World War II made a greater per capita contribution, and no group was changed more by the war."

When the Japanese attacked Pearl Harbor on December 7, 1941, there were 5,000 Indians in the U.S. military. By the end of the war in August, 1945, over 24,500 reservation Indians and another 20,000 off-reservation Indians had served. The combined figure of 44,500 was more than 12.5 percent of the entire Native American population at the time and represented approximately one-third of all able-bodied Indian men from 18 to 50 years of age. In some tribes, as many as 70 percent of their men served in the military. Many more served at home. Approximately 40,000 Indian men and women between the ages of 18 and 50 left reservations for the first time and found work in defense industries.

This extraordinary military and civilian service had an impact on Indians and non-Indians alike. It took many Indians away from the reservations and into mainstream American society. Even for those who returned to the reservation, it had demonstrated to them and to non-Indians that they were capable of making the adjustment to a non-Indian way of life. It increased the average annual income of Indians to $2,500, up 250 percent from 1940. The impact on American public opinion was also profound. Most Americans believed that World War II was proof that the process of integrating Indians into the mainstream of American life was complete and that it was time to terminate the tribes. Congress took notice and responded.

In addition to the termination policies initiated by House Concurrent Resolution 108, Congress responded by enacting Public Law 280. This act mandated five states (California, Nebraska, Minnesota [except for the Red Lake Reservation], Oregon [except for the Warm Springs Reservation], and Wisconsin [except for the Menominee Reservation]) to enforce their criminal laws on reservation lands in their borders and to exercise adjudicatory jurisdiction over civil causes of action (e.g., torts, breaches of contract, etc.) on reservation lands in their borders. (In 1954, Congress extended mandatory jurisdiction to all reservations in Wisconsin, and in 1958, it extended mandatory jurisdiction to the Territory of Alaska.) It should be noted, however, while Public Law 280 was assimilationist in its goals, it did not terminate the trust status of reservation lands.

Public Law 280 also authorized other "non-mandatory" states to assume criminal and civil jurisdiction if they so chose — and to do so without tribal consent. Acting on that invitation, ten additional states claimed all or some of the jurisdiction that Public Law 280 allowed before Congress passed the Indian Civil Rights Act (ICRA) on April 11, 1968. Section 402 of the ICRA required that "non-mandatory" states obtain tribal consent before they could assume Public Law 280 jurisdiction, and since its adoption, no Indian tribe has given its consent.

Section 403 of the ICRA was also important; it allowed states that so wished to retrocede their mandated or assumed jurisdiction back to the federal government. Public Law 280 was very unpopular in Indian country; it replaced federal and tribal courts with state courts, brought a state presence onto reservation lands, and was symbolic of Congress's goal of tribal termination. It was also unpopular with a number of the "mandatory" states. The act was a classic "unfunded mandate" imposing on them the personnel and other financial costs of enforcing their criminal and (limited) civil jurisdiction in Indian country. By 1968, public support for tribal termination and assimilation had faded. The ICRA, with its authorization of the United States "to accept a retrocession by any State of all or any measure of the criminal or civil jurisdiction," marked the end of the nation's last assimilationist era and the beginning of the current era of tribal self-determination and self-governance.

The ICRA did more, however, than deal with the failures of Congress's termination policy and the political problems of Public Law 280. Its provisions helped lay the foundation for the policies that were in place during the *Cabazon Band* litigation and subsequently. It is called the Indian Civil Rights Act, because it imposed many of the provisions of the Bill of Rights on tribal governments.

Until the ICRA, tribal governments had not been subject to the restrictions of the Bill of Rights with regard to freedom of speech and press, free exercise of religion, or the various criminal procedural protections afforded defendants in Amendments 4 through 8. In its 1896 opinion in *Talton v. Mayes*, the Supreme Court had explained why in a case involving an Indian defendant living in the Oklahoma Territory (not covered by the Major Crimes Act of 1885) who challenged his conviction for murder in a Cherokee tribal court because it was initiated without a grand jury indictment as required by the Fifth Amendment: "The powers of local self-government enjoyed by the Cherokee Nation existed prior to the Constitution, they are not operated upon by the Fifth Amendment, which . . . had for its sole object to control the powers conferred by the Constitution on the national government."

In particular, § 202 of the ICRA declared that

No Indian tribe in exercising powers of self-government shall —
(1) make or enforce any law prohibiting the free exercise of reli-

gion, or abridging the freedom of speech, or of the press, or the right of the people peaceably to assemble and to petition for a redress of grievances;

(2) violate the right of the people to be secure in their persons, houses, papers, and effects against unreasonable search and seizures, nor issue warrants, but upon probable cause, supported by oath or affirmation, and particularly describing the place to be searched and the person or thing to be seized;

(3) subject any person for the same offense to be twice put in jeopardy;

(4) compel any person in any criminal case to be a witness against himself;

(5) take any private property for a public use without just compensation;

(6) deny to any person in a criminal proceeding the right to a speedy and public trial, to be informed of the nature and cause of the accusation, to be confronted with the witnesses against him, to have compulsory process for obtaining witnesses in his favor, and at his own expense to have the assistance of counsel for his defense;

(7) require excessive bail, impose excessive fines, inflict cruel and unusual punishments, and in no event impose for conviction of any one offense any penalty or punishment greater than imprisonment for a term of six months or a fine of $500, or both;

(8) deny to any person within its jurisdiction the equal protection of its laws or deprive any person of liberty or property without due process of law;

(9) pass any bill of attainder or ex post facto law; or

(10) deny to any person accused of an offense punishable by imprisonment the right, upon request, to a trial by jury of not less than six persons.

In so doing, Congress both implicitly affirmed the principle of tribal sovereignty and explicitly recognized the tribes as units of self-government appropriately obliged to act in conformity with Bill of Rights protections in the same way as the federal and state governments. By its recognition of tribal governments through its enactment of the ICRA, Congress demonstrated its intention to preserve tribal sovereignty and autonomy — and the Indian culture the previous assimilationist era had sought to destroy.

Soon thereafter on July 8, 1970, in a Special Message to Congress, President Richard Nixon declared that "the time has come to break decisively with the past and to create the conditions for a new era in which the Indian future is determined by Indian acts and Indian decisions." He pronounced the policy of forced termination to be wrong for three reasons.

To begin with, Nixon argued that termination implied that the federal government had taken on a trusteeship responsibility for Indian communities "as an act of generosity toward a disadvantaged people and that it can therefore discontinue this responsibility on a unilateral basis whenever it sees fit." But, he insisted, "the unique status of Indian tribes does not rest on any premise such as this." Rather, it rested on "solemn obligations which have been entered into by the United States Government. Down through the years through written treaties and through formal and informal agreements, our government has made specific commitments to the Indian people."

Nixon's second reason for rejecting forced termination was that "the removal of Federal trusteeship responsibility has produced considerable disorientation among the affected Indians and has left them unable to relate to a myriad of Federal, State and local assistance efforts. Their economic and social condition has often been worse after termination than it was before."

And Nixon's third argument against forced termination concerned "the effect it has had upon the overwhelming majority of tribes which still enjoy a special relationship with the Federal government." Efforts to terminate the tribes "created a great deal of apprehension among Indian groups and this apprehension, in turn, has had a blighting effect on tribal progress. Any step that might result in greater social, economic or political autonomy is regarded with suspicion by many Indians who fear that it will only bring them closer to the day when the Federal government will disavow its responsibility and cut them adrift."

Nixon therefore proposed a "new national policy toward the Indian people to strengthen the Indian's sense of autonomy without threatening this sense of community. We must assure the Indian that he can assume control of his own life without being separated involuntarily from the tribal group." In subsequent years, the Congress passed four major pieces of legislation consistent with Nixon's "new national policy."

In the Indian Education Act of 1972, Congress recognized that Native Americans had unique educational and culturally related academic needs and distinct language and cultural needs; dealt in a comprehensive way with American Indian education from preschool to graduate-level education and reflected the diversity of government involvement in Indian education; focused national attention on the educational needs of American Indian learners and reaffirmed the federal government's special responsibility related to the education of Native Americans; and provided services to Native Americans that were not provided by the Bureau of Indian Affairs.

In the Indian Financing Act of 1974, Congress declared it to be the policy of the United States to provide capital on a reimbursable basis to help develop and utilize Indian resources, both physical and human, to a point where the Indians would fully exercise responsibility for the utilization and management of their own resources and where they would enjoy a standard of living from their own productive efforts comparable to that enjoyed by non-Indians in neighboring communities. More specifically, it provided new moneys for reservation economic development and individual entrepreneurship, created a loan guarantee and insurance fund that partially subsidized loan costs, and provided grants for new businesses.

In the Indian Self-Determination and Education Assistance Act of 1975, often referred to simply as the Indian Self-Determination Act, Congress authorized the Departments of Interior and Heath, Education, and Welfare to enter into contracts with and make grants directly to federally recognized Indian tribes, thereby enabling them to have greater control over management of funds and decisions regarding their welfare. This act made self-determination rather than termination the focus of the federal government's actions.

And, finally, in the Indian Child Welfare Act (ICWA) of 1978, Congress adopted legislation governing the jurisdiction over adoption and custody of Native American children. It gave to tribal governments an exclusive jurisdiction in all Indian child custody proceedings, including adoption, voluntary and involuntary termination of parental rights, and removal and foster care placement of Indian children when Indian children are domiciled on the reservation, and a concurrent, but presumptive, jurisdiction in similar Indian child custody proceedings over nonreservation Indian children. Congress passed the ICWA because it wanted to protect Indian culture and tribal integrity from the unwanted removal of Indian children by state and federal officials. It was reacting to the high removal rate of Indian children from their traditional homes and therefore from their exposure to Indian culture as a whole. Before the ICRA was enacted, as many as 25 to 35 percent of all Indian children were being removed from their Indian homes and Indian culture and placed in non-Indian homes. Congress worried that if this rate of removal continued and these Indian children were assimilated into non-Indian culture, the very survival of the tribes would be threatened.

Sixteen years later, Congress passed the Tribal Self-Governance Act of 1994. In it, Congress recognized the inherent sovereignty of the tribes, permanently established tribal self-governance as the policy of the federal government, and stated that it was the goal of the United States to negotiate with tribes on a government-to-government basis while retaining the federal trust relationship.

The *Cabazon Band* case required an interpretation of Public Law 280, passed at the height of the last era of assimilationist thinking, by the Supreme Court in the midst of the current era's strong congressional and presidential endorsement of the principles of tribal self-determination and tribal self-government. The Marshall Trilogy's admonition to focus on what was in the best interests of the Cabazon and Morongo Bands was centrally before the Court. So, too, was the Marshall Trilogy's generation of the unique canons of construction of federal Indian law.

Public Law 280

An Assimilationist Law in an Era
of Self-Determination

Prior to *Cabazon* in 1987, the entire federal court record to which the parties were able to turn for the meaning of any aspect of Public Law 280 was relatively scant. In the thirty-four years since its passage, it had been addressed in only sixty-six opinions by all federal courts: seven by the Supreme Court, thirty by the federal courts of appeals, twenty-eight by federal district courts, and one by the U.S. Court of Claims.

Of these sixty-six opinions, nineteen involved questions of a state's jurisdiction over hunting, fishing, and water rights in Indian country in which the issues were whether certain traditionally exercised tribal rights could be connected to some treaty, statute, or agreement so as to come within the exceptions of Public Law 280 (three Supreme Court cases, six court of appeals cases, nine district court cases, and the one Court of Claims case); fifteen involved routine and uninteresting questions of the state's criminal jurisdiction in Indian country (eleven court of appeals cases and four district court cases); five involved questions of retrocession of state jurisdiction (two court of appeals cases and three district courts cases); and five involved tax questions (one Supreme Court case, one court of appeals case, and three district court cases).

Only eleven of the sixty-six cases involved questions on the important issue of the states' civil jurisdiction in Indian country (three Supreme Court cases, four court of appeals cases, and four district court cases). Another eleven involved questions of tribal gaming, i.e., questions at the intersection of a state's criminal and civil jurisdiction (five court of appeals cases and six district court cases). And, of these sixty-six opinions, only six proved to be at all relevant to the parties as they prepared to argue *Cabazon* before the Supreme Court: one Supreme Court tax case — *Bryan v. Itasca County*, much relied on by

Judge Anderson in the Ninth Circuit's *Cabazon* decision, and five court of appeals cases — two involving the reach of a state's civil jurisdiction (both related to zoning and land use) and three involving tribal gaming.

In its 1976 unanimous opinion in *Bryan v. Itasca County*, the Supreme Court addressed the question of the reach of a state's tax powers under Public Law 280's conferral upon it of civil jurisdiction in Indian country. Russell Bryan, an enrolled member of the Minnesota Chippewa Tribe, resided in a mobile home on land held in trust by the United States for the Chippewa Tribe on the Leech Lake Reservation in Minnesota. In June 1972, he received notices from Minnesota's Itasca County that he had been assessed personal property tax on his mobile home. Three months later, he brought suit in Minnesota District Court seeking a declaratory judgment that the State and County were without authority to levy such a tax on personal property of a reservation Indian on the reservation and that imposition of such a tax was contrary to federal law. The Minnesota District Court invoked Public Law 280, rejected his contention, and entered judgment for Itasca County. The Minnesota Supreme Court affirmed. The U.S. Supreme Court granted certiorari and reversed.

Justice William Brennan began by noting that previous case law precluded the levying of such a tax in the absence of congressional consent and, he continued, § 4 of Public Law 280 provided no such consent. He mentioned that, of "special significance for our purposes," there was a "total absence of mention or discussion regarding a congressional intent to confer upon the States an authority to tax Indians or Indian property on reservations." He noted that neither the Senate or House Committee Reports nor the floor discussion in either chamber mentioned such authority. "This omission has significance in the application of the canons of construction applicable to statutes affecting Indian immunities, as some mention would normally be expected if such a sweeping change in the status of tribal government and reservation Indians had been contemplated by Congress."

Relying heavily on an article published just one year before in the *UCLA Law Review* by Professor Carole Goldberg, Brennan pointed out that nothing in the legislative history of Public Law 280 suggested that Congress intended the act's extension of civil jurisdiction to the states to "result in the undermining or destruction of such tribal governments as did exist and a conversion of the affected tribes into little more than 'private, voluntary organizations' — a possible result if tribal governments and reservation Indians were subordinated to the full panoply of civil regulatory powers, including taxation, of state and local governments." For the Court to recognize such a state power would establish an assimilationist policy beyond anything that Congress intended. "Today's congressional policy toward reservation Indians may less clearly than in 1953 favor their assimilation, but Public Law 280 was plainly not meant to effect total assimilation." He concluded, therefore, that the primary intent of the statute was simply to grant jurisdiction over private civil litigation involving reservation Indians in state court. He did so because

> in construing this "admittedly ambiguous" statute, we must be guided by that "eminently sound and vital canon" that "statutes passed for the benefit of dependent Indian tribes . . . are to be liberally construed, doubtful expressions being resolved in favor of the Indians." This principle of statutory construction has particular force in the face of claims that ambiguous statutes abolish by implication Indian tax immunities. "This is so because . . . Indians stand in a special relation to the federal government from which the states are excluded unless the Congress has manifested a clear purpose to terminate [a tax] immunity and allow states to treat Indians as part of the general community."

Of the five relevant court of appeals opinions, two dealt with regulation of land and three with tribal gaming. The first of the land regulation cases was *Santa Rosa Band of Indians v. Kings County* (1975).

In the *Santa Rosa* case, the Ninth Circuit affirmed a decision of the U.S. District Court for the Eastern District of California that held that local governments could not enforce their land use ordinances in Indian country. Judge Montgomery Oliver Koelsch wrote for a unanimous panel when he invoked the canons of construction of federal Indian law: "To resolve that ambiguity in Public Law 280, we begin with the fundamental postulate, enunciated in *Worcester v. Georgia*, that ambiguities in Federal treaties or statutes dealing with Indians must be resolved favorably to the Indians." He noted that "this principle is somewhat more than a canon of construction akin to a Latin

{ *Chapter 4* }

maxim, easily invoked and as easily disregarded." He declared that it was "an interpretive device, early framed by John Marshall's legal conscience for ensuring the discharge of the nation's obligations to the conquered Indian tribes." He observed that "the Federal government has long been recognized to hold, along with its plenary power to regulate Indian affairs, a trust status towards the Indian – a status accompanied by fiduciary obligations," and he continued that "while there is legally nothing to prevent Congress from disregarding its trust obligations and abrogating treaties or passing laws inimical to the Indians' welfare, the courts, by interpreting ambiguous statutes in favor of Indians, attribute to Congress an intent to exercise its plenary power in the manner most consistent with the nation's trust obligations."

Judge Koelsch responded to King County's argument that because Public Law 280, and particularly the legislative history of the act, was assimilationist in tone, a congressional intent to make the broader grant of jurisdiction must be found. He declared: "We cannot agree; we are unpersuaded by such general statements of assimilationist intent in the context of the specific problem at hand." He declared that "there is nothing specific in the legislative history shedding any light on whether or not Congress intended to subject reservation trust lands to local civil or criminal ordinances. If anything, the legislative history indicates that Congress gave the problem little, if any, thought."

Judge Koelsch noted that the original impetus for the act was a perceived need to extend state criminal jurisdiction to certain California reservations and that civil jurisdiction was extended almost as an afterthought. "There is very little in the legislative history indicating the congressional rationale for extending civil jurisdiction, or to indicate the extent of that jurisdiction." He concluded that "in light of the absence of more specific guidance in the statute or legislative history, we decline to extend jurisdiction to the County solely on the basis of general expressions of sentiment regarding the desirability of terminating Federal paternalistic supervision of tribes or the need for making Indians equal first class citizens – a construction denying the County jurisdiction probably serves those purposes as well or better than one granting it." And, he continued, neither the legislative history nor the statute itself were "altogether assimilationist in character" or "passed against a substantial backdrop of Indian legislation and policy with which it must be integrated." Public Law 280, he asserted, was "a compromise measure" that "awaited the decision by Congress, on a case-by-case basis, that termination of a particular tribe, with consequent imposition of all aspects of state jurisdiction, was appropriate." The broad language in the legislative history relied on by Kings County merely announced "the congressional objectives of the entire termination process, but was not meant to describe the interim status of Indians or trust lands before completion of the process."

For the panel, Judge Koelsch recognized an obligation to follow Congress's intent when construing Public Law 280, but, he declared, "we are not obliged in ambiguous instances to strain to implement a policy Congress has now rejected, particularly where to do so will interfere with the present congressional approach to what is, after all, an ongoing relationship." The Ninth Circuit was clearly hesitant to give full force to an assimilationist measure in what had become a self-determinationist era.

The second land regulation case was *Hoopa Valley Tribe v. Humboldt County* (1980). Humboldt County in northern California challenged an injunction of the federal district court of the Northern District of California in favor of the Hoopa Valley Tribe, the Hoopa Valley Housing Authority, and the United States that prevented it from enforcing its zoning and building codes against four tribal construction projects on tribal land held in trust by the federal government. The Ninth Circuit affirmed the district court's injunction and held that the County lacked jurisdiction to enforce its zoning ordinance on Indian reservation trust lands and that Public Law 280 did not grant the County the jurisdiction to do so. For a unanimous panel, Judge Benjamin Cushing Duniway declared that, "on the merits, we find the case of *Santa Rosa Band of Indians v. Kings County* squarely on point and therefore controlling." He agreed that Humboldt County, just as Kings County, "was without jurisdiction to enforce its zoning ordinance or building code on Indian reservation trust lands, and that Public Law 280 did not grant the county jurisdiction to do so."

The first of the relevant court of appeals cases that dealt with tribal gaming was *Seminole Tribe of Florida v. Butterworth* (1981) coming out of the Fifth Circuit. (In 1982, Congress split the Fifth Circuit into the Fifth Circuit and a newly created Eleventh Circuit; Florida, along with Georgia and Alabama, became part of the new Eleventh Circuit.)

In this decision, the Fifth Circuit affirmed the decision of U.S. District Court Judge Norman C. Roettger, who in May 1980 had permanently enjoined Broward County Sheriff Robert Butterworth and all his deputies and employees from enforcing a Florida bingo statute on Seminole Indian land. The statute limited organizations sponsoring bingo games to providing them no more than two days a week, proscribed more than one jackpot on any given night and limited it to a value of $100, required all other prizes to be limited to no more than $25, and prohibited the use of paid employees by the bingo organizer. The Seminole Tribe violated all of these statutory provisions in the newly constructed bingo hall on its reservation.

Judge Roettger began his opinion by recalling the "general proposition that Indian nations have always been dealt with exclusively by the Federal Government," unless Congress has expressly delegated that power to the states, and by then turning to the question at hand, namely, did Public Law 280 "permit the State of Florida to enforce its bingo statute on Seminole reservation land?" But, before proceeding, he announced that "as a preliminary matter, the court will have to determine if Florida's statute can be classified as criminal/prohibitory or civil/regulatory."

As Judge Roettger explored that question, he noted that "the law of Florida concerning gambling activities is clear. They are generally forbidden by the State Constitution . . . [and] Florida Statutes." Yet, he observed, "it seems plain that Florida, in permitting bingo to be run by certain groups in a restricted manner, has acknowledged certain benefits of bingo and has chosen to regulate rather than prohibit." So, he classified the Florida bingo statute "as a civil/regulatory scheme," and he declared that his task of determining if "Congress had authorized Florida to impose its civil regulatory schemes on Indian land" had been made "simpler," because the Supreme Court in *Bryan v. Itasca County* had declared that "the answer is clearly no." In that case, he pointed out, the Supreme Court had held that Public Law 280 did not "confer general state civil regulatory control over Indian reservations," and, therefore, "Florida could assume no more jurisdiction than was ceded to it by Public Law 280."

Judge Roettger conceded that "the question presented in this case is a close one," as "all laws do regulate, civil and criminal. Many regulate by prohibiting certain conduct." However, given the canons of construction of federal Indian law, he felt obliged to "resolve a close question in favor of Indian sovereignty."

Judge Roettger was the first to introduce the criminal/prohibitive–civil/regulatory dichotomy that would figure prominently in the *Cabazon* litigation. The Fifth Circuit Court of Appeals utilized it as well in *Seminole Tribe of Florida v. Butterworth* (1981) when it affirmed his decision. In a 2-1 decision, Judge Lewis R. Morgan acknowledged that the "difficult question" was whether Florida's bingo statute represented "an exercise of the state's regulatory or prohibitory authority," but interestingly he then immediately cited *Hoopa Valley Tribe v. County of Humboldt* and *Santa Rosa Band of Indians v. Kings County*. He noted that under "a civil/regulatory versus criminal/prohibitory analysis," he had to "consider the Florida statute in question to determine whether the operation of bingo games is prohibited as against the public policy of the state or merely regulated by the state." He observed that the Florida bingo statute did not apply to prevent "nonprofit or veterans' organizations engaged in charitable, civic, community, benevolent, religious or scholastic works or other similar activities . . . from conducting bingo games or guest games, provided that the entire proceeds derived from the conduct of such games shall be donated by such organizations to the endeavors mentioned above." He acknowledged that while the statute's inclusion of "penal sanctions" for its violation made it "tempting at first glance to classify the statute as prohibitory, the statute cannot be automatically classified as such." As he continued, "a simplistic rule depending on whether the statute includes penal sanctions could result in the conversion of every regulatory statute into a prohibitory one." The classification of a statute was "more complex," he insisted, and required "a consideration of the public policy of the state on the issue of bingo and the intent of the legislature in enacting the bingo statute."

Pursuing that line of thought, he invoked *Greater Loretta Improvement Association v. State ex rel. Boone*, a 1970 Florida Supreme Court case that recognized that bingo was one of the forms of gambling, along with horse racing, dog racing, and jai alai, excepted from the lottery prohibition and permitted to be regulated by the state — the Florida Supreme Court based its decision on the fact that since the bingo statute was enacted during the same year that the State Constitution was revised, it "did not violate the Constitution of Florida."

Conceding that this language suggesting that the Florida legislature had chosen to regulate and not prohibit bingo was not binding on the Fifth Circuit, Judge Morgan insisted that the language made it clear that "the game of bingo is not against the public policy of the state of Florida." Therefore, he declared that "bingo appears to fall in a category of gambling that the state has chosen to regulate by imposing certain limitations to avoid abuses. Where the state regulates the operation of bingo halls to prevent the game of bingo from becoming a money-making business, the Seminole Indian tribe is not subject to that regulation and cannot be prosecuted for violating the limitations imposed."

Having concluded that the Florida bingo statute could not be enforced against the Seminole tribe, Judge Morgan proceeded to reject Sheriff Butterworth's contention that the restrictions of the statute could be applied to non-Indians. He did so for two reasons. First, "as respondent strongly points out, the argument was never presented below. The issue presented to the district judge on stipulated facts involved only the question of whether the statute could be enforced to prevent the Indians from violating its restrictions. As a general rule the court of appeals need not address issues raised for the first time by a party on appeal." But second and more importantly, he noted that the Florida bingo statute made "no reference to violations of its restrictions by the players of bingo." He concluded by asserting that "the bingo statute does not prohibit the playing of bingo games in violation of its restrictions, and if the legislature of the state of Florida desires to prohibit such, then it must act accordingly." (Judge Paul H. Roney dissented. He did so "on the ground that the State of Florida has prohibited, not regulated, the precise kind of bingo operation which the plaintiff seeks to conduct.")

The second relevant court of appeals decision that construed Public Law 280 in the context of tribal gaming was *Barona Group of the Capitan Grande Band of Mission Indians v. Duffy*, decided by the Ninth Circuit just two and a half months after the Fifth Circuit's decision in *Seminole Tribe*. When the U.S. District Court for the Southern District of California denied the Baronas' request for declaratory and injunctive relief from the enforcement against them of bingo measures enacted by the State of California and the County of San Diego pertaining to the operation of bingo games by John Duffy, the Sheriff of

San Diego County, and instead entered summary judgment in favor of the County, the Barona Group appealed to the Ninth Circuit. Nine months later, for a unanimous panel, Judge Robert Boochever reversed, finding "persuasive" the Fifth Circuit's determination in *Seminole Tribe* that whether a statute is regulatory or prohibitory depends on whether the legislature deemed the activity to be contrary to the public policy of the state. He admitted that "the test for determining when a state statutory scheme such as the present one should apply to tribal members on their reservation is not susceptible of easy application," but he concluded for his colleagues that "for a number of reasons . . . the County's bingo laws are regulatory and of a civil nature."

To begin with, he noted that California law authorized bingo operations by tax-exempt organizations including, for example, fraternal societies, recreational clubs, senior citizen organizations, real estate boards, and labor and agricultural groups. "As in *Butterworth*, the California statute regulates bingo as a money making venture by limiting size of prizes, requiring that all proceeds be applied to charitable purposes, and requiring that the game be operated by volunteers from the authorized organization." If so many diverse organizations were permitted to conduct bingo operations—although under "strict regulation," it was clear to Judge Boochever that such operations did not violate California public policy. Second, he noted that the general public was allowed to play bingo at will in an authorized game, which also "cuts against a public policy prohibition." Third, he invoked the "rules of construction applicable to statutes affecting Indian affairs," observing that they "undercut application of the bingo laws in this case"; he mentioned in particular the canon that "ambiguities in statutes concerning dependent tribes are to be resolved in favor of the Indians." Finally, he examined the Barona Group's bingo ordinance and found that its stated purpose was to collect money "for the support of programs to promote the health, education and general welfare" of the Tribe. He made the interesting argument that "this intent to better the Indian community is as worthy as the other charitable purposes to which bingo proceeds are lawfully authorized under the California statute." He acknowledged that the Baronas' bingo operation clearly did not comply with the letter of California's statutory scheme, but, he insisted, it did "at least fall within the general tenor of its permissive intent."

The third and final relevant court of appeals decision that construed Public Law 280 in the context of tribal gaming was, of course, the Ninth Circuit's decision in *Cabazon*. It was extensively discussed in Chapter One, and so the pieces are now all in place to explore *Cabazon* as it was argued before the U.S. Supreme Court.

CHAPTER 5

Cabazon

The Appeal to the Supreme Court

Having lost before the Ninth Circuit, on April 17, 1986, the State of California appealed to the U.S. Supreme Court. In its Jurisdictional Statement, it asked "whether state and local laws prohibiting commercial gambling apply to Indian gambling operations, conducted on Indian reservations, that are patronized primarily by non-Indians."

Under the Judiciary Act of 1925, the Supreme Court was mandated to review certain kinds of decisions, including federal court of appeals decisions denying the constitutionality or validity of state statutes. In 1988, Congress passed the Judicial Improvements and Access to Justice Act that virtually eliminated mandatory review by the Supreme Court and replaced it with unlimited discretionary certiorari review. But even under the Judiciary Act of 1925, the Court had construed the act's terms to allow it a fair amount of discretion — the party appealing to the Court (the appellant) had to establish to the Court in its Jurisdictional Statement that the decision below posed a "substantial federal question" requiring further consideration by the Court. If the appellant was unable to do so, the Court would dismiss the appeal "for want of a substantial federal question." Therefore, California's entire Jurisdictional Statement was written to establish the "reasons for granting plenary review."

To that end, the Office of the Attorney General of California made a number of arguments. First, it insisted that "this case raises a significant federal question of national importance, and a conflict exists among lower courts concerning the question." It noted that *Cabazon Band* raised "the question whether state and local gambling laws apply on Indian reservations, a question never decided by this Court." That question, it noted, had gained "national significance and attention," as tribal bingo operations were proliferating in California and nationally. "As of mid-1985, at least 100 tribal bingo operations were in effect in 19 states, and

{ 84 }

the number has increased since then. At least 26 such operations are now in effect in California alone." This proliferation, it asserted, had occurred because of the recent Fifth Circuit decision in *Seminole Tribe* and Ninth Circuit decision in *Barona* holding that state and local gambling laws do not apply to tribal bingo operations. These decisions, it observed, were contrary to recent decisions of the Maine Supreme Judicial Court in *Penobscot Nation v. Stilphen* (1983) and the Oklahoma Supreme Court in *Oklahoma v. Seneca-Cayuga Tribe* (1985), thereby creating a conflict "among lower courts concerning the issue here."

California's second argument for why *Cabazon Band* presented a substantial federal question was that it conflicted with the Supreme Court's decisions in *Washington v. Confederated Tribes of the Colville Reservation* and *Rice v. Rehner.* In *Colville* and *Rice*, the Court had adopted a general rule that was "a form of federal common law, in that it is a judicial doctrine rather than a constitutional or statutory one." That rule held that state laws would apply on Indian reservations unless preempted by federal law or inconsistent with tribal self-government; it required a balancing of state, federal, and tribal interests. Under that rule, the tribal interest was strongest, and the state interest weakest, when "a sovereign tribe's 'tradition' existed under the particular circumstances"; by contrast, the state interest was strongest when the tribal activity involved non-Indians.

It noted that by applying the balancing test, the Court in *Colville* had upheld the State of Washington's right to tax cigarette sales by Indian retailers to non-Indians on a reservation and in *Rice* had upheld California's right to regulate liquor sales by federally licensed Indian traders to non-Indians on a reservation. The Court in both cases had held that state "regulation of sales to non-Indians . . . simply does not 'contravene the principle of tribal self-government' " because Indian Tribes had "no vested right to a certain volume of sales to non-Indians, or indeed to any such sales at all," and because the Tribes were "marketing an exception" to state laws. By contrast, the Ninth Circuit had held that State and local gambling laws did not apply on Indian reservations because Indian tribes had a sovereign right to conduct gambling operations patronized by non-Indians and because tribal sovereignty turned not on whether Indian tribes had "historically engaged in a particular activity" but on whether the tribes were "engaged in a traditional governmental function of raising revenue."

The conflict between the Ninth Circuit decision in *Cabazon Band* and the Supreme Court decisions in *Rice* and *Colville* was obvious and direct, California's Jurisdictional Statement asserted, and concerned "the fundamental question — vital to the essence of tribal sovereignty — whether the tribal sovereign 'tradition' is measured by the tribal activity or by tribal economic interests." The Ninth Circuit, it continued, "had departed from the modern 'trend' of federal Indian law, announced by the Supreme Court in *McClanahan v. Arizona State Tax Commission* (1973), under which federal preemption rather than tribal sovereignty was the focal point in determining state jurisdiction over Indian reservations," and had rested "its decision instead on tribal sovereignty grounds." California concluded its second argument as follows: "This Court should grant review because the lower decision 'has decided a federal question in a way in conflict with applicable decisions of this Court.'"

California's third argument for why the Supreme Court should hear its appeal elaborated on its first argument and focused exclusively on how the Ninth Circuit's decision in *Cabazon Band* directly conflicted with the Maine Supreme Judicial Court's decision in *Penobscot Nation v. Stilphen* and the Oklahoma Supreme Court's decision in *Oklahoma v. Seneca-Cayuga Tribe*. The Jurisdictional Statement noted that since the Supreme Court had dismissed the Tribe's appeal in *Penobscot* "for want of a substantial federal question," and since "the dismissal of an appeal on such grounds is a disposition 'on the merits,' *Penobscot* is the law of the land, not just of Maine. The Ninth Circuit decision conflicts not only with the State court decision in *Penobscot*, but also with this Court's disposition of *Penobscot* on its merits."

The fourth argument of California's Jurisdiction Statement for why the Supreme Court should hear this appeal was the need for the Court to resolve the uncertainty caused by its decisions in *Bryan v. Itasca County* and *Rice v. Rehner*. *Bryan* introduced the civil/regulatory–criminal/prohibitory distinction, but, California insisted, it did so as "dictum," because the property tax laws involved were not regulatory. *Rice* applied a "common law balancing test" to determine state jurisdiction in Indian country and thus created an "anomaly."

In *Rice*, California noted, the Supreme Court "held that state *regulatory* laws are applicable on Indian reservations, assuming that the balancing test supports this result." But according to "the *Bryan* dictum," Public Law 280 did not authorize state *regulatory* laws to be applied on Indian reservations under any circumstances. California suggested that the two decisions could be "superficially reconciled" since *Bryan* interpreted a statute while *Rice* applied the common law. But that created an anomaly. Public Law 280 was intended "to *broaden* state jurisdiction over Indian reservations, but *Bryan* interpreted the statute as affording *less* regulatory jurisdiction than all states have under the common law balancing test applied in *Rice*. In other words, a federal statute intended to broaden state jurisdiction actually confers less jurisdiction than states already have under the federal common law." Since *Rice* "cast doubts on *Bryan*'s 'civil regulatory–criminal prohibitory' dictum," California declared that the Court should grant review "to end the confusion caused by *Rice* and *Bryan*."

Finally, California argued that even if the Court were to preserve the validity of *Bryan*'s "civil regulatory–criminal prohibitory" distinction, it should grant review to determine whether the Ninth Circuit's "public policy" test properly differentiated between state " 'civil/regulatory' and 'criminal/prohibitory' laws." The Ninth Circuit assumed that, because California excepted charitable bingo from its general prohibition against gambling, bingo was not contrary to the public policy of California.

In its Jurisdictional Statement, California faulted that assumption, because it focused "on the form of the state criminal scheme rather than its purpose." The purpose of the California scheme, it insisted, was "to prevent organized criminal infiltration in California, and to provide exceptions only where such infiltration is unlikely to occur." Charitable bingo created little risk of criminal involvement, because the games featured low stakes (no jackpots over $250) and were regulated by strict statewide standards backed by the State's law enforcement apparatus. Tribal bingo was different; it created a substantial risk of organized criminal infiltration because the Tribes featured high stakes that were not regulated. The federal government did not regulate, supervise, or monitor the games, and, California continued, the tribes lacked the law enforcement capability to ensure that the games were honestly run. California noted that the Cabazon Band had "only 25 members" and could not undertake "the screening and auditing necessary to guard against criminal infiltration." The Jurisdictional Statement concluded by declaring that "California 'public policy,' to use the Ninth Circuit test, is offended by the tribal games because they invite the very risks which California gambling policy is intended to prevent. Therefore, California laws are included under Public Law 280, even assuming the validity of *Bryan*'s 'civil regulatory–criminal prohibitory' distinction."

One month later, on May 16, two amici curiae briefs were filed by a total of twenty states in support of California's appeal. One was filed by nineteen states that had "Indian lands located within their borders" and tribes that had or were considering opening bingo parlors. It urged the Court to grant review and affirm *Rice*'s common-law balancing approach. The states' interests in prohibiting high-stakes tribal bingo were great, because "the tribal gambling operations cater to non-Indian patrons who cannot lawfully play high stakes bingo elsewhere" in their jurisdictions and because the states have "an interest in preventing organized criminal elements from gaining control of the tribal games" involving "large numbers of fast moving cash transactions" and where "opportunities for 'skimming' and 'laundering' are enormous." It directly addressed the Ninth Circuit's argument that California's interest was "weak" because there was no evidence that tribal games were controlled by organized crime by asserting that the states have an interest "in *preventing* criminal infiltration, not simply *correcting* the problem after it has taken root."

It criticized the *Bryan* "civil regulatory–criminal prohibitory" dichotomy as "a highly mechanical standard that fails to consider the state's legitimate interest in regulating certain kinds of conduct. Indeed, the standard absolutely prohibits state regulation of conduct on Indian reservations, no matter how compelling the state interest or how tangential or remote the tribal interest." The balancing test adopted in *Rice*, it argued, accommodated far better the "legitimate state law enforcement and policy concerns" by assuring that those concerns are "weighed against tribal concerns." It invoked the general canon of construction that requires ambiguities in federal laws to be construed favorably to Indians, declaring that it provided sufficient protection of tribal interests, without additionally prohibiting state regulation of on-reservation conduct regardless of the legitimacy of the state interest.

The second amicus brief was filed by the State of Washington, in which were located twenty-five Indian reservations, several with bingo parlors operating contrary to state law. It urged the Court to note probable jurisdiction and grant plenary review for several of the reasons in the other amicus brief, but added an important new reason: the limited regulatory power of the states in Indian country recognized by the Ninth Circuit in *Cabazon Band* would allow tribes to shelter "non-Indian businesses from state environmental laws, *e.g.*, laws controlling disposal of hazardous wastes." It was a back-door attempt to get the Supreme Court to overturn at the same time the Ninth Circuit's decision in the *Santa Rosa* case.

On May 19, 1986, the Cabazon and Morongo Bands responded, filing a Motion to Dismiss Appeal or Affirm Judgment. Their motion, filed jointly by Glenn Feldman for Cabazon and Barbara Karshmer for Morongo, made three arguments for why it was "both unnecessary and inappropriate for the Court to grant plenary review in this case."

First, it argued that the case was not within the Court's appellate jurisdiction. Second, it argued that the Court should decline to hear the case because the Congress was in the process of enacting comprehensive legislation dealing with tribal gaming activities. Third, the decision of the Ninth Circuit was "correct both as to the method of analysis used and result reached" and therefore presented "no substantial federal question requiring further consideration by this Court." It then elaborated on each.

Concerning the claim that the case was not within the Court's appellate jurisdiction, the appellees argued that because the Ninth Circuit did not invalidate any state law, "consideration of this case as an appeal is clearly improper." The appellate court decision merely held that the State of California and the County of Riverside could not apply their laws in Indian country "because application of these laws would infringe upon the right of the tribes to make their own laws and be governed by them." They cited the Supreme Court's recent decision in *Silkwood v. Kerr-McGee Corporation* (1984), in which it had observed that it had consistently distinguished between those cases in which a state statute is expressly struck down on constitutional grounds (thereby giving the Supreme Court appellate jurisdiction) and those in which an exercise of authority under state law is invalidated without reference to a state statute (thereby denying the Court appellate jurisdiction). Since California laws were left untouched, the appeal was not within the Supreme Court's appellate jurisdiction, and "the appeal should be dismissed."

Concerning their second claim, the appellees argued that Congress was studying this issue and was moving rapidly to enact legislation reaffirming the right of tribes to operate bingo free from state jurisdiction. They reminded the Court of its limited institutional capacity to make social policy: "This Court has recognized that Congress is better equipped than the judiciary to investigate and study matters involving difficult policy considerations, and that legislative rather than judicial solutions are often preferable in such cases."

And, concerning their third claim, the appellees argued that the case was consistent with all federal court decisions and therefore did not present any substantial federal question that warranted plenary review. They noted that every federal court that had addressed the issue of tribal bingo had upheld the right of tribes to operate bingo games free from state jurisdiction, and they contended that the appellants were attempting "to create an illusion of conflict where none exists" by invoking the decisions of the Supreme Courts of Maine and Oklahoma. "Obviously, neither court is the highest court of the State of California; neither case concerns the applicability of California or Riverside County bingo laws; neither case arises in a Public Law 280 state; and both cases involve states whose relationships with tribes are very different from those of other states in this country." They denied that there was any confusion between *Bryan* and *Rice*, insisting that the two cases did not conflict with each other and caused "no uncertainty or confusion except in the minds of those who would misread them, as do appellants herein." *Bryan*, they noted, was "the seminal case interpreting Public Law 280, a statute not in question or reviewed in *Rice*."

The appellees continued by arguing that California's public policy with respect to bingo did not raise a substantial federal question warranting further review. "The State's more general argument that commercial gambling is contrary to California's public policy . . . rings somewhat hollow in light of the fact that Californians are betting $8.6 million per day on the new State Lottery; that Californians bet more than $2 billion in 1982 on horse races; and that there are over 400 public poker casinos throughout the state where card players can win or lose unlimited amounts of money."

The appellees concluded by arguing that, as a matter of federal common law, the Ninth Circuit had engaged in a "particularized inquiry" into the respective federal, tribal, and state interests involved and, "after carefully analyzing and balancing the respective interests at issue," had "concluded that the federal and tribal interests clearly outweighed the state interest." The only state interest asserted was the potential for intrusion of organized crime. But, the appellees noted that "the Morongo Band terminated one bingo operation with which it was dissatisfied and successfully brought action in federal court to terminate another bingo operating in violation of its tribal bingo ordinance. The Cabazon Band has a tribal security force and a tribal court through which it controls activities on its reservation. Thus, both tribes have the capability of controlling activities within their jurisdiction." The federal interest was, the appellees insisted, much weightier—allowing tribal bingo was "a legitimate means of raising tribal revenues and providing reservation employment opportunities."

They denied that the tribes were "marketing an exception" from state law. Unlike in *Colville*, where the Court had upheld the State of Washington's right to tax cigarette sales by Indian retailers to non-Indians on a reservation, even the State of California had conceded that the appellees' bingo revenues were derived from value generated by on-reservation activities.

And they denied the appellants' claim that there was no "tradition" of commercial gaming by the appellees on their reservations and that, absent such a tradition, California was authorized to regulate their high-stakes bingo operations. They introduced a declaration from Lowell Bean, Professor of Anthropology at California State University at Hayward, who had lived on the Morongo Reservation, conducted extensive original ethno-historical research, and published extensively on Cahuilla Indian culture, which includes both the Cabazon and Morongo Bands. Bean declared that "traditional gambling techniques have continued among these people from time immemorial until the present. Gambling has at no time in the history of the Cahuilla peoples ceased as a significant activity, including today." And, he insisted, this gambling involved "wagers of significant amounts of money." Bean also noted that "after Indians began to deal socially and economically with non-Indians throughout the Spanish, Mexican and American periods, non-Indians were encouraged to come to [gamble]."

So, gaming was a traditional tribal activity, which therefore outweighed the state's interest in its regulation. But, the appellees continued, even if it were not, federal and state courts had routinely upheld the rights of tribal governments to engage in vehicle registration, air quality regulation, zoning, and automobile repossession. "They have done so because Indian tribes are governments and these are 'traditional governmental functions.' " Indian cultures, like all cultures, the appellees noted, continue to "evolve and develop." However, "the position advanced by the State here would permanently lock Indian people into the role of subsistence farmers and dip net fishermen, living in hogans and selling baskets by the side of the road." Such a " 'traditional' Indian existence for which the State argues is clearly contrary to the twin goals of current federal Indian policy: promoting tribal self-government and fostering successful reservation economic development."

The appellees closed as follows: "Because state jurisdiction over reservations is strongly disfavored, because ambiguities in statutes concerning Indian tribes are to be resolved in favor of the Indians, and for the reasons stated above, the Morongo and Cabazon Bands of Mission Indians urge this Court to let stand the court of appeals decision in this case by dismissing the appeal for lack of jurisdiction and denying the resultant petition for writ of certiorari, or affirming the judgment below."

On May 29, just ten days later, the State of California replied to the appellees' motion to dismiss. First, it insisted that the Court had appellate jurisdiction: "California gambling laws are meant to apply on Indian reservations as elsewhere, and the Ninth Circuit invalidated California laws as applied on Indian reservations." While the appellees had argued that "California laws were left untouched," California argued that "an appeal is clearly proper," because "the Ninth Circuit clearly held that California's gambling laws are invalid as applied in this case."

Second, it rebutted the appellees' claim that the Ninth Circuit's decision was consistent with an "unbroken line of federal authority" and argued that it conflicted with the common law balancing test the Supreme Court applied in *Rice*. It repeated that the Ninth Circuit's decision "squarely conflicts with the State court decisions in *Penobscot* and *Seneca-Cayuga*."

Third, it reiterated that the *Rice* balancing test supported the application of the State's gambling laws as the tribes had not traditionally engaged in high-stakes gambling, the State's interest in preventing infiltration by organized crime was great, and the public policy of California was to permit only "regulated" bingo.

Finally, it argued that pending federal Indian gaming legislation provided no basis for granting the motion to dismiss. It "would not be appropriate" to grant the motion to dismiss, the appellants insisted, on the "doubtful contingency" that Congress would approve the bill.

On June 9, 1986, the Supreme Court noted probable jurisdiction when it declared that further consideration of the question of whether it had jurisdiction to decide the issues involved would be postponed until the case was heard on the merits. The decision to proceed with the case caused great concern and even alarm in Indian country; tribes across the nation feared that the Court had agreed to hear the case in order to reverse the Ninth Circuit—the circuit the Supreme Court reverses more frequently and regularly than any other circuit.

The Supreme Court ordered California to file its Brief of the Appellant and both parties to file their Joint Appendix (which the Rules of the Supreme Court specify should contain the docket entries, pleadings, findings, conclusions, judgments, orders, and opinions in the courts below along with "any other parts of the record that the parties particularly wish to bring to the Court's attention") by July 24—both deadlines were subsequently extended by the Clerk of the Court to August 8. It ordered Feldman to submit the Brief of the Appellees thirty days after receipt of the appellant's brief, which would have been September 10. At the time, however, Feldman was in the midst of moving his legal practice from Washington, D.C., to Phoenix, Arizona, and so on August 11, he requested a fourteen-day extension until September 24. On August 15, the Clerk of the Court granted him that extension.

California began its Brief of the Appellant by attempting to reassure the Supreme Court that it did, in fact, have jurisdiction to hear its appeal. It noted that its appeal was filed under the appropriate section of the Judiciary Act of 1925, authorizing appeals from federal appellate decisions striking down state laws as "invalid" under federal law. It insisted that California's gambling laws were meant to apply on Indian reservations as elsewhere, but the Ninth Circuit invalidated those laws as applied on Indian reservations. "The Ninth Circuit clearly intended to invalidate California laws as applied; the court described the nature of California's gambling laws; made repeated references to California's 'bingo statute,' 'bingo law,' and 'gambling laws'; and concluded that California could not apply its 'gambling laws' on Indian reservations and enjoined California from so applying its 'gambling laws.'" The Ninth Circuit, California asserted, had "clearly struck down California laws as applied."

California's opening brief observed that the Supreme Court had held that appeals were proper under the Judiciary Act where a state statute was struck down "as applied to the facts of the case," even though the statute was unaffected as applied in other contexts. And, therefore, "an appeal is proper here." It challenged the Tribes' reliance on *Silkwood* in its Motion to Dismiss and found it "not controlling," because "while the award itself was struck down, the statute authorizing such awards was left untouched." As it reminded the justices, in its opinion in that case, the Supreme Court had commented on the fact that "the appellate court had not mentioned the state statute in its decision." Nonetheless, California prudently concluded that if the Court were to determine "that an appeal is improper here, it should review the matter by [granting a discretionary] writ of certiorari."

As in its Jurisdictional Statement, California presented the question before the Court as "whether state and local laws prohibiting commercial gambling apply to Indian gambling operations, conducted on Indian reservations, that are patronized primarily by non-Indians." And, again, as in its Jurisdictional Statement, California's principal argument in its opening brief was that the federal common law balancing test of *Colville* and *Rice* supported the application of its gambling laws on the tribes' reservations.

In their 2008 book, *Making Your Case: The Art of Persuading Judges*, Justice Antonin Scalia and Bryan A. Garner urge lawyers appearing before courts to "think syllogistically." They contend that "the most rigorous form of logic, and hence the most persuasive, is the syllogism." Scalia and Garner could have pointed to California's brief as an example of a well-crafted syllogistic legal argument. Its major premise was: the common law balancing test authorizes state gambling laws to apply in Indian country when the state interest in prohibiting tribal high-stakes bingo outweighs competing tribal and federal interests. Its minor premise was: the state interest in prohibiting its non-

{ *Chapter 5* }

Indian residents from playing high-stakes bingo and in preventing organized criminal infiltration of unregulated tribal games is great; the tribal interest in conducting gambling operations that are not part of their tradition but rather solicit and depend on non-Indian patronage and in "marketing an exception" from the state's gambling laws to non-Indians "is entitled to little deference"; and the federal interest is "at most neutral," as "Congress has not authorized Indian tribes to conduct gambling operations in violation of state law." Its conclusion, as stated at the end of its "Summary of Argument" was: "Therefore, the common law balancing test supports application of State and County gambling laws in this case."

Unlike the Ninth Circuit opinion that began with and primarily focused on Public Law 280, California's forty-four-page opening brief spent only six pages on Public Law 280 (and a mere two pages on the Organized Crime Control Act), and essentially the rest on the common law balancing test. It did so not because it believed Public Law 280 weakened its claim that it should be allowed to apply its gambling laws in Indian country, but because it was merely icing on the cake. "Public Law 280 was intended to broaden California's jurisdiction over Indian reservations, but not to deprive California of jurisdiction retained by non–Public Law 280 states." It noted that "if the result were otherwise, California would have less jurisdiction over Indian reservations than non–Public Law 280 states, where such jurisdiction is supported by the common law but has not been specifically addressed in Public Law 280 itself. This result would conflict with the purpose of Public Law 280 to broaden California's jurisdiction over Indian reservations."

California's argument in its opening brief largely tracked its argument in its Jurisdictional Statement. It was longer, however, allowing it to go into significantly greater detail on key points. What follows describes both its new and its more refined points.

It began by challenging not only the continued viability of Chief Justice John Marshall's holding in *Worcester v. Georgia* that Indian reservations are analogous to foreign nations whose borders are impenetrable by state law but also the canons of federal Indian law and their insistence that federal laws relating to Indians are to be given a liberal construction and that doubtful expressions are to be resolved in favor of the interests of the tribes whose members are wards of the nation and dependent on the federal government for their protection. It cited the Supreme Court's decisions in *Rice* and especially *McClanahan v. Arizona State Tax Commission* (1973) in support of its contention that "today, a more flexible view prevails," holding that "state laws are applicable on Indian reservations unless they are preempted by federal law or infringe on tribal self-government." The Court's jurisprudential focus in those cases, it reminded the justices, was "on federal preemption rather than tribal sovereignty." It quoted *McClanahan*, in which the Court unanimously embraced Justice Thurgood Marshall's words that "the trend has been away from the idea of inherent Indian sovereignty as a bar to state jurisdiction and toward reliance on federal preemption." The modern cases, Justice Marshall argued, "tend to avoid reliance on platonic notions of Indian sovereignty and to look instead to the applicable treaties and statutes which define the limits of state power." Thus, even though in *McClanahan* the Court rejected Arizona's efforts to impose its personal income tax on a reservation Indian whose entire income was derived from reservation sources, it did so not by invoking tribal sovereignty but by asserting that Arizona's efforts interfered with matters that the relevant statutes and treaties had left to the exclusive province of the federal government and the Indians themselves, i.e., Arizona had been preempted from imposing its income tax on reservation Indians by federal statutory and treaty law.

California's opening brief continued to quote from *McClanahan*: "The Indian sovereignty doctrine is relevant, then, not because it provides a definitive resolution of the issues in this suit, but because it provides a backdrop against which the applicable treaties and federal statutes must be read." And, when the Court in *McClanahan* proceeded to read the "relevant treaty and statutes" against the "backdrop" of tribal sovereignty, it concluded that "we think it clear that Arizona has exceeded its lawful authority by attempting to tax appellant."

McClanahan became a critical linchpin in California's argument. Since "no treaties exist[ed]" between the United States and the Cabazon and Morongo Bands, preemption of the State's power to impose its gambling laws in Indian country could occur only by federal statute, but there were no federal statutes that "preempted or displaced state gambling laws as applied on Indian reservations," and therefore no "backdrop" against which to consider tribal sovereignty.

The Ninth Circuit, California insisted, "rested its decision on tribal sovereignty grounds," and, on that basis, held that the Tribes had a "sovereign" interest in raising revenue — regardless of the form of "activity" by which the revenue was raised — and that the tribal revenue-raising interest outweighed the State's interest in preventing organized criminal infiltration. California argued that the Ninth Circuit failed to follow modern Supreme Court precedent by treating tribal sovereignty not as a "backdrop" in analyzing whether any federal law preempted the State from enforcing its gambling laws in Indian country but rather as "an absolute bar to State jurisdiction," an outmoded and no longer viable concept.

McClanahan and its treatment of tribal sovereignty, as a merely a "backdrop" against which federal preemptive laws were to be assessed were critical for establishing California's major premise. By asserting that the modern view that state laws are enforceable in Indian country unless Congress has preempted them (a position absolutely contrary to the Marshall Trilogy's insistence that state laws are not enforceable unless Congress expressly authorizes their enforcement), California's opening brief sought to render Public Law 280 and OCCA — so important in the Ninth Circuit's analysis — irrelevant as they were clearly intended to grant new powers to the mandatory states, not to preempt them from exercising powers they already had. It also sought to persuade the Supreme Court that its only task was to engage in *Rice*'s common law balancing test and to weigh the overwhelming interests of the State against the lesser interests of the Tribes and the federal government.

In his book *The Nature of Legal Argument*, Professor Otis C. Jensen declared that "legal reasoning revolves mainly around the establishment of the minor premise," and, accordingly, after establishing why the Supreme Court had jurisdiction to hear the case and powerfully introducing its major premise concerning the appropriateness of applying the balancing test, California devoted the bulk of its opening brief to establishing to the Court that, under that balancing test, California's interest in enforcing its gambling laws in Indian country far outweighed the interests of the Tribes and the federal government in conducting tribal gaming.

It argued powerfully, and for the first time, on "moral grounds." It argued that its interests would be frustrated if the Tribes could establish "zones of immunity where non-Indians can play high stakes bingo in defiance of State law." If the Ninth Circuit's decision were affirmed, California worried that it would become "dotted with islands of Indian commercial gambling activity, thriving because of the 'market' that California policy itself has created." Invoking the principles of popular sovereignty, the brief contended that "the people of California, through their common law and constitutional policy, have chosen not to adopt Las Vegas–style gambling as a way of life. The people should have the right, through their elected representatives, to determine the kind of society in which they live."

It elaborated on this point: tribal gaming frustrated California's "legitimate interest in preventing its non-Indian citizens from playing high stakes bingo" and made it more difficult for California to protect this interest even in off-reservation areas. "If non-Indians can play high stakes bingo on Indian reservations, there is little reason for California to prohibit such games off the reservation." The opening brief continued by noting that if California's gambling prohibitions could be so easily circumvented, there would be little reason for the prohibitions to be maintained. "Legitimization of tribal commercial endeavors that take advantage of state restrictions against non-Indians — whether the restrictions apply to bingo or other commercial activity — makes it logically difficult for the state to maintain the restrictions, and places improper pressure on the state to remove the restrictions altogether." By exploiting California's policy against high-stakes gambling, the Tribes' gaming efforts rendered that policy "largely pointless. The effect of the tribal activity here is thus not confined to the reservation, but rather 'spills over' into off-reservation areas by undermining the State's general policy against high stakes gambling."

California added a final point to its objection to tribal gaming on "moral grounds": it quoted from the 1970 report of the Commission on the Review of the National Policy toward Gambling that declared that "bingo is one of the more regressive forms of gambling — that is, those in the lower income groups spend proportionately more of their income playing it than those in higher income categories." Adding all of these factors together, California concluded that its "interests are significant here."

In addition to these new and compelling arguments, California also reiterated its "vital" interest in preventing "organized criminal infiltration in California." It insisted that tribal bingo games created a substantial risk of organized criminal infiltration that did not arise with respect to State-regulated charitable bingo. Not only did the tribal games feature high stakes that generate huge profits attractive to organized crime, but there was no federal government regulation, monitoring, or supervision of these tribal games, and there were no federal standards that applied to them. Rather, each tribe adopted and administered its own standards, if they had "adopted any at all." It noted that the secretary of the interior had not even approved the tribal standards . . . [of] the Cabazon games involved here." And it emphasized that the Tribes lacked the law enforcement capability to ensure that their games were honestly run. It repeated the point it made in its Jurisdictional Statement that the Cabazon Tribe had "only 25 members" and therefore could "not undertake the screening and auditing procedures necessary to guard against criminal infiltration"; it also added the important point that the "Tribes lacked criminal jurisdiction over non-Indian players."

Having established how "vital" its interests were, California addressed the Tribes' interests, and found them wanting. It began by repeating its argument from its Jurisdictional Statement that, since the Tribes were "selling exemptions from California's gambling laws to non-Indians," their interest in doing so was unsupportable. High-stakes bingo, it asserted, "has value only because it is illegal under State law. The tribal games are patronized by non-Indians who cannot lawfully play high-stakes bingo elsewhere in California." But, it then went on and challenged the Tribes' interest in gaming, laid out in their reliance on Professor Lowell Bean's declaration in their Motion to Dismiss, by contending that commercial high-stakes gaming had never been part of a "tribal tradition" and was not an interest that needed to be weighed by the Court under its *Rice* federal common law balancing test. "According to *Rice*, if a sovereign tribal tradition exists, state laws generally cannot be applied on Indian reservations unless Congress expressly authorizes their application. If, however, a sovereign tradition does not exist, or if the balance of state, federal, and tribal interests otherwise requires, the 'backdrop' of tribal sovereignty is accorded 'less weight.' " While California acknowledged that "ambiguities in federal Indian law are generally construed in favor of Indian tribes," it quoted *Rice* that "this canon of construction does not apply in the absence of a sovereign tribal 'tradition.' "

With that argument in place, California declared that "the tribal activity here is well outside the tribal 'tradition.' Indian tribes have not traditionally conducted high stakes gambling operations that solicit and depend on non-Indian patronage, particularly where the operations are successful because they violate state law." It insisted that the kind of gambling activity involved on the Cabazon and Morongo reservations was "not indigenous to Indian custom or culture, nor [was it] a traditional Indian practice." It set up a battle of dueling expert witnesses by quoting from a sworn declaration by William J. Wallace, a professor emeritus of anthropology at California State University, Long Beach, who had done extensive anthropological work on the cultural life of early (pre–nineteenth century) California Indian tribes. In his declaration, Professor Wallace acknowledged that Indians had often gambled for ceremonial, religious, and recreational purposes but stated that "the Indians of California have not, to any significant degree, traditionally engaged in gambling with non-Indians on either a commercial or non-commercial basis." He described the high-stakes bingo parlors of the Cabazon and Morongo Bands as "attracting players from surrounding towns and cities by offering large cash prizes. Undertakings of this sort find no precedent in native California Indian life and culture. The game itself (a lottery), the building of special gaming halls, tribally organized gambling and dependence on its revenue as an economic base, attempts to lure outsiders, particularly non-Indians, to play, — all these things fall well outside the boundaries of traditional native gambling." (Before Judge Waters, the Tribes unsuccessfully sought to strike Wallace's declaration because he made no reference in it to the Cabazon and Morongo Bands in particular and because his research focused on California tribes prior to their exposure to European explorers and western settlers.) California also quoted from the work of Alfred L. Kroeber, a very famous professor of cultural anthropology at the University of California, Berkeley, who in his classic 1925 *Handbook of the Indians of California* had observed that California Indians were known for engaging in small-scale gambling with other Indians on festive occasions, such as dances or mourning ceremonies, but who presented no evidence that they engaged in high-stakes gambling with non-Indians.

{ *Chapter 5* }

Finally and quite perplexingly, California's opening brief defended not modern tribal self-determination but rather a nineteenth-century understanding of Indian reservations. "Indeed, the Ninth Circuit decision is inconsistent with the historic purposes of the reservation system itself. The reservation system was intended to provide Indians with a homeland for preservation of their traditional culture, and to separate them from non-Indians who were migrating westward." Tone-deaf to the Tribes' argument in its Motion to Dismiss, California argued that "the purpose of the reservation system was to allow Indians to live together, to create governmental and social organizations, to pursue agriculture, to hunt and fish, and even to commercially exploit the physical resources of the reservation." It seemed curiously oblivious to the fact that the Cabazon and Morongo reservations were located in a harsh desert with a punishing climate providing no agriculture to pursue and no game to hunt or fish to catch — and no natural resources to exploit. But it persisted in this line of argument, embracing this understanding of the life that tribal members should live and attacking the Ninth Circuit's decision because it "encourage[d] a breakup of tribal culture rather than its preservation."

California then moved to a consideration of the federal interest in allowing the Tribes to engage in high-stakes bingo in violation of state law. It insisted that "Congress had never expressed a policy favoring tribal economic development in the field of commercial gambling." It contrasted Congress's adoption of a comprehensive scheme for the regulation of timber harvesting on Indian reservations, which the Court upheld in its rejection of Arizona's attempt to tax non-Indian logging operations on Indian reservations, with Congress's failure to have authorized, directly or implicitly, Indian tribes to conduct commercial gambling operations that violate state laws. This failure, California insisted, indicated that this case was "bereft of the federal involvement and concern that has posed an obstacle to state jurisdiction over Indian reservations in other cases." Nothing in the federal policy favoring tribal economic development suggested that this "laudable goal" should be achieved by "non-traditional gambling operations that market exemptions from state law." California's opening brief became more explicit: "Congress has never expressed a policy favoring tribal economic development in the field of commercial gambling."

Having completed its common law balancing-test analysis, California turned briefly to Riverside County's prohibition of card clubs. It noted that California law did not directly prohibit card games, but it observed that California law authorized local governments to adopt more stringent gambling restrictions than those provided in state law. It then ritualistically repeated that the common law balancing test supported the county's right to prohibit the card games on the Cabazon reservation and that the absence of state and local control created a risk of organized criminal infiltration.

With its principal syllogistic balancing test argument complete, California then turned to a consideration of Public Law 280. It began as follows: "Since Public Law 280 does not preempt California's authority under the federal common law, this Court . . . need determine the effect of Public Law 280 only if it determines that California's authority is deficient under the balancing test." But, it continued, "assuming *arguendo*" that its authority were deficient, it proceeded to offer an argument for why Public Law 280 authorized the application of its gambling laws on Indian reservations.

First, it labeled the Court's introduction in *Bryan* of a "civil regulatory–criminal prohibitive" distinction in Public Law 280 as mere "dictum," i.e., as having only incidental bearing on the case in question and therefore not binding as precedent. "The property tax laws involved in *Bryan* were not regulatory; they raised revenue but did not regulate conduct." Indeed, California's opening brief continued, "*Bryan* focused primarily on legislative history showing that Congress did not mean to authorize state 'tax' laws to be applied on Indian reservations, indicating that its focus was not on state regulatory laws."

Not only was the distinction in *Bryan* dictum, but it also introduced an "anomaly." "Public Law 280 was intended to broaden state jurisdiction over Indian reservations," but, as a result of *Bryan*, it is interpreted "as conferring less jurisdiction than states already have under the common law balancing test applied in *Rice*." California urged the Supreme Court to "resolve the anomaly" by making it clear that *Bryan* applied only to state tax laws and by rejecting *Bryan*'s dictum that state regulatory laws are not included under Public Law 280.

California continued by arguing that *Bryan*'s "civil regulatory-criminal prohibitive" distinction was contradicted by the legislative history of Public Law 280. In its opening brief, it noted that on June

29, 1953, shortly before Public Law 280 was enacted, the U.S. Department of the Interior transmitted a report to the House Committee on Interior and Insular Affairs on the bill that became Public Law 280. This report recommended that the bill be amended to provide that state "civil laws . . . of general application" are applicable on Indian reservations, and explained the reasons for the proposed change as follows: "The revisions incorporated in the enclosed draft would . . . make it clear that the effect of the bill would be, not merely to permit the State courts to adjudicate civil controversies arising on Indian reservations in [the mandatory States], but also to extend to those reservations the substantive civil laws of the State[s] insofar as those laws are of general application to private persons or private property." The proposed change was included in the bill finally approved by Congress, and, California continued, Public Law 280 was therefore meant "to provide for the application of state 'substantive civil laws' on reservations." California proceeded by declaring that the "Interior report makes clear that Congress contemplated no distinction between state 'regulatory' and 'prohibitory' laws."

And, continuing to build its case against *Bryan*'s "civil regulatory-criminal prohibitive" distinction, California pointed out that "it is often difficult to determine whether state criminal laws are 'regulatory' or 'prohibitory' because many criminal laws contain both regulatory and prohibitory aspects." For example, it asked, are state traffic laws that prohibit drivers from exceeding certain speed limits "regulatory or prohibitory?" And, it wondered, "What classification applies to state liquor laws prohibiting minors from consuming alcoholic beverages?" Most state laws regulate social conduct by "selectively prohibiting certain kinds of conduct," and therefore "virtually all prohibitory laws are 'regulatory,' for they achieve social goals by prohibitory means. To classify them as one way or the other involves an often arbitrary exercise that loses sight of the objective of the criminal scheme itself."

Despite these many problems, California appreciated that the Court might nevertheless persist in its belief that the "civil regulatory–criminal prohibitive" distinction was valid. And so, California argued "alternatively" that California's gambling laws were essentially "prohibitory" rather than "regulatory" and thus were included under Public Law 280. It insisted that it "absolutely prohibit[ed] a specific form of conduct—high stakes, non-charitable bingo—rather than licens[ing] or regulat[ing] it," and therefore its gambling laws were "'prohibitive' within the meaning of *Bryan*." It faulted the Ninth Circuit's assumption that its gambling laws were "civil regulatory," and that its "public policy" is not violated, because it provided an exception from a general prohibition against criminal conduct. This assumption, it declared, was "a mechanical one" because it focused on "the form of the state criminal scheme" rather than on "its purpose and effect." The purpose of California gambling laws was to prohibit high-stakes, unregulated gambling that would attract organized crime; it provided an exception for low-stakes, regulated charitable bingo, because it posed no risk of criminal involvement. Thus, to the extent that the "public policy" inquiry had any relevance, it should turn on whether California regulated and controlled high-stakes, commercial bingo that related directly to an organized crime risk, not on whether it provided an exception for low-stakes, charitable bingo that created no organized crime risk. "The distinction is not, as the Ninth Circuit held, between commercial and charitable bingo, but between regulated and unregulated bingo."

California concluded its Public Law 280 discussion by observing how the Ninth Circuit's "mechanical" analysis compounded the already mentioned difficulties of distinguishing between state prohibitory and regulatory laws. Most prohibitory laws, it argued, could be construed as "regulatory" because they provided exceptions. "For instance, state statutes prohibiting intentional homicide provide exceptions for homicide committed in self-defense." It offered another: "State statutes prohibiting fireworks provide exceptions for publicly-controlled fireworks displays." It noted that while these state prohibitions were clearly "prohibitory," the Ninth Circuit's "mechanical" analysis suggested the opposite conclusion and illustrated "the difficulties arising from the prohibitory-regulatory distinction and the general irrelevance of the distinction in measuring state and tribal interests."

California then briefly addressed OCCA, which prohibited gambling operations "in violation of the law of a State or political subdivision in which it is conducted." By its terms, California insisted, OCCA "makes state gambling laws applicable on Indian reservations." The Ninth Circuit extended *Bryan*'s "civil regulatory–criminal prohibitory" distinction to OCCA and on that basis held that OCCA does not apply because California's gambling laws are "civil regulatory" in that the tribal bingo games do not violate the "public policy" of California. The opening brief insisted that nothing in the text of OCCA, or in its legislative history, supported that distinction.

California concluded by asserting that it could not effectively protect its interests if Indian tribes were permitted to provide gambling havens for non-Indians who seek refuge from state gambling laws; that the tribal games flagrantly exploited its gambling laws and were profitable only because they did so; that the "accommodation" of state, federal, and tribal interests appropriately weighed by *Rice*'s balancing test supported the application of its gambling laws; and "therefore, this Court should reverse the lower decision."

On August 8, 1986, the same day California submitted its opening brief, three amici curiae briefs in support of the appellants were also filed: One by the States of Washington, Wisconsin, and Connecticut; another by the States of Arizona, Nevada, and New Mexico; and a third (technically, an amicus curiae brief because filed only by one party) by the State of Minnesota. They added nothing new. All three repeated California's criticisms of *Bryan*'s "civil regulatory–criminal prohibitory" distinction; the brief of Arizona, et al., also urged the application of the *Rice* balancing test and closed with a bit of special pleading: even if the Supreme Court were to affirm the Ninth Circuit's decision, it urged the Court to confine its opinion "to the gambling activities under consideration in the State of California and not be extended by implication to other gambling operations conducted or proposed to be conducted elsewhere, particularly in States, such as the Amici Curiae States, where Public Law 280 does not generally apply."

On September 24, the Tribes replied in the Brief of the Appellees. It began, as California's opening brief had begun, by posing the "Question Presented." It did so for the same reason: the Rules of the Supreme Court require of the party briefs that "the questions shall be set out on the first page following the cover, and no other information may appear on that page." Unsurprisingly, the Tribes posed the question before the Court very differently than had California: "Whether a state law and a local ordinance regulating the operation of bingo games, and a local ordinance prohibiting certain card games that are permitted under state law, can be applied to prevent feder-ally-recognized Indian tribal governments from conducting such games on their reservations, where those activities are sanctioned by the Department of the Interior and provide the sole source of revenue and the main source of employment for the tribes?"

The Brief of the Appellees then addressed the Court's jurisdiction and argued, as the Tribes had in their Motion to Dismiss, that the Court lacked jurisdiction to hear the appeal of California. Respond-ing to California's claim that the Ninth Circuit had found California's gambling laws unconstitutional as applied, it asserted that the *Cabazon* court found California to have "no lawful authority to attempt to apply the statutes at all," and, therefore, the Judiciary Act of 1925 did not confer appellate jurisdiction in this case.

It then introduced the justices to the significance of this litigation, and in a way that tied it to the question it claimed was posed by it. "Although this case involves only two Indian tribes, the importance of Indian bingo to tribes elsewhere in the country cannot be over-looked. There are currently between eighty and one hundred tribes operating bingo games nationwide." It noted that tribal gaming was "begun in response to substantial cuts in federal funding for Indian programs and President Reagan's Indian Policy Statement of January 24, 1983, which 'encouraged the tribes to reduce their dependence on Federal funds by providing a greater percentage of the cost of their self-government.'" The Department of the Interior, it observed, regarded tribal bingo as "an appropriate means by which tribes can fulfill this federal policy objective" and was actively involved in sup-porting and promoting tribal bingo activities by approving tribal bingo ordinances and providing over $8 million in direct grants and loan guarantees to tribes for the construction of bingo facilities. The resulting revenues from tribal bingo activities were being used to fund a wide variety of important tribal programs and services, and the bingo facilities provided significant employment opportunities for economically depressed reservations.

In turning to bingo in order to raise governmental revenues, the Brief of the Appellees declared, the tribes were merely responding "as have many states, including California, which have recently turned to state lotteries, numbers games and other forms of gambling as a con-venient form of voluntary taxation." By so doing, it offered an initial challenge to California's "moral grounds" argument, while simultaneously suggesting that tribes were the equivalent of states and not subject to their jurisdiction. Connecting once again the significance of this case to the legal question it posed, the Tribes' brief emphasized that on many reservations, the jobs and revenues that bingo was providing were giving tribes "their first real chance at economic self-sufficiency. The loss of this opportunity would be devastating not only to the Cabazon and Morongo Bands, but throughout Indian country generally." It also reminded the Court that every federal court that had addressed the issue, including the Ninth Circuit in the case below, had upheld the right of Indian tribes to sponsor bingo games free from state jurisdiction.

Scalia and Garner's *Making Your Case* advises that "if your brief is filed second, begin by 'clearing the underbrush' — responding to your opponent's seemingly persuasive points that would entirely bypass your principal point." Consistent with that advice, the Tribes' brief began in earnest by arguing that California's reliance on *Colville* and *Rice* was misplaced. "Upon careful analysis, however, it is apparent that both cases are readily distinguishable from the factual and legal issues presented here, and that neither case can justify the unprecedented reach of state jurisdiction over the tribes for which the appellants argue."

Colville permitted the application of Washington's cigarette tax, but, the Tribes observed, its legal incidence "specifically fell on the non-Indian purchasers." They noted that in contrast to the tobacco products tax at issue in *Colville*, the legal incidence of the state and local bingo laws at issue in this case fell directly on the tribes. "California's statutory bingo scheme is directed at, regulates and controls only the organization sponsoring the bingo game, not the individual bingo players." And additionally, in *Colville*, the Court held that even though the tribes were "marketing an exemption from state tax laws," the state could not prohibit the tribes from selling tobacco products but merely held that the tribes had to pay the tax. Finally, in *Colville*, the Court found that the revenue interest of the tribes did not outweigh the competing state revenue interests because the value being marketed was "not generated on the reservations by activities in which the tribes have a significant interest" and because the tribes did not have a "vested right" to any such sales. But in this case, "neither of these limiting conditions" was present. Even California had conceded that the "recreational activities" being provided by the Tribes in this case constituted "value generated by on-reservation activities," as the Tribes offered these "recreational opportunities in large, permanent facilities which they have built"; operated and regulated the games under tribal ordinances; provided ancillary services including security protection to their patrons; and used the revenues derived to provide on-reservation services to their members. And, unlike *Colville*, the Tribes had a "vested right" to conduct bingo games with non-member participants, because these games have been "expressly authorized, sanctioned, funded, and promoted by the federal government." Their brief continued: "Under these circumstances, the Tribes here are not merely marketing an exemption from state tax laws, but have a federally-recognized 'vested right' to sponsor bingo games on their reservations for the purpose of raising needed tribal revenues."

Rice, the tribal brief argued, was also "readily distinguishable"; it involved the interpretation of a federal statute "not relevant here," which provided that the sale of liquor on Indian reservations had to be " 'in conformity both with the laws of the state' and with a tribal ordinance." Based on a textual analysis and a review of its legislative history, the Court concluded that the statute was "an express congressional delegation to the state of concurrent authority over liquor sales" and that California could therefore require a licensed Indian trader operating a store on a reservation to obtain a state liquor license. It was "a narrow decision" that did not support California's "principal argument that the State can exercise regulatory jurisdiction over the tribes themselves in the absence of a congressional grant of such authority."

And, *Rice* did not hold, as California asserted it did, that the principle of tribal self-government is not implicated when a state asserts jurisdiction over activities on the reservation in which non-Indians are participants. Rather, it was consistent with the Court's repeated recognition that current federal Indian policy not only strongly supported the twin goals of strengthening tribal self-government and promoting reservation economic development but also is predicated on the knowledge that "the only way that Indian tribes can achieve economic self-sufficiency and reservation development is through commercial interaction with the non-Indian community. No Indian tribe, no matter how resource-rich its reservation, can hope to develop its economy by marketing goods and services only to its own members."

Finally, the Tribes argued that California was "wrong both as a matter of fact and law" when in its opening brief it contended that since there is no "tribal tradition" of commercial gaming with non-Indians on the Cabazon and Morongo reservations, *Rice* authorized the State to regulate these tribal activities. First as the facts: California, they noted, relied on a declaration by Professor William Wallace who asserted that Indians did not engage in commercial gambling and did not "traditionally" engage in gambling with non-Indians. "But Professor Wallace's report and opinions were restricted to aboriginal or prehistoric California Indian cultures (i.e., before Indian contact with non-Indians)." They pointed out that, using Dr. Wallace's definition, "it would have been impossible for Indians to have 'traditionally' gambled with non-Indians, because 'traditional' activities were practiced only before Indian/non-Indian contact." They noted that Professor Alfred L. Kroeber likewise reported only on this early period. They insisted that "far more authoritative" was the declaration and report of their expert, Professor Lowell Bean, whose research revealed that the tribes "received monies and/or goods for services provided to visitors or participants who came to gamble, wager, or observe gaming" and that once Indians interacted with non-Indians in the Spanish, Mexican, and American periods, non-Indians were encouraged to participate in gambling games, which included card and dice games and horse races. They quoted Professor Bean's conclusion based on his nearly thirty years of research on the Cahuilla that the Cabazon and Morongo tribal bingo enterprises are "a present day adaptation of the traditional ways of the Cahuilla people, e.g., the use of tribal lands for gaming, recreation, and generating an income from gambling and spending by outsiders for the benefit of the reservation." They also used Professor Wallace to their own advantage, noting that when he was deposed, he "acknowledged that his report covered an earlier time period than Dr. Bean's, and that he had 'no reason to dispute' Dr. Bean's findings and conclusions as to Cahuilla tribal gambling since the end of the 18th Century, the time of Western contact."

Having addressed how California was wrong on the facts, the Brief of the Appellees turned to how the State was also wrong as to the law when it read *Rice* as "requiring a tribe to demonstrate a clear historical record of engaging in a particular activity in order to assert tribal powers of self-government over that activity today." If the State were correct, "every case involving tribal jurisdiction would be reduced to a battle of anthropological experts, quibbling over historical minutia"; many federal and state court decisions that had upheld tribal self-government activities that were clearly not "traditional" such as zoning and vehicle registration would be called into question; all the federal legislation of the last twenty years directed at making Indians economically self-sufficient would have to be negated; and Indians would have to be forever relegated "to the status of dip-net fisherman, living in tepees and selling baskets by the side of the road."

The Tribes then launched into their argument on the merits. They denied that the common law balancing test could be applied to grant California jurisdiction in this case. They asserted that the Court had never authorized the direct assertion of state jurisdiction over a tribe on its reservation in the absence of a treaty or statute expressly conferring such authority. Yet, they observed, California was asking the Court to ignore this "immutable principle of federal Indian law" and to grant it jurisdiction though the application of a federal common law balancing test. They acknowledged that common law principles had been applied to give states "jurisdiction over non-Indians on the reservation," but, they insisted, these principles had never previously been applied where, as here, "the state seeks jurisdiction over the tribe itself." California had cited as the linchpin to its argument *McClanahan v. State Tax Commission of Arizona* and its language that tribal sovereignty was merely a "backdrop" against which to interpret federal treaties and statutes. The Tribes cited *McClanahan* as well, but a different passage: "State laws are generally not applicable to tribal Indians on an Indian reservation except where Congress has expressly provided that State laws shall apply." And, while it conceded that in the past 150 years the absolute barrier to state jurisdiction found in *Worcester v. Georgia* had been "modified in some respects," it insisted that the Supreme Court had "uniformly held that a state lacks jurisdiction over Indians in Indian country in the absence of an Act of Congress expressly conferring such jurisdiction." As Congress had not granted California such jurisdiction to enforce its gambling laws on Indian reservations, the State's effort was "barred under the basic principles espoused in *McClanahan* and its progeny."

The Tribes agreed with California that Congress had the power to preempt or displace the federal common law balancing test on which the State relied. And that, they argued, is exactly what Congress did when it passed Public Law 280. California had denied Public Law 280's preemptive effect because the result would be that California would have less jurisdiction in Indian country than non–Public Law 280 states, an anomalous result because Public Law 280 was intended by Congress to give the mandated states more jurisdiction. But, as the tribes remarked, "This Court has never upheld state jurisdiction over tribes or reservation Indians if not obtained in compliance with Public Law 280 or some other applicable federal statute. Therefore, the 'anomaly' complained of by the appellants is simply non-existent."

The Tribes' brief then addressed the possibility that the Court might nonetheless apply the common law balancing test in this case, and it argued that California still would not have jurisdiction. Both "federal law" and "current federal Indian policy" encouraging and fostering tribal self-government and promoting reservation economic development preempted California's gambling laws. It denied California's contention that the federal government played no role in the oversight of tribal bingo: the secretary of the interior had approved the tribal bingo ordinances of the Cabazon and Morongo Bands, had other "extensive substantial regulatory authority" over tribal bingo activities, and had imposed "detailed guidelines" requiring, among other things, FBI investigation and background checks on all non-Indian bingo management personnel for the express purpose of prohibiting criminal infiltration into any tribal bingo enterprise.

Finally concerning the balancing test, the Tribes' brief argued that even if federal law and policy did not preempt California's gambling laws, on balance, the federal and tribal interests in supporting and promoting tribal bingo enterprises were strong, because they raised revenue for tribal governments to provide essential programs and services on their reservations, and the state interest was weak, because the threat of criminal infiltration of tribal games was potential, not actual; because both the tribes and the federal government shared "a substantial interest" in keeping tribal games free from criminal involvement; and because there were no "off-reservation effects that necessitate State intervention." It noted that "despite its pious pronouncements, it is important to note that California not only makes commercial gambling widely available to its residents, through race tracks and card rooms, but it is now itself in the gambling business, by operation of the new State Lottery. Thus, its argument against tribal bingo based on 'moral grounds' is somewhat hypocritical."

The Brief of the Appellees then moved on to a focused consideration of Public Law 280. It argued initially, and for the first time in this litigation, that Public Law 280 did not confer any state jurisdiction over the Tribes themselves and their governmental activities. It quoted the Supreme Court's words in *Bryan*: "There is notably absent any conferral of state jurisdiction over the tribes themselves." Public Law 280 was not, it insisted, intended to "undermine or destroy existing tribal governments." Rather, it was intended to "subject individual Indians to state judicial proceedings, as criminal defendants or voluntary civil litigants." Even though Public Law 280 was passed at the height of the last period of assimilationist sentiment, its language contrasted strikingly with the contemporaneous language of various Termination Acts, in which Congress declared that state law "shall apply to the Tribe and its members." Congress clearly knew how to subject tribal governments to state jurisdiction, but, the Tribes' brief continued, it did not employ language that did so in Public Law 280. And, it reminded the Court, even if it found that it still had some doubt about this, " 'the eminently sound and vital canon' that ambiguities in federal statutes passed for the benefit of Indians" obliged it to resolve them in the Tribes' favor.

The Appellees' brief sought to assure the Court that tribal governmental immunity from state jurisdiction under Public Law 280 "would not allow Indian tribes to operate Las Vegas–style casinos, or traffic in narcotics, or operate reservation-based brothels with impunity." Such activities would be subject to federal prosecution under the Johnson Act of 1951, which made it unlawful in Indian country "to manufacture, recondition, repair, sell, transport, possess, or use any gambling device [defined as any slot machine or mechanical device, employing a drum or wheel, used for a game of change entitling the winner to receive any money or property]." This was an important concession: the Tribes were not arguing that they were free from federal regulation, only state regulation.

We are not arguing here that Indian tribes, or individual tribal members, are free to engage in criminal conduct under the guise of tribal self-government. Rather, we contend that Public Law 280 does not authorize the State of California to prohibit tribal activities that are in furtherance of federal Indian policy and, in fact, sanctioned by the Secretary of the Interior, and treat them as 'criminal' activities because they differ in minor ways from the manner in which the State authorizes the same conduct. Congress intended no such result when it enacted Public Law 280.

The Brief of the Appellees then argued that, if the Court were to find that Public Law 280 did, in fact, subject tribal activities to state jurisdiction, *Bryan*'s civil/regulatory–criminal/prohibitive distinction nevertheless prohibited California from enforcing its gambling laws on their reservations because they were civil regulatory in nature. It observed that even the California Supreme Court had recognized and adopted precisely the same civil/regulatory–criminal/prohibitory distinction under Public Law 280 that the Ninth Circuit had made in *Cabazon* in its *People ex rel. Department of Transportation v. Naegele Outdoor Advertising Company* (1985) – California petitioned the U.S. Supreme Court for review of the California Supreme Court decision, but the U.S. Supreme denied certiorari in 1986. In that case, California's highest court held that California could not regulate billboards located on Indian reservations by applying the California Outdoor Advertising Act, because Public Law 280 gave the State jurisdiction to hear private civil litigation involving tribal members but not to enforce its civil regulatory laws, like the Outdoor Advertising Act, on the reservation. And, the brief continued, "Like its bingo laws, the State's Outdoor Advertising Act authorized some billboards, regulated them in certain ways, and included a criminal penalty for violations of the statutory scheme."

It denied California's claim that the civil/regulatory–criminal/ prohibitive distinction was arbitrary or unworkable. It was, in fact, required by the language and structure of Public Law 280 and represented a straightforward determination that federal and state courts routinely make in many contexts. It noted that state and local governments are frequently given, under various state constitutions and statutes, the power to "regulate" – as opposed to "prohibit" – a given activity, obliging state courts to draw "this distinction in determining the propriety of state or local governmental action." And additionally, various constitutional guarantees, such as those prohibiting compelled self-incrimination or double jeopardy, apply in criminal but not civil proceedings, which, it pointed out, again require the courts "to distinguish between the two in determining whether the protections apply."

Finally, it branded as "incorrect" California's contention that "a revisionist approach to Public Law 280" was warranted on the basis of "previously unknown legislative history." The 1953 Interior Department letter upon which appellants relied was clearly part of the record before the Supreme Court when it decided *Bryan*. Thus, there is "no newly discovered legislative history and no reasoned basis upon which to reconsider *Bryan*."

The Brief of the Appellees briefly addressed OCCA. It noted that despite the fact that various tribal bingo enterprises had been in operation since 1980, and that there were currently more than eighty bingo parlors in operation around the country, the federal government had never attempted to enforce OCCA against a single tribal bingo enterprise. "This fact alone belies any contrary interpretation of OCCA by the appellants."

It also briefly addressed Riverside County's claim to jurisdiction over the Cabazon Band's card room by pointing out that in *Bryan*, the Court had cited and relied on the Ninth Circuit's opinion in *Santa Rosa Band of Indians v. Kings County* that had held that Public Law 280 did not subject reservation Indians to local jurisdiction and that a tribal government on the reservation was "more or less the equivalent of a county or local government" and therefore empowered "to regulate matters of local concern within the area of its jurisdiction." In this case, the brief continued, "the Cabazon Band is seeking local decision-making authority within the parameters of State law to operate a card room for the purpose of generating tribal revenues. If the congressionally mandated goal of Indian self-determination has any substance whatsoever, it must include at least this minimal level of self-governance over the reservation." And it denied that the Cabazon Band was "marketing an exception" by permitting various card games to be played on its reservation, for those specific games were not prohibited under state law and were widely played throughout California and in five other card rooms in other cities in Riverside County. "Nor is there any significance to the fact that non-Indians may come onto the reservation to play these games," for nonresidents of these other

Riverside cities "can readily" travel to them to play poker. Finally, it challenged California's claim that Cabazon's card games were more prone to criminal infiltration than the other identical games being played elsewhere in Riverside County. "All of the[se] factors . . . preventing criminal involvement in tribal bingo games, including the resources of the federal government, are equally applicable to the[se other] card games. For these reasons, the Court should affirm the right of the Cabazon Band to operate its tribal card room."

The Brief of the Appellees concluded with one brief sentence: "For all of the foregoing reasons, the Cabazon and Morongo Bands of Mission Indians respectfully urge this Court to dismiss this appeal for lack of jurisdiction or, alternatively, to affirm the judgment of the Ninth Circuit Court of Appeals."

Eight amici curiae briefs were filed on behalf of the Tribes; seven on September 24, the same date the Tribes submitted their Brief of the Appellees, and one, jumping the gun on September 22 by the San Manuel Band of Serrano Mission Indians. These eight briefs, representing seventy-one tribes or tribal associations that were already engaging in tribal gaming or that were preparing (or wanted to preserve the option) to engage in tribal gaming, repeated many of the points found in the Brief of the Appellees. Three emphasized the federal government's commitment to tribal self-sufficiency and economic development and quoted President Ronald Reagan's "Statement on Indian Policy" to that effect; two stressed how the Supreme Court's decision in *Bryan* was controlling; one (the San Manuel brief) emphasized that the "charitable" bingo games California authorized were not controlled by the State "in a way that would have any meaningful impact on organized crime control or criminal activity in general"; one (the brief of the Barona Band of Mission Indians, the Pala Band of Mission Indians, the Rincon Band of Mission Indians and thirty-nine other tribes) repeated the important argument of the Tribes' brief that the Cabazon and Morongo Bands were engaged in gaming operations for the same reasons as California, i.e., to raise revenue; one (the brief of the Seminole Tribe of Florida and the Fond du Lac Band of Lake Superior Chippewa of Minnesota) insisted that the supposed "serious risk of organized crime infiltration" was "unsupported by the record, unsupported by the literature, and unfounded in fact"; one (the brief of the Agua Caliente Band of Cahuilla Indians and thirteen other tribes) emphasized that "this case is controlled by the rule in *McClanahan* that state laws are not applicable to Indians on reservations absent express federal consent"; and one (the brief of the Jicarilla Apache Tribe and two others) made the unique and important point that if the Court accepted California's balancing test argument, the result would "necessarily generate an enormous amount of litigation to determine the continued validity of many treaties, federal statutes intended to benefit Indian tribes, and other federal policies that affect Indian tribes."

On October 20, California submitted its closing brief in which it recapped its case and replied to the argument of the Brief of the Appellees. It began by defending the balancing test and by responding to the Tribes' contention that the balancing test did not apply here because the State was attempting to assert jurisdiction over Indians rather than non-Indians in Indian country: "The tribal games solicit and depend on non-Indian patronage. . . . Further, the games are operated by non-Indian professional operators who have entered into management contracts with the Tribes. In effect, non-Indian operators are conducting bingo games played by non-Indian patrons in circumvention of State law. In light of the extensive non-Indian involvement here, the balancing test is particularly appropriate in determining the jurisdictional issue."

It rejected the Tribes' effort to distinguish *Colville* because they were providing "value" to non-Indians who played the games. The games had "value," it noted, only because the Tribes were offering a product that was unlawful in California and that non-Indian enterprises could not similarly offer. "In other words, the tribal product has 'value' only in the sense that contraband has 'value,' because it is marketed to buyers who cannot lawfully obtain it under state law. The value of the tribal product depends less on tribal efforts than on state laws prohibiting the product. Such 'value' is not entitled to judicial cognizance."

It reminded the Court that in *Rice*, it had held that California—a Public Law 280 state—had the right to regulate liquor sales on Indian reservations. If Public Law 280 preempted state regulatory jurisdiction as the Tribes insisted, California would have lacked the authority to regulate such liquor sales, and *Rice* "would have been wrongly decided."

California denied that federal policy, articulated by President Reagan and various members of the Department of the Interior, favoring tribal economic development preempted California's gambling laws. The presidential policy statement did "not mention gambling or bingo as a means to achieve tribal economic development." It also noted that unlike in *Rice*, the federal government had not filed an amicus brief supporting the tribal position here. "In any event, the statements cited by the Tribes lack the force of law and cannot have a preemptive effect."

It proceeded to deny the Tribes' claim that the secretary of the interior maintained oversight authority by approving tribal bingo ordinances, and that the exercise of this authority preempted state and local laws, pointing out that the secretary's approval of tribal bingo ordinances was not a prerequisite for tribal operation of the games, and that many games were operating without such approval:

> The Cabazon Tribe here, for example, although commencing its bingo operation in or around March 1983, did not seek or obtain secretarial approval until September 16, 1986, barely a week before the Tribe filed its brief on the merits. This scenario suggests that the Tribe was attempting to improve its position in this litigation rather than comply with a prerequisite, and in any event shows that the Secretary maintains little or no regulatory control over the games.

If anything, according to the closing brief, this "scenario" showed that the Tribes were operating in a "regulatory void," and it offered many concrete examples: the secretary did not regulate operating personnel, the size of jackpots, the days or hours of operation, or the distribution of revenues. The games were wholly unregulated, and each tribe controlled its own games. The tribes could "hire any operating personnel, offer jackpots in any amount, commingle bingo revenues with other revenues, and use revenues for any purpose." They could even use these tribal revenues "to enrich individual tribal members rather than fund tribal programs."

It faulted the Tribes for "seriously underestimat[ing]" the organized crime risk their unregulated games created and thereby underscored the State's vital interest in prohibiting them. It also discounted the Tribes' interest in offering high-stakes bingo, calling it "simply economic," and it noted that the Court in *Colville* had held that the generation of revenues for tribal services was an insufficient justification to outweigh the enforcement of state tax laws. It insisted that "unless Congress specifically legislates in favor of the tribal interest asserted here," California's interest in protecting the integrity of its gambling policy and in preventing organized criminal infiltration "outweighs any tribal economic interests, however compelling."

California repeated its arguments that OCCA and Public Law 280 authorized the application of its gambling laws and that *Bryan*'s civil/regulatory–criminal/prohibitory dichotomy was mere "dictum." It parried the Tribes' argument that Public Law 280 did not provide for state jurisdiction over Indian tribes, as opposed to individual Indians, by declaring that "nothing in Public Law 280 or its legislative history supports this limitation." It argued that both Public Law 280 and the common law balancing test allowed Riverside County to enforce its card game ordinance in Indian country. And it concluded that "for the foregoing reasons, it is respectfully requested that this Court reverse the decision below."

CHAPTER 6

Cabazon

Oral Argument and the Supreme
Court's Decision

In a letter to the parties dated October 6, 1986, the Supreme Court announced that it had scheduled one hour of oral argument for *California v. Cabazon Band of Mission Indians* for 2:00 p.m. on Tuesday, December 9. On October 14, Feldman filed a motion with the Court to allow additional counsel to argue for the Tribes (Barbara E. Karshmer, attorney for the Morongo Band); on November 3, the Court denied his motion, with only Justice Blackmun noting his support. On November 18, Karshmer filed on behalf of the Tribes a "Request to Take Judicial Notice" of two things: the first was a just-released Senate Report, No. 493, that contained "material that is germane to this case"; the second was the fact that "although the 99th Congress adjourned before Senate action could be completed on . . . the Indian Gambling Regulatory Act, which had already passed the House of Representatives, the Senate Select Committee on Indian Affairs favorably reported the bill, with an amendment, to the full Senate on September 26, 1986."

Four cases were heard by the Supreme Court on December 9; *Cabazon* was the last of the day. Before Roderick E. Walston, Supervising Deputy Attorney General for the State of California and Counsel of Record for the Appellants, could begin with the famous words employed by all attorneys who appear before the Supreme Court: "Mr. Chief Justice, and may it please the Court," the justices had already heard oral argument in a case involving the statutory construction of the Federal Unemployment Tax Act (*Wimberly v. Labor & Industrial Relations Commission*, decided 8-0 on January 21, 1987) and in two cases addressing the question of whether criminal defendants had voluntarily waived their *Miranda* rights (*Connecticut v. Barrett* and *Colorado v. Spring*, both decided by identical 7-2 votes on January 27).

In their book, *Making Your Case: The Art of Persuading Judges*, Scalia and Garner note that "many lawyers view oral argument as just a formality, especially in courts [such as the U.S. Supreme Court] that make a practice of reading the briefs in advance." "What," these lawyers wonder, "can a half hour of oral argument add to what the judges have already learned from reading a few hundred pages of briefs, underlining significant passages, and annotating the margins?" This skepticism, Scalia and Garner assert, "has proved false in every study of judicial behavior we know." Oral argument does not change the mind of a well-prepared judge; however, "what often happens is that the judge is undecided at the time of oral argument (the case is a close one), and oral argument makes the difference. It makes the difference because it provides information and perspective that the briefs don't and can't contain."

Scalia and Garner continue, specifying "in descending order of importance" an attorney's objectives in oral argument: (1) "to answer any questions and satisfy any doubts that have arisen in the judges' mind"; (2) for attorneys for the appellees, "to answer new and telling points" raised in the appellant's reply or closing brief ("oral argument is your only chance"); and, (3) "to call to the judges' minds and reinforce the substantive points made in your brief." With those objectives in mind, Roderick Walston, attorney for the State of California, began, formulating the question before the Court as "whether state laws prohibiting high stakes gambling are applicable to tribal gambling operations, most of which feature bingo."

Before beginning his argument that California's gambling laws do apply, Walston provided a brief summary of California's "main argument before the Court" — one that focused exclusively on the federal common law balancing test and never even mentioned Public Law 280.

Our view is that four major factors support state jurisdiction here as those factors are relevant under the balancing test, and I would like to briefly mention them. First, in our view the tribal games here are successful primarily because they are illegal under California law in that they allow non-Indians to play high stakes bingo in circumvention of state law, and therefore the value of the games essentially derives from restrictions that the state places against its own non-Indian citizens. Second, the states, not Indian tribes, have traditionally regulated gambling. Therefore the activity in this case falls within the traditional province of states, not Indian tribes, and therefore as we view it the principle of tribal sovereignty is not implicated in this case. Third, the federal government does not in any way regulate or supervise these games. They are wholly unregulated. Fourth, because of the high stakes and lack of regulation the tribal games create in our view a serious risk of infiltration by organized criminal elements.

Before he could state his conclusion, Walston was interrupted by Justice John Paul Stevens, who asked, "What do you mean by high stakes?" ($250, he was told), and who wondered what the maximum stakes for winning were ("a $15,000 maximum prize under the Morongo games," he learned). But after two minutes of questioning by several justices curious about the details of tribal bingo, Walston completed his opening summary: "Our conclusion from the four factors is that if these games are legalized they should be regulated and therefore the conclusion as we view it is that if there is to be bingo by the Indian tribes here the authorization must come from Congress. Congress has the power to impose regulations upon these games. Until Congress does that we think it is impermissible for this Court to uphold the games in their present form."

At this point, the justices became more active in their questioning. Chief Justice William Rehnquist suggested that the games were already regulated — by the tribes. Walston replied: "The tribes claim that but in actuality we feel that there is no regulation at all. Each tribe makes its own decision in terms of how the games are operated. There is no uniform federal standard that applies. The Secretary of Interior does not regulate the games. There is no uniform intertribal standard that applies." Rehnquist, however, wondered what was wrong with a lack of uniform standards and with each tribe having its own gaming regulations. "If you think of tribal sovereignty as compared to state sovereignty, California wouldn't regulate the same way that Arizona does." Revealing the State's low regard for the principle of tribal sovereignty, Walston dismissed the comparison and argued that the tribes did not have "the same relation to the State as other states do." State sovereignty, he noted, is "spelled out in the Tenth Amendment," while tribal sovereignty depends on "the balance of competing tribal, federal, and state interests." He emphatically rejected any equating of tribal sovereignty with state sovereignty; the Cabazon Band, he stated, "has only 25 members, and it is difficult for us to imagine that an Indian tribe with 25 members can be equated with, say, the sovereign state of California or, for that matter, any other sovereign state."

Justice Sandra Day O'Connor then asked whether under the balancing test the State was advocating, the federal interest in promoting tribal gaming would not predominate over the State's interest: surely, she said, he would "concede" that there is "certainly no question but that the federal government has supported and encouraged the tribes to engage in these bingo operations." Walston refused to do so. He insisted that "a pronounced ambivalence" existed at the federal level with respect to tribal gaming. He elaborated on this when O'Connor asked: "Isn't there legislation pending in the Congress now that would that would authorize these games and regulate them, too?" Walston agreed that an Indian gambling bill had passed the House and the Senate Select Committee, but he noted that it had not been approved by the full Senate. When O'Connor added: "That's because it was the end of the session, wasn't it?" Walston insisted that "there was more to it than that," declaring that there was strong opposition on the floor of the Senate to the bill. He informed her that the Department of Justice had stated that the bill "did not go far enough in establishing regulatory safeguards" and had labeled it "an anti–law enforcement device that failed to adequately protect against the intrusion of organized crime on Indian reservations." When Chief Justice Rehnquist then asked him if the federal government had filed a brief on this case, Walston was allowed to underscore his point: "No, the federal government has not, and I think that the failure of the federal government to file a brief in this case speaks volumes concerning the ambivalence of the federal position in this case."

When Justice Stevens then inquired if the federal government supported the pending bill in the Congress, Walston was able to highlight this federal ambivalence one more time by replying: "I understand that the Interior Department supported the bill. The Justice Department opposed it, and the views of the President, I understand, were closer to those of the Justice Department than Interior."

Justice Harry Blackmun then asked if it was not true that the tribes heavily relied on the proceeds from these games for support of tribal programs. Walston conceded that fact but argued that the tribes had an interest only in the revenue, not an interest in high stakes gambling, which, he insisted, had never played a part of Indian historical development, was not indigenous to tribal culture or custom, and was not a traditional Indian practice.

Chief Justice Rehnquist wondered if Walston's characterization was accurate: "The Ninth Circuit. . . said that there had been a tradition of Indian gambling for a long time, didn't they, in their opinion?" Walston was unfazed: "No, the Ninth Circuit didn't say that, Mr. Chief Justice. I think that the Ninth Circuit said that the tribes had a sovereign interest in raising revenue and that that was a traditional government function, and that therefore the tribes . . . should be allowed to raise revenue by any type of activity at all, and therein lies the difference, one of the major differences between the Ninth Circuit and us." He reminded the Court of *Rice*, which he said was consistent with past Supreme Court decisions that had "always looked to the activity of Indian tribes, not their revenue raising interest, in determining whether the principle of tribal sovereignty applies."

He was then asked by Justice Lewis Powell if there was any evidence that organized crime had infiltrated the appellants' bingo operations. He replied that there was no evidence "on the record" but repeated his arguments from the State's opening brief that the possibility that the bingo operations may be taken over by organized crime is a very serious concern to the State of California and that it is better to prevent organized criminal infiltration before it takes place rather than attempt to eradicate a criminal operation after it has actually occurred. Justice O'Connor chimed in: "Well, I suppose nothing would prevent the Department of Interior from adopting some kind of further regulation." Walston agreed. "If Interior adopted regulations, presumably the regulations would be effective in resolving or at least reducing the organized crime problem, and to the extent that the regulations would have that effect, then many of the concerns that I have expressed today would be mitigated." But, he continued, to date, neither the Interior Department nor Congress had acted.

Justice Stevens then questioned whether California had any other interest in passing its gambling laws than the prevention of organized crime. Walston answered "No, that is the major interest that California has in placing limits on charitable bingo." Stevens seemed incredulous: "Just to keep organized crime out?" But Walston insisted: "Yes, our view is that if the low-stakes limits were eliminated and if charitable organizations were allowed to hire outside operators rather than conduct the games themselves, then under those circumstances organized crime may well take control of charitable bingo operations in California."

Unsatisfied, Justice Stevens persisted in his line of questioning and forced Walston to address what he had emphasized in California's opening brief but what he now seemed interested in ducking: the moral objections to gambling. Stevens asked him: "Do you think historically that the only basis for state prohibition or regulation of gambling is to keep organized crime out of the business? . . . It has been a long time that gambling was considered contrary to public policy." Walston conceded, "I suppose there is another element," prompting a sarcastic Stevens to respond: "You just happened to think of that?" Somewhat sheepishly, Walston then admitted that "I suspect that what you are leading to is the possibility that the state may have some moral objections to unregulated gambling." Stevens had made his point: "Protecting its citizens against their appetites, isn't it?"

Walston's reasons for wanting to sidestep the "moral grounds" on which California had steadfastly stood in its opening brief soon became clear, for Justice Antonin Scalia then asked him to describe the "other sorts of gambling" allowed in California. When he had finished mentioning the state lottery, card clubs, pari-mutuel betting on horseracing, and low-stakes bingo, Scalia provoked general laughter in the courtroom by quipping: "It is sort of hard to get moral when you hit bingo."

Walston then admitted that he had "deliberately not tried to advance a moral argument before this Court." While California had initially regulated gambling for primarily moral reasons, "the recent adoption of the state lottery and other types of state-authorized gambling activities" led him to conclude that "the state's moral objections to gambling have diminished." Finishing on this topic, Walston supposed that many people in California support California's anti-gambling laws primarily on moral grounds, "but as I say, that is not the argument that we address before this Court today."

Justice Byron White then took the argument in a different direction and challenged California's argument that tribes were marketing an exception to the State's gambling laws. He described "California's efforts here as going beyond preventing the Indians from offering this service or marketing this gambling to non-Indians. You want them to quit entirely." When Walston replied that California wanted the Tribes' bingo games to comply with state law, White asked: "Suppose the Indians said, all we want to do is have a bingo game for Indians." Would California still have the right to regulate them, he wondered. Walston replied that "the factors, the elements, and the dynamics of the case would be vastly different if Indians were playing bingo on the reservation with other Indians," and he conceded that "where Indians engage in a purely internal activity on the reservation I think a stronger argument can be made by the tribes that they have a sovereign right to engage in that kind of activity." But that response brought the following query from Justice Scalia: "Even though that might attract criminal elements just as well. If you have enough Indians on the reservation you can have a pretty big bingo game, and organized crime might be attracted to it." When Walston replied that while that was true, "still the balance of interest we think might indeed support that kind of tribal operation." Justice White caught him in this contradiction and showed that Walston was not as clear on the theory of his case as he should have been by declaring that "California law on its face would prevent that." Walston confessed that was true and then sought to extricate himself by reminding the justices that "the situation before the Court is not one where Indians are playing bingo amongst themselves."

Justice White concluded this colloquy by summarizing California's argument as follows: "This is just Indians dealing with a non-Indian situation, and if you can keep them from selling cigarettes to non-Indians you ought to be able to keep the non-Indians out of their bingo game." Walston agreed: "I think that is essentially much of our argument."

Chief Justice Rehnquist then observed that "one reason the state approves and regulates horseracing is that it gets a lot of revenue," and asked "is that true of its regulation of bingo, too? Does it get any revenue from bingo games that are conducted in compliance with its laws?" Walston replied that California received no money from charitable bingo, but it did receive money from the lottery and the state horseracing act. And, he used this question as the opportunity to snipe at the Tribes' argument that because of the lottery, gambling was not contrary to the public policy of California. "I should add that part of the moneys from the state lottery do indeed inure to the benefit of Indians themselves." He told the Court that "about $6.5 million of state lottery funds" had been expended "just for the education of Indian children. So the Indian children themselves receive the benefits of California's state lottery, and it is therefore difficult for us to understand the tribal argument that somehow the existence of the state lottery militates against the state position here."

This statement was met with stony silence by the justices, and after a long and embarrassing pause, Walston briefly addressed OCCA and how it expressed "a federal policy we think in favor of state regulation of gambling and against unregulated gambling." He then reserved the rest of his time (six minutes) for rebuttal.

Glenn M. Feldman then approached the lectern to argue on behalf of the Tribes. He was irritated that Walston was now arguing that all California wanted was for the Department of the Interior to adopt regulations that would reduce the organized crime problem and thereby "mitigate" the State's concerns. He began in the customary fashion but then immediately launched into his attack: "Mr. Chief Justice, and may it please the Court, I think we have seen a bit of equivocation on the part of the state here this afternoon. Let there be no mistake that what the state is asking for here is full jurisdiction over these tribal activities to shut them down and put them out of business."

He got no further when Justice Stevens interrupted him with a question: "Well, Mr. Feldman, is that fair . . . if you just put a $250 limit on the game they wouldn't want to shut you down, would they?" Feldman replied: "No, that is not correct, Your Honor. Under California law a great number of organizations can sponsor charitable bingo, but Indian tribes are not among those groups, so under California law Indian tribes are not able to sponsor even charitable bingo in California." Feldman also argued that the tribes were also prohibited by California's bingo law from restricting the games to tribal members because it affirmatively required that the bingo games must be open to the general public and not restricted solely to members of the authorized organization.

Justice O'Connor then got to the heart of the matter: "Mr. Feldman, I guess the most obvious concern about your position in the case is the concern we would have that the tribes are marketing an exemption from state law and the analogy to the cigarette tax situation as in *Colville*." Feldman was quick to point out how "considerably different" tribal gaming was from the issue presented in *Colville*. "I would note at the outset that in the cigarette tax case that the incidence of the tax at issue there was on non-Indians. In this case the incidence of the state's jurisdictional scheme is directly on the tribes themselves. So the question of whether the state has jurisdiction to regulate these activities is a considerably different one." He also pointed out that the non-Indians who came onto the reservation to play bingo violated no state law and evaded "no state obligation by doing so"; by contrast, in *Colville*, the cigarette purchasers were evading a legal obligation to pay Washington cigarette taxes. Finally, he noted, in *Colville*, the tribes did not provide "what was called value generated on the reservation." They were in fact marketing an exception, for "there you had people coming onto the reservation, buying cigarettes which had been imported from elsewhere, and then taking the cigarettes off and evading the obligation to pay state taxes." In this case, Feldman insisted, the situation was quite different. "What the tribes are offering here are recreational services, plain and simple."

His argument that the tribes were providing recreational services prompted Justice O'Connor to ask if he thought the tribes could open casino gambling on the reservation? His answer was "clearly no." He pointed out that under the Johnson Act of 1951 the use or possession of certain mechanical gambling devices such as slot machines, roulette wheels, and wheels of fortune on Indian reservations is a federal offense. "So in no instance could those activities take place on an Indian reservation. They would be immediately in violation of federal law."

Justice Stevens continued in the same vein. "Mr. Feldman, with reference to recreational services on the reservation, what if the services were the opportunity to consume drugs on the reservation?" Feldman replied that the Tribes' position was "pretty straightforward" and that "if the activity is prohibited by the state, then under Public Law 280 that prohibition applies equally on the reservation." Stevens responded by asking if the Tribes' high-stakes bingo games were not prohibited by the state, to which Feldman answered, "No, the question is what activity is involved, and in this case bingo is permitted but regulated under California law."

Chief Justice Rehnquist then jumped in and repeated the arguments of California's opening brief: "You can really get into some hairsplitting about, you know, whether something is prohibited or whether it is regulated." Feldman acknowledged that the civil/regulatory–criminal/prohibitive dichotomy would not "result in absolute clarity in every instance," but the dichotomy had been applied by "every federal court that has considered" it and was "consistent" with *Bryan*, in which the Court had unanimously held that states had no civil regulatory jurisdiction over tribal government.

Justice Stevens then asked: "Mr. Feldman, supposing a state authorized prostitution subject to certain regulation. If they regulated it, then you could have it on an Indian reservation unregulated under your argument." Because Stevens then went on to mention Nevada in particular, Feldman used the occasion to remind the Court of the sovereign status of the Tribes: "If the state permits local option on prostitution, then yes, our view is that a tribal government is equivalent to a city or state or county government." Stevens interrupted him, "No, I didn't say local option. I said they permit it throughout the state but they regulate it. But you would say on the tribe it could go forward unregulated." Feldman replied that it could go forward but "subject to federal and tribal regulation." Stevens asked: "By analogy to the bingo . . . yes." Feldman indicated his irritation with the hypothetical: "I think there has got to be an element of common sense provided here." He reminded the Court that the tribes are under the direct control and supervision of the secretary of the interior, and "the Secretary is not going to allow outrageous activities on the reservation."

A break in the questioning allowed Feldman to say: "Let me make a couple of points here that I think need to be made." First, he pointed out that Indian tribes are governments, and like all governments they need a source of revenue in order to function. Next, he noted that most tribes do not have a natural resource base. "The Cabazon and Morongo bands have reservations out in the middle of the desert, and until there is a commercial market for sand or sagebrush they do not have any sort of natural resources to generate tribal income." Consequently, they and more than 120 other tribes around the country had turned to bingo. "In doing this they have been acting very much like the 28 states, including California, that have established state lotteries. The purpose is the same, to provide governmental revenues for public purposes. This is in essence a form of voluntary taxation."

A question from Scalia provided Feldman the opportunity to inform the Court that in 1984 the average jackpot on the Cabazon reservation for their bingo games was $184.89, well below the limit on state-regulated charitable bingo. "Now, that is not to say that in some games they don't offer larger prizes." But, he continued, the amount of money "actually being awarded" is "considerably less" than what is trumpeted on the big billboards along the freeway. Just as "the D.C. Lottery doesn't award $20 million every week," so the tribal bingo parlors do not award huge jackpots every game. Feldman was in the midst of describing the billboards as "something that is designed to improve the number of people" attending, when Scalia once again elicited laughter from spectators in the courtroom by interrupting him and asking: "Do you think the state has an interest in regulating the kind of disclosure that is made to prospective customers?"

Learning the modest size of the average jackpot, Chief Justice Rehnquist was puzzled: "Why do people drive 70 or 80 miles then to play this game, if they do that, when they could just drive a couple miles to a charitable game closer to home?" Feldman answer was direct: "We think that what we are providing are better services, frankly. Bingo players don't require very much. Bingo players want a chair with a little padding and Smoke-Eaters that will clear the air and get the cigarette smoke out. And if you can provide that better than the guy down the street, then you are going to attract more people to your bingo."

Feldman was then able to segue to the concern of organized criminal infiltration of tribes. "What we are dealing [with] here on the part of the state of California is at most a hypothetical concern." The State had stipulated to the fact that there is no evidence of organized crime involvement on either the Cabazon or Morongo reservation. When Justice Stevens noted that California said there was nonetheless a real danger, he replied that "I suppose at some point you have to determine how realistic, how credible is the danger. Here Congress has studied the issue extensively over the last two years. They have conducted field hearings around the country, including California, and both the Senate and the House reports on [the] legislation [pending before the Congress] conclude with no qualifications that there is no organized crime involvement anywhere."

Justice Scalia then returned to mechanical gambling devices and led Feldman through a grueling set of questions. It started easy: "Suppose California doesn't allow roulette wheel gambling. Would the reservations be able to have roulette wheel gambling?" Feldman answered no, because it would be a criminal offense under both the Johnson Act, as he had previously noted, and Public Law 280. Scalia continued: Why is the difference between roulette wheels and bingo cards more significant as to whether it constitutes a prohibition as opposed to merely a regulation than the difference between bingo for under $250 and bingo for $1 million. . . . I am asking, are you sure that this is just a regulation and not a prohibition? California prohibits bingo for more than $250. It is just like prohibiting roulette wheels."

Feldman replied that California flatly prohibited roulette wheels but permitted through its regulations the playing of bingo, but Scalia declared: "Not for over $250." Scalia continued on this theme: "Why isn't it realistic here in light of the interest involved to consider bingo for more than $250 as absolutely prohibited in California." Feldman responded, arguing that California had to demonstrate that it has some "authority" or "reasoned basis" to exercise jurisdiction over the tribes, especially since "the whole concept under California law is that bingo is going to be widely permitted throughout the state." Scalia continued to bear down: "Maybe you know gamblers better than I do, but I think a real gambler would probably consider the difference between a $250 roulette game and a $250 bingo game as less significant than the difference between a $1 million bingo game and a $250 bingo game. I think California is prohibiting high-stakes bingo and the tribes are offering high-stakes bingo." Feldman replied that the question becomes this: "Does the inclusion of a penal sanction in their regulatory scheme give them jurisdiction over these tribal activities?" The Tribes' answer under *Bryan* was "absolutely not. If that were the law, *Bryan* would be gutted. *Bryan* says states were not authorized to exercise general regulatory jurisdiction over Indians."

When Chief Justice Rehnquist then interjected: "All *Bryan* held was that a tax statute couldn't be applied in Itasca County," Feldman was quick to point out that while "that was the issue, the Court used the phrase civil regulatory jurisdiction, including taxation, four times."

Rehnquist continued, raising another issue present in California's opening brief. "Well, California prohibits the intentional taking of a human life but allows it in the case of self-defense. Does that mean intentional killing is prohibited or regulated?" Feldman was quick to reply: "It is prohibited," prompting Rehnquist to provoke general laughter when he declared, "Good." Unflustered, Feldman acknowledged that "all regulation involves some aspect of prohibition," but defended the civil/regulatory–criminal/prohibitory dichotomy as a "meaningful way" by which courts can protect tribal self-government from unauthorized assertions of state jurisdiction. "We think the fact that every single federal court that has considered the question, and there are now ten decisions over the last five years, every single federal court has concluded in this manner. We think there must be something to those decisions." The dichotomy "must be workable or all these federal courts wouldn't have decided to adopt [it]."

Justices Stevens and Scalia then asked a series of questions that expressed their concern about the Tribes' ability and willingness to dismiss bingo employees who were shown to have associations to organized crime. Feldman responded emphatically that "the tribes are governments, and they have an interest in seeing that these games are run as effectively and as efficiently and as honestly as they can. They have the most to lose. So there is no reason why a tribe would knowingly employ or continue to employ somebody who is going to provide trouble for them." He insisted that the tribes had been very effective in regulating these activities, that their ordinances were very clear as to what was or was not permitted, that they had employed security personnel to avoid any problems, that "even the smallest tribes ha[d] the ability to regulate their games," that they were able to bar access to the reservation to any non-Indian they choose, that they could seek judicial relief if there was a problem, and finally, that they could close their games entirely until the matter was resolved.

Feldman was then able to complete his argument by addressing the federal government's support for and involvement in tribal bingo. There was, he insisted, "a very clear shared understanding among all three branches of the federal government that these activities are a legitimate means by which tribes can raise revenues." There was "an unbroken line of federal authority" that supported these activities against state and local jurisdiction. While Congress had not yet completed action on a bill, it had issued reports that "provide a pretty clear factual record as to the benefits that bingo is providing to these tribes." The tribes were using their revenues for governmental services, providing programs on the reservation that had not previously been provided. And, they were "doing this without relying on federal funds, and that is the whole idea of what tribal self-sufficiency is supposed to be about." For over a century, the federal government had been telling the tribes, "Don't rely on the federal government. Go out and raise the money yourselves and then provide services to your members, just like any government." However, the tribes had "never been able to do it until now. Bingo is providing 100 or more tribes around the country with that ability." These bingo games, he insisted, were "not a nefarious activity" and "not threatening." They were "subject to close scrutiny by the Secretary of the Interior," and, he closed, "the federal government is strongly supportive of these activities."

Walston returned to the lectern for rebuttal. In *Making Your Case*, Scalia and Garner describe the purpose of rebuttal as allowing the appellant to respond to "the appellee's significant oral attacks on your oral presentation or your brief." This is exactly what Walston did. He "very strongly" differed with Feldman's claim that under California law the Indian tribes in this case could not conduct charitable bingo. The State's revenue and taxation code provided an exemption for a not-for-profit entity that is engaged in promoting the social welfare, and, Walston argued, "our view is that Indian tribes can qualify as charitable organizations within the meaning of that section and therefore can conduct charitable bingo on the same terms as other charitable organizations in California."

He also attacked Feldman's argument that *Colville* was not applicable because the incidence of state regulation there fell on non-Indians. The incidence of state regulation here, he insisted, fell on both the tribes and the non-Indian patrons. He pointed to § 320 of the California penal code that specifically prohibited both the operation of and the participation in a lottery. Since bingo is a form of a lottery, he concluded that "it is illegal for non-Indians to participate in these games."

Before he could address other points, Justice White wondered who "complain[ed] about these Indian lotteries," prompting the Riverside County District Attorney to prosecute them. "I wouldn't think a local prosecutor would get so excited unless there might be a question of votes or something." Walston pointed to the "vast opposition" to tribal gaming by nonprofits engaging in charitable bingo. He mentioned an example from Arizona involving the St. Keno Learning School that was heavily dependent upon the proceeds from charitable bingo and that was forced to "shut down simply because of the competition from the tribal games in Arizona."

Walston then attempted to rebut one more point made by Feldman, namely, that tribes needed high-stakes bingo in order to obtain revenue for tribal purposes and had no real options other than tribal bingo. With his time expiring, he insisted that "other types of options" were available to the tribes including "manufacturing, agri-business, and modern technology." Before he could elaborate, he declared: "I am sorry. My time is up."

Chief Justice Rehnquist then concluded the oral argument in *California v. Cabazon Band of Mission Indians* with customary language: "The case is submitted."

But, while the case was submitted, the parties were not done arguing before the Court. On December 17, in a highly unusual move, Feldman filed simultaneously a "Motion for Leave to File Post-Argument Brief" and the "Post-Argument Brief."

The motion argued that Walston had made a "misstatement of fact" during his rebuttal during oral argument that related to a significant issue and was "directly contrary to the stipulated facts in the case. Because it was made in rebuttal, counsel for the appellees had no opportunity to respond during oral argument." The Post-Argument Brief then elaborated. During rebuttal, Walston stated that the Cabazon and Morongo Bands could qualify as organizations authorized to sponsor bingo games under California laws. But, the brief noted, California had stipulated to Judge Waters during the District Court's consideration of this case that "the appellees tribes are 'not among the enumerated entities authorized to operate bingo games' under California law."

On December 22, California responded with its "Motion for Leave to File Response to Post-Argument Brief" and its accompanying "Response to Post-Argument Brief." Its motion to file a response asserted that if the Court granted the Tribes' motion, that it be allowed to respond, and its response argued that "in stipulating that the appellees tribes are 'not among the enumerated entities authorized to operate bingo games,'" the State "meant only to stipulate that the appellees tribes have not undertaken the necessary procedures to obtain authorization under California law, not that the appellees tribes could not operate the games if such procedures were undertaken."

On Wednesday, February 25, 1987, Chief Justice Rehnquist began the Court's session by calling upon various justices to announce the decisions of the Court in those cases for which they had been assigned the writing of the Opinion of the Court. He called upon Justice White to announce the Court's decision in *California v. Cabazon Band of Mission Indians*. Justice White was characteristically brief. "In the *Cabazon* case which is here from the Court of Appeals for the Ninth Circuit, we affirm the judgment of that court and remand the case. Justice Stevens has filed the dissenting opinion; Justices O'Connor and Scalia have joined that opinion."

Cabazon was one of six cases decided that day. The other five were *U.S. v. Paradise*, in which, by a 5-4 vote, the Court upheld an affirmative action plan that forced the Alabama State Police to promote one black trooper for every white promoted until blacks comprised 25 percent of upper-rank officers; *Hobbie v. Unemployment Appeals Commission*, in which, by an 8-1 vote, it ruled that states may not deny unemployment benefits to workers fired for refusing to work on their Sabbath; *FCC v. Florida Power*, in which the Court held unanimously that the federal government may put limits on the rates cable television companies must pay for attaching their wires to utility company poles; *Martin v. Ohio*, in which, by a 5-4 vote, it held that Ohio's law placing the burden of proof on a murder defendant to prove self-defense did not violate due process; and *Springfield v. Kibbe*, in which, by a 5-4 vote, it declined for procedural reasons to decide whether the City of Springfield, Massachusetts, could be forced to pay damages in the death of a fleeing motorist killed by a policeman's bullet.

Justice White's majority opinion in *Cabazon* was joined by Chief Justice Rehnquist and Justices William Brennan, Thurgood Marshall, Harry Blackmun, and Lewis Powell. This by itself was interesting. Chief Justice Rehnquist and Justices White and Powell had typically voted against tribal interests in previous cases; White had in fact written the majority opinion in *Colville*, Rehnquist had joined the majority in *Rice*, and Powell had joined the majority in both. Without their three votes, *Cabazon* would have been a 6-3 decision not for but against the Tribes.

Justice White's opinion, as his announcement from the Bench, was fairly brief, taking up only eighteen pages. The structure of its legal argument closely followed the structure of the Ninth Circuit's opinion.

In his introduction of the case, he mentioned that the tribal ordinances allowing for bingo games on the reservation had been approved by the secretary of the interior and that the games in question were open to the public, were played predominantly by non-Indians, and were the major source of employment for tribal members and the sole source of income for the Tribes. He also noted that the statute California was attempting to apply to the Tribes did not entirely prohibit the playing of bingo but rather permitted it when the games were operated and staffed by designated charitable organizations that limited prizes to no more than $250 per game. In a footnote, he addressed Deputy Attorney General Walston's rebuttal statement in oral argument that "contrary to the position taken in the merits brief and contrary to the stipulated facts in this case," the Tribes were among the charitable organizations authorized to sponsor bingo games under the statute. Without referencing the post-argument briefs, but clearly acknowledging them, he declared that it was "unclear whether the State intends to put the tribal bingo enterprises out of business or only to impose on them the staffing, jackpot limit, and separate fund requirements." But in any case, he noted, the tribal bingo enterprises were "apparently consistent" with other provisions of California's statute. Finally, in another footnote, he addressed the fact that the Court had postponed the question of whether it had jurisdiction in this case until a hearing on the merits. He asserted that "since it is now sufficiently clear that the state and county laws at issue were held, as applied to the gambling activities on the two reservations, to be 'invalid as repugnant to the Constitution, treaties or laws of the United States' within the meaning of [the Judiciary Act of 1925], the case is within our appellate jurisdiction."

He then launched into the core of his argument. He observed that the Court had consistently recognized that tribes retained "attributes of sovereignty over both their members and their territory," and that "tribal sovereignty is dependent on, and subordinate to, only the Federal Government, not the States." While state laws could be applied to tribal Indians on their reservations if Congress expressly so provided, the question before the Court was whether Congress had in fact given its express consent. California, he noted, argued that Congress had expressly consented twice: "first in Public Law 280 in 1953 and second in the Organized Crime Control Act in 1970." But, he continued: "We disagree in both respects."

White first took up Public Law 280. He affirmed the Court's decision in *Bryan* and its interpretation that Public Law 280 granted the mandated states jurisdiction over private civil litigation involving reservation Indians in state court but did not grant them general civil regulatory authority. Since a grant to the states of general civil regulatory power over Indian reservations "would result in the destruction of tribal institutions and values," he concluded that the Court must determine whether a law that a state seeks to enforce within an Indian reservation under the authority of Public Law 280 "is criminal in nature, and thus fully applicable to the reservation, or civil in nature, and applicable only as it may be relevant to private civil litigation in state court."

While the Minnesota personal property tax at issue in *Bryan* was "unquestionably civil in nature," he acknowledged that the California bingo statute at issue here was "not so easily categorized." California law permitted bingo games conducted only by charitable and other specified organizations and then only by their members who volunteered their efforts; it limited prizes and required that receipts be segregated and used only for charitable purposes. Violation of any of these provisions was a misdemeanor, and so California insisted that these are criminal laws which Public Law 280 permitted it to enforce on the reservations.

But, White noted, in both *Barona*, and before it, *Butterworth*, federal courts of appeals had built on what they "thought to be the civil/ criminal dichotomy drawn in *Bryan*" and introduced

> a distinction between state "criminal/prohibitory" laws and state "civil/regulatory" laws: if the intent of a state law is generally to prohibit certain conduct, it falls within Public Law 280's grant of criminal jurisdiction, but if the state law generally permits the con-

duct at issue, subject to regulation, it must be classified as civil/ regulatory and Public Law 280 does not authorize its enforcement on an Indian reservation. The shorthand test is whether the conduct at issue violates the State's public policy.

White endorsed this approach: "We are persuaded that the prohibitory/regulatory distinction is consistent with *Bryan*'s construction of Public Law 280."

He confessed that the civil/regulatory–criminal/prohibitory distinction was "not a bright-line rule," and that "an argument of some weight" could be made that California's bingo statute was prohibitory rather than regulatory. But, he continued, "we are reluctant to disagree with [the Ninth Circuit's] view of the nature and intent of the state law at issue here," for California clearly did not prohibit all forms of gambling. "California itself operates a state lottery and daily encourages its citizens to participate in this state-run gambling. California also permits parimutuel horse-race betting." Although California prohibited "certain enumerated gambling games," it permitted "games not enumerated, including the card games played in the Cabazon card club," and it allowed to "flourish" more than 400 card rooms similar to the Cabazon card club. And concerning bingo, California permitted charitable bingo but imposed no limit on the number of games an eligible organization could operate, the amount of revenues it could generate, the number of games a participant could play, or the amount of money a participant could spend, either per game or in total. "In light of the fact that California permits a substantial amount of gambling activity, including bingo, and actually promotes gambling through its state lottery, we must conclude that California regulates rather than prohibits gambling in general and bingo in particular."

White then addressed the California argument that "high-stakes, unregulated bingo, the conduct which attracts organized crime, is a misdemeanor in California and may be prohibited on Indian reservations." He rejected the proposition that regulatory law enforced by criminal as well as civil means is thereby converted into a criminal law within the meaning of Public Law 280. Otherwise, he pointed out, the civil/regulatory–criminal/prohibitory distinction "could easily be avoided and total assimilation [of the tribes] permitted" — a result at odds with the canons of construction of federal Indian law. Accordingly, he concluded for the six-member majority that that Public Law 280 did not authorize California to enforce its gambling laws on the Cabazon and Morongo Reservations. (In a footnote, he added the following: "Nor does Public Law 280 authorize the County [of Riverside] to apply its gambling ordinances to the reservations.")

White turned next to OCCA and the claims of California and Riverside County that it authorized the application of their gambling laws to the tribal bingo enterprises. The Ninth Circuit had rejected their claims below on the basis of *Farris* and *Barona*. In these two cases, earlier Ninth Circuit panels had held that whether a tribal activity is "a violation of the law of a state" within the meaning of OCCA depended on whether it violated the "public policy" of the State, i.e., the same test for application of state law under Public Law 280; on that basis, they had concluded that bingo was not contrary to the public policy of California. White's additional commentary was brief: Neither accepting nor rejecting the Ninth's Circuit's analysis, he simply declared that OCCA was "a federal law that, among other things, defines certain federal crimes over which the district courts have exclusive jurisdiction. There is nothing in OCCA indicating that the States . . . are authorized to make arrests on Indian reservations that in the absence of OCCA they could not effect."

White then turned to California's federal common law argument. Even though *McClanahan* had declared that "[state] laws generally are not applicable to tribal Indians on an Indian reservation except where Congress has expressly provided that State laws shall apply," White observed that the Court had never "established an inflexible *per se* rule precluding state jurisdiction over tribes and tribal members in the absence of express congressional consent." *Colville* was "illustrative," for he had held for the Court majority in that case that, even in the absence of express congressional permission, Washington could require tribal smoke shops on Indian reservations to collect state sales tax from their non-Indian customers.

For White, the federal common law question of whether California could prevent the Tribes from making available high-stakes bingo games to non-Indians coming onto their reservations turned on whether state authority was preempted by the operation of federal law; that, in turn would be determined by employing a balancing test, with state jurisdiction being preempted if it interfered or was incompatible with federal and tribal interests as reflected in federal law, unless the state interests at stake were sufficient to justify the assertion of state authority. That balancing of interests would, however, proceed "in light of traditional notions of Indian sovereignty and the congressional goal of Indian self-government, including its 'overriding goal' of encouraging tribal self-sufficiency and economic development."

These, White emphasized, were important federal interests. Relying on arguments from the Tribes' briefs, he invoked President Reagan's 1983 Statement on Indian Policy and noted that the Department of the Interior, which had the primary responsibility for carrying out the federal government's trust obligations to Indian tribes, had sought to implement these policies by promoting tribal bingo enterprises. Under the Indian Financing Act of 1974, the Secretary of the Interior had made grants and guaranteed loans for the purpose of constructing bingo facilities. Likewise, the Departments of Housing and Urban Development and Health and Human Services had also provided financial assistance to develop tribal gaming enterprises. Additionally, the secretary of the interior had approved tribal ordinances establishing and regulating the gaming activities involved, had exercised authority to review tribal bingo management contracts, and had issued detailed guidelines governing that review. These policies and actions were particularly relevant to the case and demonstrated to White's satisfaction the federal government's "approval and active promotion of tribal bingo enterprises." He noted that the Cabazon and Morongo Reservations contained no natural resources that could be exploited, and that the tribal games provided "the sole source of revenues for the operation of the tribal governments and the provision of tribal services" and the major source of employment on the reservations. "Self-determination and economic development are not within reach if the Tribes cannot raise revenues and provide employment for their members. The Tribes' interests obviously parallel the federal interests."

White next addressed California's assertion that the tribal interests were weak because they merely marketed an exemption from state gambling laws. He contrasted the bingo parlors here with the smoke shops in *Colville*. Repeating Feldman's argument in the Brief of the Appellees and what Feldman had said in reply to Chief Justice Rehnquist's questions during oral argument, White declared that the Tribes were not merely importing a product onto the reservations for immediate resale to non-Indians. "They have built modern facilities which provide recreational opportunities and ancillary services to their patrons, who do not simply drive onto the reservations, make purchases and depart, but spend extended periods of time there enjoying the services the Tribes provide. The Tribes have a strong incentive to provide comfortable, clean, and attractive facilities and well-run games in order to increase attendance at the games." The Cabazon and Morongo Bands were "generating value on the reservations through activities in which they have a substantial interest." He found California's reliance on *Rice* equally unavailing. *Rice* was predicated on the fact that Congress had never recognized any sovereign tribal interest in regulating liquor traffic and "had plainly anticipated that the States would exercise concurrent authority to regulate the use and distribution of liquor on Indian reservations." But, he insisted, there was "no such traditional federal view governing the outcome of this case, since, as we have explained, the current federal policy is to promote precisely what California seeks to prevent."

Finally, he addressed California's claim that its interest in imposing its bingo laws was strong because of the need to prevent the infiltration of the tribal games by organized crime. He was unpersuaded, to say the least: "To the extent that the State seeks to prevent any and all bingo games from being played on tribal lands while permitting regulated, off-reservation games, this asserted interest is irrelevant and the state and county laws are pre-empted. Even to the extent that the State and county seek to regulate short of prohibition, the laws are pre-empted." California insisted that high-stakes tribal bingo was attractive to organized crime, whereas the low-stakes charitable games authorized under California law were not. While this was "surely a legitimate concern," he remained unconvinced as California did not allege any present criminal involvement in the Cabazon and Morongo enterprises, and the Ninth Circuit discerned none.

In a footnote, White responded powerfully to Justice Stevens's identification of another state interest in prohibiting or regulating tribal bingo, i.e., the state's interest in restricting the proceeds of gambling to itself and the charities it favored. He found this "strange," noting that California had asserted no such interest and that it was "pure speculation" on Stevens's part to argue that, "in the absence of tribal bingo games, would-be patrons would purchase lottery tickets or would attend state-approved bingo games instead." But, quite apart from that, White insisted that California had no legitimate interest in allowing potential lottery dollars to be diverted to non-Indian owners of card clubs and horse tracks while denying Indian tribes the opportunity to profit from gambling activities. Neither was it entitled "to prefer the funding needs of state-approved charities over the funding needs of the Tribes, who dedicate bingo revenues to promoting the health, education, and general welfare of tribal members."

White concluded: "We therefore affirm the judgment of the Court of Appeals and remand the case for further proceedings consistent with this opinion. It is so ordered."

Unsurprisingly, given the questions they asked during oral argument, Justice Stevens filed a dissenting opinion in which Justices O'Connor and Scalia joined. Stevens proceeded from what White described in his majority opinion as an entirely "opposite presumption," which he laid out in the very first sentence of his dissent. "Unless and until Congress exempts Indian-managed gambling from state law and subjects it to federal supervision, I believe that a State may enforce its laws prohibiting high-stakes gambling on Indian reservations within its borders." Stevens appreciated that gambling provided needed employment and income for Indian tribes, but, he insisted, these benefits did not justify tribal operation of currently unlawful commercial activities. Building on a line of questioning he had pursued during oral argument, he declared that accepting the majority's reasoning would require "exemptions for cockfighting, tattoo parlors, nude dancing, houses of prostitution, and other illegal but profitable enterprises." As he understood the law, "tribal entrepreneurs, like others who might derive profits from catering to non-Indian customers, must obey applicable state laws."

Addressing Public Law 280, he held that its "plain language" authorized California to enforce its prohibition against commercial gambling on Indian reservations. The State prohibited bingo games that were not operated by members of designated charitable organizations or that offered prizes in excess of $250 per game, and Public Law 280 "expressly provided that the criminal laws of the State of California 'shall have the same force and effect within such Indian country as they have elsewhere within the State.'"

He found "curious" the Court's reasoning that the operation of high-stakes bingo games did not run afoul of California's public policy because the State permitted some forms of bingo. California's policy concerning gambling was clear: it was to authorize certain specific, carefully regulated gambling activities that provided revenues either for the State itself or for certain charitable purposes and to prohibit all unregulated commercial gambling operated for private profit. He drove his point home with a powerful analogy: "To argue that the tribal bingo games comply with the public policy of California because the State permits some other gambling is tantamount to arguing that driving over 60 miles an hour is consistent with public policy because the State allows driving at speeds of up to 55 miles an hour."

He was not persuaded that the Tribes were not marketing an exception to state law. The only value he saw the Tribes as generating by their "asserted exemption" from California's gambling laws was the "primary attraction" it provided "to customers who would normally do their gambling elsewhere." He cited the Declaration of William J. Wallace, expert witness for California (and whose declaration the Tribes had made a concerted effort at the District Court level to have stricken from the record) and argued that the Cabazon Band had "no tradition or special expertise in the operation of large bingo parlors." And, he found it a "mystery" how "this small and formerly impoverished" band with only twenty-five enrolled members "could have attracted the investment capital for its enterprise without benefit of the claimed exemption."

While California had argued in its opening brief that it had two interests in prohibiting tribal gambling (preserving the moral character of its residents and preventing the infiltration of organized crime), and while later during oral argument it had somewhat clumsily insisted that its only interest was the fear of criminal infiltration, Stevens on his own added still a third interest: "The State's interest is both economic and protective. Presumably the State has determined that its interest in generating revenues for the public fisc and for certain charities outweighs the benefits from a total prohibition against publicly sponsored games of chance." For Stevens, the revenues the Tribes received from their bingo operations drained revenues from the state-approved recipients of its lottery, "just as the tax-free cigarette sales in [*Colville*] diminished the receipts that the tax collector would otherwise have received."

While during oral argument Stevens had pressed Walston to address the morality of gambling and California's interest in "protecting its citizens against their appetites," he did not advance that state interest in his dissent but turned instead to California's concern that these unregulated high-stakes bingo games could attract organized criminal infiltration. "Comprehensive regulation of the commercial gambling ventures that a State elects to license is obviously justified as a prophylactic measure even if there is presently no criminal activity associated with casino gambling in the State." The threat was sufficient for him to conclude that unless Congress authorized and regulated these tribal gambling operations, "the State has a legitimate law enforcement interest in proscribing them."

Stevens concluded by acknowledging that, "in the abstract, gambling facilities are a sensible way to generate revenues that are badly needed by reservation Indians." But, consistent to the end in his rejection of the canons of construction of federal Indian law, he insisted that the decision to adopt "such a course of action, and thereby to set aside the substantial public policy concerns of a sovereign State, should be made by the Congress of the United States. It should not be made by this Court."

What *Cabazon* Has Wrought

Reactions to the *Cabazon* Decision

Justice White concluded his Opinion for the Court in *Cabazon* by affirming the Ninth Circuit's decision on behalf of the Tribes and remanding the case for further proceedings consistent with his opinion. The only remaining issue to be resolved at that point was the Cabazon Band's damages claim for $12,500,000 against Riverside County for violating 42 U.S.C. § 1983 by acting under color of law to deprive the rights, privileges, and immunities of the Tribe to govern itself on its own reservation as secured by the Constitution, laws, and policies of the United States and by denying the Tribe the equal protection of the laws by closing its card club when it allowed other non-Indian card clubs to operate unimpeded. (A similar damages claim by the Morongo Band – the amount sought by the Tribe had been left unspecified – was dismissed by stipulation by Judge Waters on October 15, 1985.) In late December 1986, after the *Cabazon* case had been submitted but before the Court had ruled in the Tribes' favor, Judge Waters had completed his review of Cabazon's damages suit and had dismissed it with prejudice.

Undaunted, and flush with its victory before the Supreme Court, the Cabazon Band appealed to the Ninth Circuit. In its pleadings before Judge Waters, the Tribe was able to show a loss of revenue of $106,182.33 when its card club had been closed for a month after the County's raid of its operations. But it wanted not just compensatory damages but punitive damages for the County's violation of the Tribe's sovereign rights under 42 U.S.C. § 1983, which provides that "every person who, under color of any statute, ordinance, regulation, custom, or usage, of any State or Territory or the District of Columbia, subjects, or causes to be subjected, any citizen of the United States or other person within the jurisdiction thereof to the deprivation of any rights, privileges, or immunities secured by the Constitution and laws, shall be liable to the party injured in an action at law, suit in equity, or other proper proceeding for redress." So, on May 27, 1987, the Tribe filed a fifty-page Brief of the Appellant with the Ninth Circuit. On July 10, Riverside County filed a twenty-nine-page Brief of the Appellee, and on August 10, the Tribe filed a twenty-nine-page Reply Brief. All three briefs explored at length the meaning of § 1983, its application to the facts involved, and the question of whether it provided the Riverside County Sheriff and his deputies with either absolute or qualified immunity from this suit.

Simultaneously, behind-the-scenes negotiations between the County and the Tribe were under way, and on September 29, one week before oral argument was schedule before the Ninth Circuit, a tentative agreement was reached. It was not for millions of dollars, but it was one that Feldman wrote to the Business Committee of the Cabazons and recommended the Tribe to accept. Riverside had agreed to settle for $85,000 — $59,500 to the Cabazon Band and, even though its damages claim had been dismissed two years before, $29,500 to the Morongo Band. With the recovery of other court costs and lawyers fees, and with the very distinct possibility that the Tribe might lose its case before the Ninth Circuit, Feldman argued that accepting the agreement seemed the prudent thing to do. It went a considerable way toward covering the Tribe's actual lost card club revenues, and it brought finality to what was an eight-year legal battle. The Tribe agreed that very day; the Ninth Circuit was notified of the settlement by the parties, at which point it dismissed the cross-pleadings by the Tribe and the County with prejudice; a Riverside County warrant was issued to the Tribe on October 26 and immediately deposited; and, at long last, on November 13, Judge Waters approved the settlement and closed the book on this extraordinary case.

Press reactions to the Supreme Court's *Cabazon* decision, at least in the Southwest, were immediate. On the very day of the decision, Wednesday, February 25, 1987, the local *Indio Daily News* ran a banner headline on page one announcing that the "Supreme Court Upholds Cabazon Bingo." It quoted Tribal Chairman Arthur Welmas as saying: "It's like Jack against the Giant." Also on February 25, *The Desert Sun*, published in nearby Palms Springs, declared in its banner headline, "Court

Upholds Indian Gambling." Welmas was again quoted: "We knew all along we have sovereign rights. It's the last thing we have on the reservation." He talked about how the decision assured tribal economic independence. "I'm sure the Indians want a piece of the American dream. [This decision] is going to help us economically — so we can provide employment, health care, and day care for our people. It's just a plus!" His comments reflected a cultural view of tribal sovereignty; he saw the decision as vindicating tribal sovereignty from infringements from all levels of government, not just from state infringements. He ignored, for example, the significant limitations on tribal sovereignty that the Congress had imposed on the ability of the tribes to engage in gaming through its passage of the Johnson Act of 1951 and that Glenn Feldman, operating from a constitutional and legal view of tribal sovereignty, had readily acknowledged during oral argument.

Feldman was also quoted: "Other people say it is raining in Phoenix [where his office was located], but I think it is bright and sunny."

Both the AP and the UPI had brief mentions of *Cabazon* along with the other five cases the Supreme Court decided that day. So did the *New York Times* wire service, which headlined its Supreme Court Roundup with what it considered the Court's most important decision that day: "Justices Rule in Florida Sabbath Case." The AP also had a brief (527-word) story entitled "Reservation Gambling Immune to Local, State Control."

On Thursday, February 26, the local *Riverside Press-Enterprise* ran a page one story headlined: "High Court Rules on Indian Bingo: Local Authority Limited on Tribal Reservations." It quoted Feldman: "This goes beyond gambling. Tribes are going to have a much broader degree of self-government under this ruling. State jurisdiction over reservations will be severely limited"; and it quoted Walston: "We're disappointed, but the Court has spoken, and we will conform to its decision." The *Phoenix Republic* also ran a page one story with the following headline and subhead: "Indian-Run Bingo OK'd by Justices: States Can't Bar or Regulate Games, Supreme Court Rules." It quoted a disappointed Arizona Attorney General Robert K. Corbin (on behalf of Arizona, he had filed an amicus brief before the Supreme Court in support of California); Corbin was worried about the infiltration of organized crime. The *Phoenix Republic* also informed its readers that Congressman Morris Udall, chairman of the House Interior and Insu-

{ *Chapter 7* }

lar Affairs Committee, was directing his committee staff to examine how the ruling could affect pending legislation to regulate tribal gaming. The *Los Angeles Times* ran a page three story announcing that the "Supreme Court Rules States Can't Regulate Indians' Bingo Games." It quoted Feldman and Barbara Karshmer, Morongo's attorney, who hailed the decision "as upholding 150 years of federal Indian law which the state wanted to change." The attorney for the San Manuel Band, a tribe that had filed an amicus brief on behalf of the Tribes and that had just opened its own 2,600-seat bingo hall, was ecstatic; he declared the Court's decision "should have long-range implications for tribes in general, and particularly on the issues of sovereignty and the relationships between tribes and other governmental entities such as cities and states." The *Albuquerque Journal* weighed in on page A-6 with a brief story entitled "High Court Bars State Regulation of Indian Reservation Gambling." On that same day, the *Indio Daily News* ran a follow-up page one story, "Cabazons Hit Jackpot with Court Victory." It quoted John Paul Nichols, the Tribe's general manager, as putting the cost of the litigation at $500,000, and Tribal Chairman Welmas as observing that this "money could have been put to better use improving tribal property and social programs."

The reaction to *Cabazon* in the legal literature was quite limited. At the time of the twentieth anniversary of the Court's decision in this landmark case, *Cabazon* had been mentioned in the law reviews only 382 times: 236 times in articles and 146 times in student notes and comments. The overwhelming percentage of these articles (83.1 percent) and notes and comments (83.5 percent) merely cited *Cabazon*, often with other related cases and without analysis or commentary. Of the articles and notes and comments that substantively addressed the *Cabazon* decision, only one argued that the Supreme Court misconstrued Public Law 280 and unjustifiably restricted state power to regulate and tax the tribal gaming industry — it found it troubling that the decision allowed tribal gaming to reduce lottery sales or cause consumers to spend money on gambling that would otherwise have been spent on goods and entertainment that generated state sales taxes. Three were neutral on the conflict between state and tribal interests and focused on the decision because of its faithful application of the canons of construction of federal Indian law. Thirteen focused on the civil/regulatory–criminal/prohibitory distinction. Ten applauded the decision's affirmation of tribal sovereignty and self-determination. Two were upset with the Supreme Court for even entertaining California's federal common law argument and applying (rather than repudiating) the balancing test and holding that California's jurisdiction was preempted by federal law because its interest was insufficient to justify the assertion of its authority. Thirty-five focused on how *Cabazon* was responsible for Congress's passage of the Indian Gaming Regulatory Act (about which, more below).

The reaction to *Cabazon* in the federal and state courts was more profound. At the time of its twentieth anniversary, *Cabazon* had been cited in 336 cases: by the U.S. Supreme Court in 9 cases, the United States Courts of Appeal in 89 cases, U.S. District Courts in 116 cases, the U.S. Bankruptcy Court in 1 case, the U.S. Tax Court in 1 case, state supreme courts in 41 cases, and lower state courts in 79 cases. In many of these cases, *Cabazon* was cited for more than one reason. These 336 cases cited *Cabazon* 213 times to indicate that federally recognized Indian tribes have ultimate sovereignty on their reservations unless specifically prohibited by Congress; they cited *Cabazon* 134 times to affirm that Public Law 280 does not grant general regulatory authority to the mandatory or discretionary states or to assert that the civil/regulatory–criminal/prohibitory dichotomy introduced in *Bryan* is controlling; they cited *Cabazon* 107 times as justification to apply the federal common law balancing test and to determine whether the federal and tribal interests in promoting tribal self-government and self-sufficiency outweigh competing state interests; they cited *Cabazon* 60 times to note that the Indian Gaming Regulatory Act was a result of the Supreme Court's decision in this case; and they cited *Cabazon* 43 times for a variety of other reasons — mostly in string citations.

In its first twenty years, *Cabazon* had also been cited in 176 briefs: 153 submitted to the U.S. Supreme Court, 5 submitted to various circuits of the United States Court of Appeals, 14 submitted to state supreme courts (9 to the California Supreme Court, 1 to the Montana Supreme Court, and 4 to the New York Court of Appeals), and 4 submitted to various districts of the California Court of Appeals. In many of these briefs, especially those submitted to the U.S. Supreme Court, *Cabazon* was cited for more than one reason. These 176 briefs cited

Cabazon 90 times to indicate that federally recognized Indian tribes have ultimate sovereignty on their reservations unless specifically prohibited by Congress (and that this principle pertains particularly to matters of state taxation); they cited *Cabazon* 38 times to affirm that Public Law 280 does not grant general regulatory authority to the mandatory or discretionary states or to assert that the civil/regulatory–criminal/prohibitory dichotomy introduced in *Bryan* is controlling; they cited *Cabazon* 59 times as justification to apply the federal common law balancing test and to determine whether the federal and tribal interests in promoting tribal self-government and self-sufficiency outweigh competing state interests; they cited *Cabazon* 19 times to note that the Indian Gaming Regulatory Act was a result of the Supreme Court's decision in this case; and they cited *Cabazon* 8 times for a variety of other reasons — ranging from the Court's affirmation in that case of the Marshall Trilogy to Congress's passage of the Dawes Act.

As mentioned above, many law review articles described the passage of the Indian Gaming Regulatory Act of 1988 (IGRA) as Congress's reaction to *Cabazon*. This is clearly an exaggeration. As early as 1983, Representative Morris Udall of Arizona had introduced H.R. 4566, the Indian Gambling Control Act, in the 98th Congress. While it died in committee, it would have recognized the right of tribes to engage in gaming so long as the games did not violate federal law or any express prohibitory state law. This is just one example of Congress's multiyear search for a regulatory scheme for Indian gaming. In their Motion to Dismiss Appeal or Affirm Judgment, the Tribes pointed to another: they offered as one reason for why the Court should deny jurisdiction in this case the fact that Congress was moving rapidly to enact legislation regulating tribal gaming and reaffirming the right of tribes to operate bingo free from state jurisdiction. Less than three weeks before oral argument, the Tribes filed a "Request to Take Judicial Notice" of the fact that while the Congress had adjourned before it could enact the Indian Gambling Regulatory Act, the House of Representatives had passed it and the Senate Select Committee on Indian Affairs had favorably reported the bill to the full Senate. Interestingly, not even the palpable anxiety felt by many tribal members and their friends in Congress when the Court noted probable jurisdiction in the *Cabazon* case – they feared that the Court had agreed to hear the case in order to reverse the Ninth Circuit – was sufficient to lead to necessary final compromises and adoption of new federal legislation prior to the Court's decision. IGRA clearly was not a direct congressional reaction to *Cabazon*. Professor Robert N. Clinton, in his superb article, "Enactment of the Indian Gaming Regulatory Act of 1988," suggests that a "more accurate description" would be that IGRA was the culmination of "parallel federal judicial and legislative responses to Indian gaming progressing relatively independent of one another." When the Court decided *Cabazon*, Congress was obviously forced to take account of *Cabazon* in its final legislation and to tailor IGRA to the Court's analysis in *Cabazon*.

Many law review articles also argue that what the Supreme Court gave the tribes in *Cabazon* – ostensibly, complete tribal authority over gaming on their reservations, Congress took away with IGRA – federal regulation of bingo and nonbanked card games (what the act called Class II gaming) and, subject to the terms of a mutually negotiated tribal-state compact, some state regulation of "Las Vegas"–style games (what the act called Class III gaming). This is an even greater exaggeration.

To begin with, *Cabazon* did not hold that the tribes had complete authority over gaming in Indian country. While it powerfully asserted that state authorities had no jurisdiction or power to challenge the Cabazon and Morongo tribal gaming operations, it did not hold that these operations were even legal or that they were in any way free from federal regulation. To begin with, there was the Johnson Act of 1951, acknowledged as governing by Feldman during oral argument, which made the use or possession of certain mechanical gambling devices such as slot machines, roulette wheels, and wheels of fortune on Indian reservations a federal offense. The Cabazon and Morongo Tribes were able to engage in high-stakes bingo and card games without violating the Johnson Act because neither involved the use of mechanical gambling devices. Were the Tribes, however, to have attempted to introduce lucrative slot machines in their facilities, they would in all likelihood have faced immediate federal prosecution. And, quite apart from the Johnson Act's ban on mechanical gambling devices, there remained the problem of even the legality of the Tribes' high-stakes bingo operations under OCCA. All that Justice White had held in his majority opinion in *Cabazon* was that California could not use OCCA to make arrests in Indian country to enforce its gambling laws against the Tribes. While the Ninth Circuit had held that OCCA was to be interpreted as preserving the same civil/regulatory–criminal/prohibitory distinction as Public Law 280, White had expressly declined to accept that position, therefore leaving open the question of whether federal authorities could prosecute the Tribes for violating California's bingo statute. White did offer the Tribes some reassurance when he observed that "we are not informed of any federal efforts to employ OCCA to prosecute the playing of bingo on Indian reservations, although there are more than 100 such enterprises currently in operation, many of which have been in existence for several years, for the most part with the encouragement of the Federal Government." But that, of course, was no guarantee against future federal prosecutions. Clearly, the Tribes had won a great victory in *Cabazon*, but it was against state regulation of their gaming operations, not against federal regulation.

It is also an exaggeration to say that IGRA took from the tribes what *Cabazon* had given them. The act began with three especially important congressional findings, including (1) "Numerous Indian tribes have become engaged in or have licensed gaming activities on Indian lands as a means of generating tribal governmental revenue"; (2) "A principal goal of Federal Indian policy is to promote tribal economic development, tribal self-sufficiency, and strong tribal government"; and (3) "Indian tribes have the exclusive right to regulate gaming activity on Indian lands if the gaming activity is not specifically prohibited by Federal law and is conducted within a State which does not, as a matter of criminal law and public policy, prohibit such gaming activity." IGRA also stated that the purposes for its enactment were the provision of a legislative basis for the operation/regulation of Indian gaming, the protection of gaming as a means of generating revenue for the tribes, the encouragement of economic development of these tribes, and the protection of their gaming enterprises from organized crime and other corrupting influences.

IGRA advanced those purposes by dividing Indian gaming into three categories and prescribing different levels of regulation for each category. Class I gaming consists of "social games solely for prizes of minimal value or traditional forms of Indian gaming engaged in by individuals as a part of, or in connection with, tribal ceremonies or celebrations." The act leaves "Class I gaming on Indian lands . . . within the exclusive jurisdiction of the Indian tribes."

Class II gaming includes bingo — "whether or not electronic, computer, or other technologic aids are used in connection therewith" — and, if played at the same location, "pull-tabs, lotto, punch boards, tip jars, instant bingo, and other games similar to bingo" as well as non-banked card games such as poker. "An Indian tribe may engage in, or license and regulate, Class II gaming on Indian lands within such tribe's jurisdiction, if such Indian gaming is located within a State that permits such gaming for any purpose by any person, organization or entity (and such gaming is not otherwise specifically prohibited on Indian lands by Federal law)." The states, however, have no formal role in the regulation of Class II games; such games are regulated by the tribes through tribal ordinances that have been approved by the chairman of the National Indian Gaming Commission (NIGC), a three-member commission also created by IGRA.

Class III gaming is any gaming not included in Classes I or II, including banked card games; casino games such as blackjack, craps, roulette, baccarat, and keno; slot machines; jai alai; and pari-mutuel wagering. The regulation of such gaming is subject to the same requirements as Class II gaming, but with one significant addition: in order to engage in Class III gaming, the tribes have to negotiate a compact with the state, subject to approval by the secretary of the interior. Addressing what was considered the likely possibility that states might simply refuse to negotiate compacts with the tribes, IGRA included provisions imposing on states a duty to negotiate in good faith with a tribe toward the formation of a compact and authorizing the tribes to sue a state in federal court in order to compel performance of that duty.

IGRA included language providing for an express exemption from the Johnson Act for compact-approved Class III gaming. It also provided that, except for assessments by a state necessary to defray the costs of regulating tribal gaming, nothing in the act

> shall be interpreted as conferring upon a State or any of its political subdivisions authority to impose any tax, fee, charge, or other assessment upon an Indian tribe or upon any other person or entity

authorized by an Indian tribe to engage in a Class III activity. No
State may refuse to enter into the negotiations . . . based upon the
lack of authority in such State, or its political subdivisions, to
impose such a tax, fee, charge, or other assessment.

IGRA also limited the authority of the secretary of the interior to
acquire land in trust for use for gaming activities.

IGRA passed the U.S. Senate by a voice vote on September 15, 1988,
the House of Representatives by a vote of 323 to 84 on September 27,
and was signed into law by President Reagan on October 17. It was the
culmination of five years of congressional efforts to address the various and conflicting interests of the federal government, the states, and
the tribes regarding the regulation of tribal gaming.

As mentioned above, the first proposed Indian gaming bill, H.R.
4566, was introduced in 1983 during the 98th Congress by Representative Udall, a Democrat from Arizona; entitled the Indian Gambling
Control Act, it would have codified the civil/regulatory–criminal/
prohibitory distinction first introduced in 1981 in the Fifth Circuit's
opinion in *Seminole Tribe v. Butterworth*; recognized the right of tribes
to game and to regulate gaming on their reservations provided the
games violated neither federal law nor any express prohibitory state
law; required tribes to adopt gaming regulations at least as restrictive
as state laws regulating gaming; authorized the secretary of the interior to approve tribal gaming ordinances; and given the secretary
access to the tribes' gaming facilities and their records. This early
effort made no distinctions between various forms of gaming and did
not modify either the Johnson Act or OCCA. The measure failed to
generate support from the Reagan Administration (the Justice Department was worried about the infiltration of organized crime, and the
Interior Department was ambivalent), the states, or the tribes, and it
died in committee. Nonetheless, this first effort was significant in one
respect: as Professor Clinton has noted, it "envisioned tribes as co-
equal regulators of gaming with the states" — it envisioned the states
regulating gaming outside of Indian country and the tribes regulating it on their own reservations.

In the 99th Congress, Representative Udall reintroduced a slightly
modified version of H.R. 4566 as H.R. 1920. (In the Senate, Senator
Dennis DeConcini, Democrat from Arizona, introduced S. 920, a bill

very similar Udall's H.R. 1920.) Interest on the subject, however, was growing in this Congress, and competing bills were also introduced. Representative Norman Shumway, a Republican from California, introduced N.R. 2404, a bill that would have restricted considerably tribal gaming by repudiating *Seminole Tribe*'s civil/regulatory–criminal/prohibitory dichotomy and allowing the enforcement of all state gambling laws, whether considered regulatory or prohibitory, in Indian country. And Representative Douglas Bereuter, a Republican of Nebraska, introduced H.R. 3130; it was not a comprehensive regulatory measure but instead was focused simply on prohibiting the acquisition of land in trust if the purpose of doing so was to provide a site for tribal gaming.

Hearings by the House Committee on Interior and Insular Affairs on these bills were held in the summer and fall of 1985. Among those testifying was the solicitor of the Department of the Interior, who proceeded to divide tribal gaming into three classes: (1) social and Indian ceremonial; (2) bingo; and (3) all other forms of gambling activity, thereby introducing for the first time the three classes of gaming ultimately adopted in IGRA. The solicitor explained that since social and ceremonial gambling were not operated for profit, involved only small stakes, and involved only tribal members, there was no need for regulation of such activities. Tribal high-stakes bingo was different, providing significant tribal revenue needed for tribal operations but also raising more significant law enforcement questions; it could, however, be safely regulated without state involvement by a "federal bingo regulatory commission," the first suggestion for the establishment of a regulatory body that ultimately became in IGRA the National Indian Gaming Commission. Finally, while acknowledging that all other forms of gambling could be economically beneficial to the tribes, the solicitor worried that "the potential law enforcement problems are so great as to outweigh the economic benefits to the tribes." This testimony proved extremely valuable; it indicated the kind of legislation that the Reagan Administration would accept and helped to shape the final outlines of what eventually became IGRA.

While the states were largely on the sidelines in the 98th Congress (not a single state representative appeared to testify on H.R. 4566), they became actively involved in the 99th Congress and came out in strong opposition to any form of Indian gaming. Arizona Attorney

General Corbin emphasized the serious law enforcement problems high-stakes bingo caused, noted that these games were illegal under OCCA, and expressed his frustration that federal law enforcement officials were unwilling to enforce its prohibitions. In his testimony, California Deputy Attorney General Rudolph Corona rejected (as the State would later reject in its arguments before the Supreme Court) *Seminole Tribe*'s civil/regulatory–criminal/prohibitory distinction and insisted that an application of the federal common law balancing test clearly favored state control of gaming in Indian country.

Horse racing and greyhound racing operators also weighed in; they worried that tribal gaming facilities, unregulated by state laws, would damage the public's belief in the integrity and honesty of their pari-mutuel betting operations. Nevada and Atlantic City casinos did not testify; since none of these bills modified the Johnson Act's ban of mechanical gambling devices in Indian country, they did not feel a competitive threat from Indian gaming operations.

During the second session of the 99th Congress, the House Committee on Interior and Insular Affairs, based on its hearings in the first session, significantly amended H.R. 1920 by introducing the solicitor's proposed division of tribal gaming into three classes; by giving concurrent federal and tribal regulation of Class II and Class III gaming; by adopting as the federal standard for Class III gaming a state's gambling law, irrespective of regulatory content; and, by expressly prohibiting any Class II and Class III gaming in Indian country in Nevada — in a major accommodation to Senator Harry Reid, Democrat of Nevada (and future Majority Leader of the Senate).

In the Senate, S. 902 was considered in hearings by the Senate Select Committee on Indian Affairs and was modified to became S. 2257; it modified S. 902 by strictly limiting Indian gaming to bingo regulated by a full-time National Indian Gaming Commission and by punting on the question of allowing Class III gaming in Indian country by imposing a four-year moratorium on any new Class III tribal gaming. It was never voted out of committee.

By a voice vote, H.R. 1920 was passed by the House of Representatives on April 21, 1986 — just four days after California submitted its Jurisdictional Statement to the Supreme Court appealing the Ninth Circuit's decision in *Cabazon*. The bill was then sent to the Senate, where the Senate Select Committee on Indian Affairs on September

26 voted 6-3 in favor of reporting out an amended version of H.R. 1920 to the full Senate. Chief among its amendments was an incorporation of a version of H.R. 3130's limitation of the authority of the secretary of the interior to acquire land in trust for use for gaming activities – a version of its language would ultimately be included in IGRA. The committee's reporting of its amended version was ill timed; it was only a month before the off-year congressional elections, and senators were otherwise engaged or distracted. The bill failed to make it to the Senate floor and died with the adjournment of the 99th Congress.

The 100th Congress came into session on January 3, 1987; fifty-three days later, the Supreme Court handed down its decision in *Cabazon* holding that states lacked regulatory power over tribal gaming facilities in Indian country. The reaction in Indian country to the Court's decision in *Cabazon* was euphoric; many tribal leaders read the decision as affirming tribal sovereignty in a cultural sense rather than as limiting state jurisdiction and, therefore, as conferring on the tribes the exclusive power to regulate and conduct any and all kinds of gaming in Indian country. They no longer saw the need for any federal legislation on the subject, as they believed the tribes were now free to authorize, regulate, and engage in gaming on their own. This view, later reflected in any number of law review articles, was incorrect. *Cabazon* did not confer on the tribes exclusive regulatory power over tribal gaming, and it did not address (and certainly did not limit) federal regulation of tribal gaming through the Johnson Act or OCCA. The need for comprehensive Indian gaming legislation remained a high priority; *Cabazon* gave urgency to Congress to complete its work, and the Court's affirmation of *Seminole Tribe*'s civil/regulatory-criminal/prohibitory distinction helped importantly to shape the final measure.

While the House of Representatives had taken the lead in the 98th and 99th Congresses, the Senate took the lead in the 100th Congress. In the summer of 1987, the Senate Select Committee on Indian Affairs conducted hearings on two competing Indian gaming bills. One bill was S. 555, offered by Senator Daniel Inouye, Democrat of Hawaii; it was similar to the Senate's amended version of H.R. 1920 that died with the adjournment of the 99th Congress. It included two especially significant modifications. It declared that the Johnson Act would not apply to any gaming conducted in conformity with its provisions (language that would also find its way into the final version of IGRA), and it banned all Class III gaming in Indian country unless the tribe consented to transfer to the state both regulatory and law enforcement jurisdiction over such gaming.

The other bill was S. 1303, offered by Senator John McCain, Republican of Arizona; it required that the national gaming commission it was proposing to establish approve tribal ordinances and license tribes to operate gaming facilities, including those offering Class III gaming, unless the commission made specific findings that the tribe could not operate the facility in accordance with the provisions of the act and the gaming codes it was charged with establishing. (Representative Udall introduced a companion bill in the House, H.R. 2057.) The proponents of S. 550 and S. 1303 agreed on many points, but they differed completely on one critical issued: Who was to regulate Class III gaming — the states or the federal government?

During the hearings it held that summer, the Select Committee received testimony from many tribal leaders generally in favor of some version of S.1303 and the federal regulation it proposed, but it also heard from some tribal leaders who challenged any form of federal regulation based on the cultural dimensions of tribal sovereignty. Roger A. Jourdain, chairman of the Red Lake Band of Chippewa Indians in Minnesota, asserted his Tribe's opposition to "S. 555, S. 1303, or any other legislation that would impose upon Indian tribes federal standards and regulations covering the conduct of gaming activities on Indian reservations"; he read *Cabazon* as conferring on the tribes the exclusive authority to regulate tribal gaming.

The committee also heard from state representatives committed to state and local regulation. John Duffy, the Sheriff of San Diego County and then serving as chairman of the National Sheriff's Association, testified. Duffy was the Sheriff involved in *Barona*, in which the Ninth Circuit for the first time embraced *Seminole Tribe*'s civil/regulatory–criminal/prohibitory distinction. He argued for state and local control of tribal gaming, declaring "the citizens of San Diego County expect — and I think should reasonably expect — that laws are applied equally throughout San Diego County." He worried that a national gaming commission, attempting to regulate hundreds of tribes from Washington, D.C., would fail at a task "best done at the local level where these sharp operations are involved."

Because of S. 555's Johnson Act exemption, Nevada gaming interests also became actively involved. Senator Reid of Nevada argued before the committee for state regulation of gaming on all lands within a state, including reservation land, and in opposition to "any exception to that rule," candidly acknowledging that the issue was "of utmost importance . . . to the future of my State's most important industry." Senator Jacob Hecht, Republican from Nevada, made much the same case, as did Representative Barbara Vucanovich, Republican from Nevada. Philip P. Hannifin, a former chairman of the Nevada Gaming Control Board and at the time a director of Riviera Holdings Corporation and executive vice president of MGM Grand, joined the chorus, urging that any Indian gaming must conform "to existing State laws and regulations." C. Stanley Hunterton, a former attorney with the U.S. Department of Justice's Organized Crime Strike Force in Las Vegas and deputy chief counsel to the President's Commission on Organized Crime during 1984–1985, also testified. He emphasized the difficulty of properly regulating gambling and keeping corrupting influences at bay and concluded by declaring that his extensive experience in law enforcement had convinced him that there was no reason to believe that the federal government would do a better job of regulation than the states.

Over a year passed before the Senate Select Committee on Indian Affairs returned to the question of regulating tribal gaming. The major sticking point to reaching a compromise all could accept had been deciding the question of whether Class III gaming in Indian country was to be regulated by the federal government or the states. But, on August 3, 1988, the Senate Select Committee voted out a much-amended version of S. 555, which addressed the question by deciding not to decide; rather than decide, once and for all, how much jurisdiction and regulatory authority the states should have over the tribes and their Class III gaming operations, the committee decided to let the parties themselves resolve those questions on a case-by-case basis through the negotiation of tribal-state compacts. In the Senate Report accompanying S. 555, the committee declared that the compacting process was perhaps the most "viable mechanism for settling various matters between two equal sovereigns."

The compact compromise was smart politically, but it posed a major threat to the tribes in one respect: what if a state simply refused to negotiate a compact with the tribes within its borders? In its Senate Report on the bill, the committee made it clear that it was not its intent for the compact requirement for Class III gaming to be used "as a justification by a State for excluding Indian tribes from such gaming or for the protection of other State-licensed gaming enterprises from free market competition with Indian tribes." But, how could the committee assure the tribes that the states would in fact come to the negotiating table?

The committee proposed an elaborate remedial scheme designed to ensure the formation of a tribal-state compact. It provided that a tribe could bring an action in federal district court showing that no tribal-state compact had been entered and that the state had failed to respond in good faith to the tribe's request to negotiate; at that point, the burden then shifted to the state to prove that it was in fact negotiating in good faith. If the district court concluded that the state was simply obstructing the process, it was required to order the state and Indian tribe to conclude such a compact within a sixty-day period. If no compact had been concluded sixty days after the court's order, then the court was to order both the Indian tribe and the state to submit to a mediator appointed by the court their proposed compacts that represented their last best offer for an agreement. The mediator would then choose from between the two proposed compacts the one that best comported with the terms of the act and any other applicable federal law and with the findings and order of the court and then submit it to the state and the Indian tribe. If the state consented to the proposed compact within sixty days of its submission by the mediator, the proposed compact would be considered as approved by the parties. If, however, the state did not consent within that time period, the mediator would notify the secretary of the interior, who was then authorized to "prescribe . . . procedures . . . under which Class III gaming may be conducted on the Indian lands over which the Indian tribe has jurisdiction" — i.e., to authorize the tribe to engage in Class III gaming on its reservation irrespective of the act's compacting requirements.

The full Senate took up debate of the amended S. 555 and its compact compromise on September 15, 1988. Not unexpectedly, Senator Reid of Nevada declared that "one of the most significant provisions of the bill," at least from his perspective, was the waiver of the Johnson Act for tribes that had successfully negotiated a compact with a state for the operation of Class III gaming. He sought confirmation that this waiver was in fact very limited. He was reassured by Senator Inouye, the floor leader of the bill, who confirmed that the waiver was in fact limited and that "the bill is not intended to amend or otherwise alter the Johnson Act in any way." Opposition to the bill came mainly from senators who thought it did not adequately protect tribal gaming. The comments of Senator Thomas Daschle, Democrat of South Dakota, were typical: "My reason for opposing the bill is that those Indian tribes from South Dakota I represent have informed me that this bill is unacceptable. The tribes strongly object to any form of direct or indirect State jurisdiction over tribal matters." Nonetheless, with minor amendments, S. 555 was approved by the Senate by a voice vote that same day.

Twelve days later, on September 27, the House voted to suspend the rules to consider S. 555 without committee action and then proceeded immediately to debate it. Some House members such as Representative Shumway wanted more state control and were unhappy with the compact compromise. Others, such as Representative Vucanovich, who said her earlier fears were now assuaged and that she would vote for it, thought it struck a "fair balance among the many parties who have interests at stake in the regulation." It passed later that same day by a vote of 323-84. IGRA was signed into law by President Reagan on October 17.

The constitutionality of IGRA was immediately challenged in U.S. District Court for the District of Columbia by the Red Lake Band of Chippewa Indians and the Mescalero Apache Tribe. The Tribes argued that by passing IGRA, Congress violated their right to self-determination and the federal government's trust responsibility to the Indians. Judge Louis F. Oberdorfer granted the motion of the Interior Department to dismiss the Tribe's complaints in *Red Lake Chippewa Tribe v. Swimmer* on June 3, 1990. A legal and constitutional understanding of tribal sovereignty trumped once again a cultural understanding of tribal sovereignty.

The suit was brought by Chippewa Chairman Roger Jourdain, who was convinced that what the Supreme Court had given in *Cabazon* in terms of full recognition of tribal sovereignty and complete tribal authority over gaming in Indian country, Congress had taken away in IGRA by subjecting Class II gaming to federal regulation and Class III gaming to regulation spelled out in a tribal-state compact. In truth, however, IGRA gave the tribes far more than it took away.

To begin with, IGRA gave the tribes an explicit exemption from the Johnson Act for Class III gaming conducted pursuant to a tribal-state compact. As Professor Robert Clinton persuasively argues: "Without this express exemption from the Johnson Act none of the slot machines, video poker machines, or, perhaps, even roulette wheels that constitute the cash cows of modern Indian gaming would have been possible since all such gambling devices were expressly prohibited in Indian country under section 5 of the Johnson Act." Second, while there was no explicit exemption from OCCA of tribal high-stakes bingo, IGRA's recognition of Class II gaming subject to the National Indian Gaming Commission constituted an implicit waiver of OCCA: what Justice White had left open in *Cabazon* — federal enforcement of state laws banning high-stakes bingo — was closed by IGRA. Third, IGRA was a statutory codification of the civil/regulatory–criminal/prohibitory distinction recognized in *Cabazon*. Fourth, IGRA went further than *Cabazon*, which had not addressed Las Vegas–style gaming, by allowing Class III gaming negotiated through a tribal-state compact. And fifth, IGRA protected the proceeds from tribal gaming from state taxation.

What IGRA took away from the tribes was, in fact, relatively modest. The tribes lost the ability to engage in Class III gaming without a compact, but without the Johnson Act exemption IGRA also provided, their Class III games would likely have been shut down by the federal government. Their Class II games were now subject to the regulation and oversight of the National Indian Gaming Commission, but the Cabazon and Morongo Bands had already sought approval by the secretary of the interior of their tribal gaming ordinances and management contracts, so little practically was changed by IGRA. IGRA also required federal approval of per capita distributions of gaming revenues to members to prevent favoritism or corruption, and provided that only tribes, rather than individual tribal members, could operate gaming facilities.

States gained much less than the tribes from IGRA. They were allowed to regulate tribal gaming only consistent with the terms of tribal-state compacts, and they were obliged to negotiate these compacts in good faith.

Interestingly, however, what the Congress in IGRA gave the tribes, the Supreme Court took away in the 1996 case of *Seminole Tribe of*

Florida v. *Florida*. When the Seminole Tribe sued the State of Florida in federal court for its refusal to enter into good-faith negotiations, Florida moved to dismiss the complaint on the ground that congressional authorization of the suit violated its sovereign immunity from suit in federal court. The district court denied Florida's motion, but the Court of Appeals for the Eleventh Circuit reversed, concluding that, under the Eleventh Amendment, the federal courts had no jurisdiction. In an opinion by Chief Justice William Rehnquist, a five-member majority of the Supreme Court agreed, holding that Congress lacked power under the Indian Commerce Clause to abrogate state sovereign immunity. As a result, the Court found unconstitutional that section of IGRA ordering the states to negotiate with the tribes in good faith; it did not, however, invalidate the language authorizing the secretary of the interior to approve tribal Class III gaming when the states are simply intransigent, as subsequent compact negotiations in Florida, discussed in the next chapter, make clear.

The fears of the tribes about the states' refusal to negotiate gaming compacts were realized. The Court in *Seminole Tribe of Florida* v. *Florida* had given the states a final veto on whether a tribe could engage in Class III gaming, frustrating the Congress's intention that the compact requirement for Class III gaming would not be used to exclude Indian tribes from such gaming or to protect other state-licensed gaming enterprises from tribal competition. As the next chapter will show, however, while Congress, after the Supreme Court's *Seminole Tribe* decision, was unable to provide a sufficient incentive for the states to negotiate tribal-state compacts in good faith, the tribes were able to achieve that all on their own; by offering various revenue-sharing proposals to cash-strapped states, a number of tribes were able to provide the monetary incentives necessary to coax the states to the negotiating table and to negotiate Class III gaming compacts that benefitted the tribes.

CHAPTER 8

Tribal Gaming under the Indian Gaming Regulatory Act

Compacting in Connecticut, California, and Florida

When the Congress passed IGRA, it effectively punted on the question of how much jurisdiction and regulatory authority the states were to have, consistent with the *Cabazon* decision, over the tribes and their Class III gaming operations; it decided instead to let the parties themselves resolve these questions on a state-by-state and a case-by-case basis through the negotiation of tribal-state compacts. This concluding chapter considers Class III tribal gaming under IGRA by examining three widely differing and not necessarily representative compacting experiences under IGRA: the straightforward and relatively uncomplicated experience in Connecticut, the contentious and protracted California experience resolved ultimately by the tribes' skillful use of the direct ballot, and the caustic and convoluted experience in Florida that took almost a quarter of a century to resolve.

Connecticut has only two tribal casinos: Foxwoods, operated by the Mashantucket Pequot Tribe, and Mohegan Sun, operated by the Mohegan Tribe. They are the largest and second-largest casinos in the United States, respectively, with their combined 13,000 slot machines generating annually close to $20 billion in gross revenues and $1.8 billion in net revenues for the tribes and approximately $420 million in annual tribal contributions to the State of Connecticut. But tribal gaming in Connecticut is interesting for other reasons as well.

Connecticut lost one of the first significant cases concerning the interpretation of IGRA. IGRA permits a tribe to conduct Class III gaming if, among other requirements, it is "located in a state that permits such gaming for any purpose by any person, organization, or entity." Connecticut permitted nonprofits to conduct annually a "Las Vegas night" to raise funds for charitable purposes subject to certain limitations and restrictions, such as limits on the size of wagers, the character of the prizes, and the use of volunteer labor. The law was passed, with great support from Mothers Against Drunk Driving (MADD), to encourage high schools to hold casino-type events following proms in order to reduce drunk driving by teenagers. The games of chance permitted by Connecticut's law at the Las Vegas nights included blackjack, poker, dice, money-wheels, roulette, baccarat, chuck-a-luck, pan game, over and under, horse race games, acey-deucey, beat the dealer, and bouncing ball. The Mashantucket Pequots contended that, since Las Vegas nights were permitted by the State, they fell within the "such gaming" language of IGRA and that the State was therefore obligated to negotiate the terms of a tribal-state compact permitting the Tribe to operate such games of chance at their casino. In the spring of 1990, they entered U.S. District Court for the District of Connecticut and sought summary judgment under IGRA to order Connecticut to negotiate in good faith concerning the terms of operation of these games of chance on their reservation and to conclude a tribal-state compact governing such activities within sixty days — this was prior to the Supreme Court's decision in *Seminole Tribe of Florida v. Florida* (1996) invalidating under the Eleventh Amendment IGRA's provisions mandating that the states negotiate with tribes in good faith and authorizing the tribes to bring an action in federal courts against the states that refused to do so.

Connecticut disagreed; it argued that IGRA's use of the phrase "such gaming," as opposed to "such type of gaming," evidenced the intent of Congress that, with regard to Class III gaming, only the actual forms of gaming that the State had legalized (i.e., specific Las Vegas games offered one night a year by a charitable organization) needed to be the subject of compact negotiations. It further asserted that its interpretation was supported by the congressional findings prefacing IGRA that "Indian tribes have the exclusive right to regulate gaming activity on Indian lands if the gaming activity is not specifically prohibited by Federal law and is conducted within a State which does not, as a matter of criminal law and public policy, prohibit such gaming activity." It argued that if the restrictions it had imposed on Las Vegas nights were removed, such gaming would amount to professional gambling which was prohibited in Connecticut as a matter of public policy and criminal law. It insisted that it was not obliged to negotiate a compact with the Tribe concerning gaming not permitted under state law.

On May 15, 1990, in *Mashantucket Pequot Tribe v. State of Connecticut*, U.S. District Court Judge Peter C. Dorsey granted the Tribe's motion for summary judgment and ordered Connecticut to enter into good-faith negotiations with the Tribe. He began by noting congressional findings in IGRA that "Indian tribes have the exclusive right to regulate gaming activity on Indian lands if the gaming activity is not specifically prohibited by Federal law and is conducted within a State which does not, as a matter of criminal law and public policy, prohibit such gaming activity," and he concluded by holding that Connecticut was impermissibly subjecting the Mashantucket Pequots to the full extent of its "Las Vegas night" regulation without negotiation. For Judge Dorsey, "The type of gaming permitted is identified by the type of play permitted, not by bet, frequency, and prize limits." Significantly, he applied the same civil/regulatory–criminal/prohibitory dichotomy to IGRA that the Supreme Court had applied to Public Law 280 in *Cabazon* and concluded that Congress intended IGRA to permit a particular gaming activity, even if conducted in a manner inconsistent with state law, if the state law merely regulated as opposed to completely barred that particular gaming activity. He concluded by observing that "IGRA balances the Tribe's autonomy as a sovereign and the State's regulatory interest over gaming operations within its borders. These interests are accommodated by requiring negotiations aimed at a Tribal-State compact governing the conduct of class III gaming activities."

Less than four months later, on September 4, 1990, Judge Dorsey's decision was unanimously affirmed by the U.S. Court of Appeals for the Second Circuit in *Mashantucket Pequot Tribe v. State of Connecticut*. Judge J. Daniel Mahoney, joined by his colleagues, Ralph K. Winter and John M. Walker, declared: "The district court concluded that the games of chance that the Tribe seeks to conduct constitute 'such gaming' as is permitted by Connecticut law at 'Las Vegas nights,' and that the Tribe's contemplated activities therefore constituted permissible Class III gaming activities in the State. In our view, the district court correctly decided the issue."

Judge Mahoney then commented importantly on the compacting process more generally and why Connecticut was obligated by IGRA to negotiate a compact in good faith with the Pequots that would allow the Tribe to offer in its casino the games mentioned in Connecticut's Las Vegas–night statute. He turned to the Senate Report accompanying S. 555 and noted that it "specifically adopted the *Cabazon* rationale . . . [and] anticipates that Federal courts will rely on the distinction between State criminal laws which prohibit certain activities and the civil laws of a State which impose a regulatory scheme upon those activities." He described the compacting process as "the ultimate legislative compromise regarding Class III gaming," and he again quoted from the Senate Report: "After lengthy hearings, negotiations and discussions, the Committee concluded that the use of compacts between tribes and states is the best mechanism to assure that the interests of both sovereign entities are met with respect to the regulation of complex gaming enterprises." He concluded that the compacting process was therefore to be followed in this case, because, "applying the *Cabazon* test," the district court and the court of appeals had both determined that Connecticut, "as a matter of criminal law and public policy," did not prohibit the Las Vegas games in question. Judge Mahoney took a "categorical" approach to the language in IGRA, holding that the Tribe was free to offer all forms of Class III gaming if the state allowed any form of Class III gaming.

Connecticut is interesting for another reason as well. IGRA prohibits states from imposing "any tax, fee, charge, or other assessment upon any Indian tribe or upon any other person or entity authorized by an Indian tribe to engage in a Class III activity." However, this no-tax clause was quickly circumvented, with Connecticut leading the way. It turns out, quite interestingly, that IGRA's language does not prohibit a state from receiving a share of tribal gaming revenues if it offers a quid pro quo for that share of gaming revenues. That quid pro quo typically is a promise of a degree of exclusivity for tribal gaming; thus, for example, if a state agrees to prohibit casino-type gaming other than by Indian tribes, the payment of a reasonable share of revenues is deemed to be a payment for exclusivity and not a tax. The first exclusivity provision in a compact agreement negotiated after IGRA's passage occurred in Connecticut.

While the Pequots were able, with the federal courts' help, to bring Connecticut to the negotiation table and negotiate a compact allowing it to offer at its casino the many games specified in Connecticut's Las

Vegas–night statute, and while those games were important for the generation of tribal revenue, the statute did not include slot machines — and why should it? Slot machines are expensive to purchase and maintain, and their use made no sense at a one-night-a-year Las Vegas–night charitable fundraiser. But, slot machines made enormous sense for the Pequots, for in most casinos — tribal or otherwise — they generate close to 90 percent of all casinos' gross revenues; all the card games, the high-stakes games, the entertainment, and the restaurants and bars are simply baubles and lures that make the casino experience attractive and inviting and that draw crowds to the cash cow (or, for tribal casinos, the "new buffalo"), the slot machine.

The Pequots wanted to amend their compact with Connecticut to allow for the operation of slot machines, and to that end, they negotiated a new compact in 1993 with Connecticut's governor, Lowell Weicker, providing the Tribe with exclusive rights to operate slot machines within the state. In return, the Tribe agreed to make yearly payments to the state of $100 million or 25 percent of their slots revenue, whichever was greater. When the Mohegan Tribe the next year gained federal recognition and signed its own compact with the governor to operate a casino, the Mashantucket Pequots granted the Mohegans permission to include slot machines in their new casino — each currently operates approximately 6,500 slot machines in its facilities. In return, Connecticut set the annual payment required from each tribe at $80 million or 25 percent of their slots revenue, whichever is greater. The revenue-sharing strategy that the Pequots pursued to bring Connecticut to the negotiating table may not have been anticipated by the Senate Select Committee on Indian Affairs when it included language in its Senate Report accompanying S. 555 that it was the committee's view that "both State and tribal governments have significant governmental interests in the conduct of Class III gaming," and that "States and tribes are encouraged to conduct negotiations within the context of the mutual benefits that can flow to and from tribe and States." But, it worked; it brought Connecticut to the table, and resulted in great financial benefits for both the Pequots and Mohegans and the State of Connecticut. And when the Supreme Court would later invalidate in the *Seminole Tribe* case those provisions of IGRA requiring states to negotiate compacts in good faith with the tribes, tribes in other states were aware that the incentive that Congress had unsuccessfully attempted to provide the tribes to prevent states from simply vetoing tribal gaming was not the only arrow in their quiver for they had another: they could by themselves offer monetary incentives sufficient to bring the states to the negotiating table and to negotiate Class III gaming compacts that benefitted both the tribes and the states. And, when the Ninth Circuit in 2003 upheld as valid a revenue-sharing agreement in *In Re Gaming Related Cases*, their confidence that this other arrow was there for them to use was greatly confirmed. Seven small Northern California tribes sued the State because California under Proposition 1A (more below) required in the compact that the tribes contribute 3 percent of slot machine revenues to a Special Distribution Fund (SDF), to be used to provide funding for gambling addiction programs and aid to local governments impacted by tribal gaming. Judge William A. Fletcher held for a unanimous panel that "in exchange for an exclusive right to conduct Class III gaming, we do not find it inimical to the purpose or design of IGRA for the State, under these circumstances, to ask for a reasonable share of tribal gaming revenues."

California's compacting experience has been very different from Connecticut's. To begin with, California has compacts with sixty-one different tribes (as opposed to two in Connecticut). Taken together, these tribes are generating revenues of more than $9 billion annually.

But, these compacts did not come easily. Shortly after IGRA's passage, California Indian tribes that were already operating casinos in the state made the first of numerous efforts to negotiate compacts initially with Governor George Deukmejian and then with Governor Pete Wilson, but they made little progress. In fact, Governor Wilson vetoed bills to establish compacts on three different occasions — once in 1993, again in 1995, and finally in 1996. During this entire time, approximately three dozen California tribes offered Class III gaming (including slot machines) in the absence of a compact with the state. Because slot machines are versions of a lottery and because California had a state lottery, they were not contrary to the public policy of the State, and California therefore lacked the authority under either Public Law 280 or IGRA to close them down. They could have been closed down by the federal government as contrary to the Johnson Act; IGRA exempted tribes from prosecution under the Johnson Act, but only for those tribes that had successfully negotiated compacts allowing for the use of slot machines. However, U.S. Attorneys in California refrained from prosecuting the tribes under the Johnson Act so long as the issue remained before the legislature. (That, at least, was their public reason. There was another as well; because the Clinton Administration was actively seeking financial contributions and political support from the tribes, the Justice Department lacked the political will to raid the casinos and seize these machines.) The gaming tribes, operating without compacts, generated approximately $1.4 billion in revenues in 1997, providing the tribes with sufficient funds to enter the political process, to contribute to candidates who supported tribal gaming, and, ultimately, to use California's direct ballot to secure the compacts Governor Wilson had refused to negotiate.

Governor Pete Wilson was unquestionably hostile to the California gaming tribes. There are several theories as to why this was the case. His hostility may have been a response to an overwhelming imbalance of Indian campaign contributions to Democratic candidates — gaming tribes gave $2.5 million to Democratic candidates in 1994, compared with only $300,000 to Republican candidates. Wilson's public position was that he was unwilling to negotiate with tribes already breaking the law, and he was determined to restrict the growth of legalized gambling in California generally. Whatever the motivation, Wilson stated that he would not negotiate with the tribes that operated "Nevada-style" slot machines, as opposed to the player-pooled, lottery-like slots he favored.

Wilson took encouragement from the Ninth Circuit's decision in *Rumsey Indian Rancheria of Wintun Indians v. Wilson* (1994), which gave the State much greater power in determining what specific Class III games would be allowable in any compact that Connecticut was able to exercise. When the Rumsey Indian Rancheria asked California to negotiate a compact permitting the use of electronic gaming devices and live banking and percentage card games, the State refused, asserting that the proposed gaming activities were illegal. The Tribe sued, convinced that on appeal, it would prevail under the Second Circuit's analysis that if a state permits any form of Class III gaming, IGRA allows the tribes to engage in all forms of Class III gaming. The U.S. District Court for the Eastern District of California awarded the Tribe summary judgment, finding that the activities were a proper subject of negotiation. California appealed, and the Tribe cross-appealed.

The Ninth Circuit reversed, holding that since California did not allow banked or percentage card gaming by anyone else, it was not obliged to negotiate a compact that allowed the Tribe to operate games that others could not offer. Judge Diarmuid F. O'Scannlain's opinion in *Rumsey* meant, for Wilson, that the State had no obligation to negotiate with tribes over some of the most lucrative forms of Class III gaming.

The Ninth Circuit's statutory construction of IGRA differed completely from the Second Circuit's categorical approach to the construction of IGRA in *Mashantucket Pequot Tribe v. State of Connecticut*. When the Second Circuit interpreted IGRA's language permitting a tribe to conduct Class III gaming if, among other requirements, it is "located in a state that permits such gaming," it focused on the words, "such gaming" and concluded that if Connecticut permitted any form of Class III gaming, it permitted all forms of Class III gaming. When the Ninth Circuit interpreted that same language, it focused on the word, "permits." By focusing on "permits," the Ninth Circuit adopted a "game-specific" approach and therefore a more restrictive definition under which only those forms of Class III gaming activities specifically authorized in the state could be the subject of compact negotiations. As Judge O'Scannlain explained: "IGRA does not require a state to negotiate over one form of Class III gaming activity simply because it has legalized another, albeit similar form of gaming." Instead, the statute says only that, if a state allows a gaming activity "for any purpose by any person, organization, or entity," then it also must allow Indian tribes to engage in that same activity. "In other words, a state need only allow Indian tribes to operate games that others can operate, but need not give tribes what others cannot have." In so arguing, Judge O'Scannlain was following the lead of an earlier Eighth Circuit decision in *Cheyenne River Sioux Tribe v. South Dakota* (1993). Interestingly, this split among the circuits was never addressed or resolved by the Supreme Court.

After several years of stalemate, Wilson finally negotiated a gaming pact with a California tribe — the Pala Band of Mission Indians. Rather than being delighted, however, the majority of the state's Indian tribes were furious. The Pala Band was a tiny tribe that had not previously engaged in gaming of any sort, and the compact enabled them to enter the gaming industry. But, and this is what angered the other tribes, Wilson tried to apply the same terms of that compact to every tribe in the state.

The compact set a limit of 975 on the number of video gambling machines that each tribe could possess, as well as a statewide limit of 19,000; it raised the legal gambling age to twenty-one from eighteen; it required the tribes to allow casino workers to unionize — something that Indian tribes are not required to do under existing federal law; and it forbade video poker and video versions of other popular card games such as blackjack.

The existing gaming tribes did not question the right of the Pala Band of Mission Indians to agree to such a compact, but they were infuriated when Wilson tried to apply the provisions of the Pala compact to all the other tribes in the state without having included them in the negotiations over the compact. Many tribes already possessed more than 1,000 slot machines and intended to grow beyond that. They were unwilling to submit to a compact that would have severely undermined the profitability of their casinos, and consequently the self-sufficiency of their tribes.

A total of eleven tribes agreed to the terms of the Pala Compact; many of these were in San Diego County and were being pressured by the local U.S. Attorney's office to do so. But thirty-one tribes, faced with the choice of accepting the Wilson pact, which they believed to be negotiated in bad faith, or having their casinos shut down by federal marshals for engaging in illegal Class III gaming, turned to a third option: they decided to change the legal environment in which they operated. They decided to place a statutory initiative on the ballot, Proposition 5, that would force Wilson to sign compacts written by the tribes.

Proposition 5 represented a wish-list of the items that California's gaming tribes had been seeking in their unsuccessful negotiations with Governor Wilson. The point of the initiative was to adopt a model gaming compact with or without the signature of the governor for any Indian tribe that requested it. The language of the compact was contained within the initiative itself. If the governor did not sign the compact within thirty days of the request, it was deemed to have been executed anyway. In general, the provisions of the compacts that Proposition 5 prescribed largely prevented regulation by the State of California, entrusting appropriate oversight to the tribes who wished to pursue Class III gaming. In the specific details, Proposition 5 permitted the use of the slot machines, so long as they were "player-pooled," did not dispense currency or coins, and were not operated by handles; instituted no limits whatsoever on the number of slot machines that any tribe could have, nor on the total number of slot machines permitted in the state; provided for revenue sharing with the state, local governments, and nongaming tribes; permitted the continuation of any games that were actually operated in a California tribal casino prior to January 1, 1998, even including games explicitly forbidden by state law; authorized any sort of lottery game, including, but not limited to, raffles, drawings, match games, and instant lottery ticket games; authorized off-track pari-mutuel horse race wagering; kept the legal gambling age set at eighteen; and made no mention of labor or environmental regulations.

Once Proposition 5 qualified for the ballot, Nevada and other nontribal California gaming interests immediately began pouring funds into the campaign opposing the ratification of Proposition 5; $25 million was spent directly by the Coalition against Unregulated Gambling (CAUG), funded by labor unions, Nevada casinos, horse racing tracks, card clubs, and the Walt Disney Company. Nevada casinos contributed substantially to CAUG and other committees opposing Proposition 5: Mirage Resorts contributed over $9 million; Hilton and Circus Circus each over $6.5 million; the Sahara $3 million, and Caesar's Palace, $1 million. The tribes answered in kind by spending a record $66,257,088 in support of Proposition 5. The investment paid off. From the start, public opinion was with the Indians in supporting the tribes' attempts at self-sufficiency, and in November 1998 Proposition 5 passed with 62 percent of the vote.

Having lost at the polls, the forces opposed to tribal gaming entered state court and argued that Proposition 5 was unconstitutional. Their principal argument was that Proposition 5 was merely a statutory initiative (it did not amend the California Constitution) and was therefore unconstitutional because inconsistent with the 1984 constitutional amendment that created the California Lottery. One provision of that amendment declared that "the Legislature has no power to authorize, and shall prohibit, casinos of the type currently operating in Nevada and New Jersey." Under California, Nevada, and New

Jersey law, they argued, slot machines, blackjack, and "banked" or percentage games constituted casino gambling.

The case challenging the constitutionality of Proposition 5, *Hotel Employees and Restaurant Employees [HERE] v. Davis*, was argued before the California Supreme Court on June 1, 1999, and decided by that Court on August 23. The Court ruled 6-1 against the constitutionality of Proposition 5. Justice Kathryn Werdegar wrote the majority opinion, concluding that the State of California could not validly enter into the compact contained in Proposition 5 because the terms of its own Constitution forbade it from doing so.

Although the ruling in *HERE v. Davis* represented a blow to the gaming tribes, they still found themselves in a much better position vis-à-vis the State than they had been prior to the passage of Proposition 5. To begin with, in the fall elections of 1998, California had elected a new governor, Gray Davis, who was much less hostile to the gaming ambitions of the tribes than Pete Wilson, and a new attorney general, Bill Lockyer, who was likewise much less hostile than his predecessor, Dan Lungren. Furthermore, with the passage of Proposition 5, the Indians proved themselves to be a significant political power, with strong public support and deep pockets in their favor — facts that were not lost upon most members of the California Legislature. These developments provided a much better environment for the tribes to negotiate compacts with the State of California, and they moved to do so immediately.

In late August 1999, representatives of over sixty tribes convened in Sacramento to negotiate the details of a new gaming compact with Governor Davis. The negotiations were heated and free-wheeling, with the tribes, still frustrated at the imposition that the IGRA compacts made upon their tribal sovereignty, frequently disagreeing with each other about the details of the compacts as much as they disagreed with Davis. After several days, however, the negotiations produced a constitutional initiative measure, Proposition 1A, that was amenable to all parties.

Proposition 1A modified California's constitutional prohibition against casinos by authorizing the governor to negotiate compacts, subject to legislative ratification, for the operation by the tribes on their reservations of slot machines, lottery games, and banked and percentage card games (including blackjack, keno, and baccarat — only roulette, craps, and sports betting would continue to be forbidden); it allowed each of California's 107 federally recognized Indian tribes to have a maximum of two casinos but limited them to a total of no more than 2,000 slot machines; it granted the tribes a monopoly to operate these slot machines in a quid pro quo for tribal contributions of 6 percent of their slot machine revenues (3 percent for a revenue-sharing program for nongaming tribes and 3 percent for local governments to mitigate the impact of the casinos on traffic, the local infrastructure, public safety, etc.); and it authorized the negotiation of future gaming compacts with federally recognized tribes.

The campaign for Proposition 1A, which appeared on California's March 2000 primary ballot, was markedly different than the one for Proposition 5. This time, rather than opposing Indian gaming, Nevada casino operators adopted an "if you can't beat them, join them" strategy. Many such operators, including Anchor Gaming Corporation, Donald Trump, and others, began signing agreements with the Indian tribes to manage Indian casinos on behalf of the tribes. As a result of this new accommodation, the "No on Proposition 1A" groups, comprised largely of church groups and gambling addiction activists, never had a chance. The pro-1A committee (Yes on 1A, Californians for Indian Self-Reliance Sponsored by California Indian Tribes) spent less than $20 million to support the initiative while the opposing committees never even managed to collect the $100,000 that made electronic campaign finance filing a requirement. On March 7, 2000, Proposition 1A passed with 64.5 percent of the vote, carrying all but two counties — El Dorado and Placer — whose economies depended heavily on the success of the nearby Nevada casinos in Lake Tahoe and Reno.

A key provision of Proposition 1A was one authorizing the negotiation of future gaming compacts with federally recognized tribes. Under this provision, in 2006, Governor Arnold Schwarzenegger, facing huge budget deficits and eager for additional income streams, entered into new compacts with four of the most successful Southern California gaming tribes (the Agua Caliente Band of Cahuilla Indians, the Sycuan Band of the Kumeyaay Nation, the Pechanga Band of Luiseño Indians, and the Morongo Band of Mission Indians) allowing them to increase the number of slot machines they could operate in their casinos to a maximum of 7,500, but on which the tribes would have to pay 25 percent of all the revenues these additional machines generated. In the summer of 2007, the legislature passed four bills approving these compact amendments, which the governor signed in July 2007.

Intense opposition to the four bills, however, mounted, coming especially from smaller gaming tribes worried about the competition these mega-casinos would create, union interests wanting the right to engage in collective bargaining on behalf of casino employees, and environmental groups using the occasion to object once again to the tribes' exemption, under Public Law 280, from the California Environmental Quality Act. And all four bills were put on hold, when, in November 2007, the opponents to these four bills were able to qualify four propositions (one for each amended compact) for California's February 5, 2008, primary ballot. These propositions were referendums intended to let the voters decide on the compact approval bills passed in the legislature. If approved, these propositions would allow the compact amendments to go into effect, subject to approval by the U.S. Department of the Interior. But, if they were rejected, the tribes would have to continue to operate their casinos under their current compacts without the new slot machines. Turnabout, it seemed, was fair play; the same direct ballot that the tribes had used to secure the passage of Propositions 5 and 1A was now being employed against them by those seeking to restrict further expansion of tribal gaming. But, in the end, all four propositions passed (two received 55.8 percent of the vote; two 55.7 percent), and the amended compacts went into effect. The four Southern California gaming tribes in question, plus the San Manuel Band of Serrano Mission Indians (another nearby tribe that subsequently agreed to the amended compact's terms as well), are therefore authorized to expand their casino operations significantly. Several have done so, but none of the tribes begins to approach the limit of the total number of additional machines they are authorized to have. These machines are very expensive, and the tribes will bring them on line only when there is player demand sufficient to justify them doing so.

Florida's compacting experience is different still. Despite the Seminole Tribe's early 1981 landmark Court of Appeals victory in the *Butterworth* case, the Tribe was not able to complete successful negotiation of a compact with the State of Florida for it legally to offer Class III gaming in its casinos until June 24, 2010.

The Seminole Tribe first sought to negotiate a Class III gaming compact in January 1991, and in September of that year, requested the State to enter into good-faith compact negotiations pursuant to IGRA. The negotiations were unsuccessful and later that year, the Tribe filed suit against the State alleging that Florida failed to negotiate a compact in good faith. The State asserted state sovereign immunity under the Eleventh Amendment, and the suit was ultimately dismissed on those grounds by the Supreme Court in *Seminole Tribe of Florida v. Florida* in a 5-4 decision in 1996.

Over the next three years, the Tribe, as provided under IGRA, continually submitted proposals to the secretary of the interior to establish Class III gaming at its casinos. Finally, in 1999, one of the Tribe's proposals was deemed by the secretary to meet the requirements of IGRA and the regulations of the Department of the Interior, and the secretary arranged for an informal conference with the Seminole Tribe and the State. At that meeting, Florida suggested a temporary suspension of the discussion to allow further time for the Tribe and State to negotiate a compact. In 2001, more than a year after the informal conference was suspended and during which time no progress had been made in the negotiation of a compact, the secretary finally issued a decision on the scope of gaming permitted in Florida. In that decision, the secretary allowed the tribe to offer a wide range of Class III games. However, five months later — and with no notice to the Tribe, the secretary withdrew the decision "in order to evaluate the important issues raised in this matter."

A delay ensued for the next five years; finally, in 2006, the secretary finally reconvened the conference and warned the State that if it did not reach an agreement with the Seminole Tribe within sixty days, consistent with the language of IGRA, the Department of the Interior would authorize the Seminole Tribe to engage in Class III gaming. When, six months later, no progress had been made, the Tribe sued the department in federal court. Prompted by that suit, the secretary warned the governor to negotiate a compact with the Tribe by November 15, 2007, or the department would approval Class III gaming for the Tribe. On November 14, 2007, one day before the deadline, Governor Charles Crist entered into the twenty-five-year compact with the Seminole Tribe authorizing the Tribe to offer Las Vegas–style slot machines and certain card games such as blackjack and baccarat. In a quid pro quo for the exclusive right to offer blackjack and baccarat and to operate slot machines and card games in the State (except for the slot machines already permitted in Broward and Miami-Dade Counties), the Tribe agreed to a revenue-sharing agreement guaranteeing Florida at least $100 million annually.

However, five days after Governor Crist entered into the compact with the Seminole Tribe, the House of Representatives and its Speaker, Marco Rubio, filed a petition to the Florida Supreme Court disputing the governor's authority to bind the State to the compact without legislative authorization or ratification. And, on July 3, 2008, the Florida Supreme Court, in *Florida House of Representatives v. Crist*, held that Governor Crist lacked the authority to bind Florida to the compact because it contradicted state law. The Court reasoned the governor did not have the constitutional authority to bind the State of Florida to a gaming compact that "clearly departs from the State's public policy by legalizing types of gaming that are illegal everywhere else in the state." Interestingly, however, the Court did not resolve the question of whether the tribal-state compact violated IGRA, addressing instead only the narrower issue of whether the Florida Constitution granted the governor the authority to bind Florida to a compact that violated the State's public policy.

In response to the Florida Supreme Court's ruling, the Seminoles filed a motion for rehearing encouraging the Court to take a categorical, as opposed to a game-specific, approach to the "permits such gaming" language under IGRA. The Tribe noted that Florida permits limited forms of Class III gaming: Florida's Constitution, for example, authorizes a state lottery and slot machines in Broward and Miami-Dade counties; permits and regulates pari-mutuel wagering on jai alai and dog and horse racing; and expressly authorizes cardroom gaming, including, among other games, poker, rummy, hearts, bridge, and dominos in which "the winnings of any player in a single round, hand, or game do not exceed $10 in value." The Tribe noted additionally that Florida permits and profits from a vast gaming cruise industry through "cruises to nowhere," operating out of many Florida ports and offering on board a full range of casino games including slot machines and table games. The Tribe argued that since Florida per-

mitted all of these games, it was regulating the games rather than prohibiting them and that it was therefore "foreclosed from imposing a
policy that prohibited banked card games or Class III slots on any
tribal lands in the state." The Tribe's petition for rehearing, however,
proved unavailing.

Nonetheless, by the time the Florida Supreme Court held that the
tribal-state compact violated state law, the secretary of the interior
had already approved the compact and provided notice to that effect
on January 8, 2009, in the *Federal Register*, and, as a general rule, once
the secretary approves a compact and publishes notice in the *Federal
Register*, it goes into effect. Thus, even though the compact was held
by the Florida Supreme Court to be in direct violation of state law,
the Seminole casinos throughout Florida continued to operate Class
III games, and the State continued to grapple with how to stop the
Tribe from operating these games.

In the wake of *Florida House of Representatives v. Crist*, several
attempts were made to halt these games, but all proved unsuccessful,
because, under *Cabazon*, the State possessed no compulsory authority
over the activities on Indian lands. As Florida Attorney General Bill
McCollum bitterly complained in a September 19, 2008, letter to the
chairman of the National Indian Gaming Commission, Florida is "in
the untenable position of having a tribal gaming operation, which
everyone acknowledges is unauthorized, ongoing without the jurisdiction to stop the illegal gaming activities." Additionally, the Tribe's sovereign immunity, together with the federal court's compulsory joinder
rule, prevented interested third parties from halting the Tribe's operation of its games. One example will suffice: In 2008, the Pompano
Harness Racing Track in Pompano Beach, Florida, a competing pari-
mutuel facility, sought both a judgment setting aside the secretary's
approval of the compact as invalid under IGRA and a permanent
injunction enjoining implementation of the compact provisions, only
to have the U.S. District Court for the Northern District of Florida
deny its motion; the Tribe was an indispensible party to the action that
needed to be joined to the suit under Rule 19 of the Federal Rules of
Civil Procedure because of its significant interest in the outcome of the
litigation. The District Court acknowledged that "although there is no
alternative forum" for the Pompano Harness Racing Track "to litigate
its claim, in equity and good conscience this case cannot proceed with-

out the Seminole Tribe." Clearly, the only authority with the power to stop the Seminole Tribe's Class III gaming activities was the U.S. Department of Justice, and, just as in California during the 1990s, it decided, for whatever reasons, not to intervene.

Efforts to negotiate a new compact to replace the one negotiated by Governor Crist and approved by the secretary failed again in October 2009, when the legislature rejected still another Crist-proposed compact—in large part because it was perceived to be unfair to the Tribe's private-sector gaming competitors. But, by the spring of 2010, the pressure was on the legislature. The Seminole Tribe continued to operate Class III games outside of a valid compact and from which the State received no sharing of revenues. Given the financial collapse of Wall Street, the Florida legislature was facing a $3.2 billion budget deficit and was desperately in need of the revenues a signed compact would provide to the State. To a lesser extent, the pressure was also on the Seminole Tribe; it wanted a valid compact so its Class III gaming operations (and the vast expansion of its facilities it wanted to undertake) would be legal and could not be closed down were the Department of Justice to have a change of mind.

Accordingly, a new compact was entered into by the Tribe and the governor and was finally agreed to by the state legislature in April 2010. It was ratified by the Seminole Tribe on April 7 and executed by Governor Crist that same day. On April 15, the Florida Senate passed a bill approving the compact; on April 15, the Florida House of Representatives concurred, and on April 28, Governor Crist signed the bill into law. On June 24, Assistant Secretary of the Interior for Indian Affairs Larry Echo Hawk formally approved the compact.

Under the agreement, the State gave the Tribe the exclusive operation of three card games—blackjack, baccarat, and chemin de fer—at five of its seven casinos (including their lucrative Tampa Hard Rock casino that was already bringing in at least half of all of the Tribe's gaming revenues) and the exclusive operation of Class III, Las Vegas–style slot machines at its four casinos outside Miami-Dade and Broward Counties. In exchange for this exclusivity, the tribe guaranteed the State $1 billion over five years and up to 10 percent of its net revenues on its exclusive games for fifteen years after that. The legislation approving the compact legalized the three card games mentioned above (refusal of the legislature to approve these games had doomed the 2008 compact). It also protected the Tribe's private-sector competitors by lowering the tax rate for horse and dog tracks and jai-alai frontons to 35 percent from 50 percent; allowing the 19 pari-mutuels outside of Miami-Dade and Broward Counties to install up to 350 bingo-style machines, vending machines that dispense lottery tickets, and historic racing machines; and giving all pari-mutuels expanded gambling hours and higher betting limits.

The Tribe guaranteed the State of Florida $150 million per year in years one and two of the compact; a minimum of $233 million in years three and four; and $234 million in year five (or, beginning in year three, 10 percent of its net revenue from the exclusive games, whichever would be greater). After five years, the legislature would be required to pass a law either allowing tribal card games to continue or ordering the games to cease. The legislature could expand private-sector casinos to other parts of Florida, but, in that case, the Tribe would be allowed to reduce the amount of money it paid to the State.

The three compact experiences discussed above are widely divergent in many respects, but in one respect, they are representative of tribal-state compacts across the country: every tribal-state compact now includes revenue-sharing language that provides the tribes with at least some degree of exclusive authorization to operate Class III gaming within the state's territory in return for paying the state a portion of its revenues from those games. Oklahoma, for example, provides the tribes with substantial exclusivity for electronic games and total exclusivity for card games; in return the tribes pay 4 percent of the first $10 million of their adjusted annual revenues, 5 percent for the next $10 million, etc. Michigan's compact requires the tribes to pay 8 percent of its net gaming revenues from Class III gaming in return for the exclusive right to operate all electronic gaming in the State. New Mexico's 2001 compact requires the tribes to pay 8 percent of all slot machine revenues (down from 16 percent in its 1997 compact) in return for the exclusive right to offer slot machines. New York's compact requires the tribes to contribute 25 percent (just as in neighboring Connecticut) of its gaming revenues in return for the exclusive opportunity to offer Class III gaming. In New York's compact, as in many other compacts, there is language that if the State breaches the tribes' promised exclusivity, the tribes' payment to the State will cease.

Other examples could be provided, but these will suffice. What these various compacts reveal is, of course, the diversity among the tribes, and the states. This was very much anticipated by Congress when it enacted IGRA. As the Senate Report accompanying S. 555 noted, compacts would be "the best mechanism to assure that the interests of both sovereign entities are met with respect to the regulations of complex gaming enterprises such as pari-mutuel horse and dog racing, casino gaming, jai alai, and so forth." What one tribe is willing to negotiate in terms of "raising revenues to provide governmental services for the benefit of the tribal community and reservation residents" and "realizing the objectives of economic self-sufficiency and Indian self-determination," another may not; and likewise, what one state considers an acceptable revenue-sharing arrangement, another may not. A one-size-fits-all tribal-state compact would fail to recognize both tribal sovereignty and state sovereignty. Thus, IGRA provided for compacts allowing the opportunity for what the Senate Report describes as "two equal sovereigns" (with different interests in part but with a common interest in securing "the mutual benefits that can flow to and from the tribe and states") to come together and resolve their specific and individual differences.

But for the intrepid members of the Cabazon and Morongo Bands of Mission Indians who secured victory in *Cabazon*, things may have turned out very differently. Their resolute defense of their sovereign right to engage in high-stakes bingo on their reservation lands raised the profile of tribal gaming. Their "Jack v. the Giant" victory before the Supreme Court, to invoke the language of Cabazon Chairman Arthur Welmas, applied enormous pressure on Congress to pass legislation concerning the regulation of tribal gaming, something it had failed to do in the past due in no small part to fundamental disagreements between the two houses and among its members concerning how much jurisdiction and regulatory authority the states were to have over the tribes and their Class III gaming operations. That pressure for a speedy resolution in turn encouraged the Congress to step aside and to let the parties themselves resolve these questions, consistent with the Court's holding in *Cabazon*, through the negotiation of tribal-state compacts. The resulting $27 billion in annual tribal gaming revenues that IGRA has made possible (that does so much for tribal self-sufficiency and the welfare of individual tribal members, and that provides critical financial support for so many state budgets) can all be said to flow from *Cabazon*, in much the same way that the Mighty Mississippi River flows from Lake Itasca. The imagery is appropriate. The source of the Mississippi is also the source of the litigation that gave us *Bryan v. Itasca County* and the Supreme Court's first use of the civil/regulatory–criminal/prohibitory distinction on which it would so fundamentally rely in *California v. Cabazon Band of Mission Indians*.

RELEVANT CASES

Antoine v. Washington, 420 U.S. 194 (1975)

Arizona v. California, 373 U.S. 546 (1963)

Barona Group of the Capitan Grande Band of Mission Indians v. Duffy, 694 F.2d 1185 (9th Cir. 1982)

Bryan v. Itasca County, 426 U.S. 373 (1976)

Cabazon Band of Mission Indians v. California, 783 F.2d 900 (9th Cir. 1986)

Cabazon Band of Mission Indians v. City of Indio, 694 F.2d 634 (9th Cir. 1982)

California v. Cabazon Band of Mission Indians, 480 U.S. 202 (1987)

Carcieri v. Salazar, 129 S.Ct. 1058 (2009)

Cherokee Nation v. Georgia, 30 U.S. 1 (1831)

Cheyenne River Sioux Tribe v. South Dakota, 830 F. Supp. 523 (D.S.D. 1993)

Chickasaw Nation v. United States, 534 U.S. 84 (2001)

County of Oneida v. Oneida Indian Nation, 470 U.S. 226 (1985)

County of Yakima v. Confederated Tribes and Bands of the Yakima Nation, 502 U.S. 251 (1992)

Ex parte Crow Dog, 109 U.S. 557 (1883)

Federal Power Commission v. Tuscararo Indian Nation, 362 U.S. 99 (1960)

Florida House of Representatives v. Crist, 990 So. 2d 1035 (Fla. 2008)

Greater Loretta Improvement Association v. State ex rel. Boone, 234 So. 2d 665 (Fla. 1970)

Hoopa Valley Tribe v. Humboldt County, 615 F.2d 1260 (9th Cir. 1980)

Hotel Employees and Restaurant Employees [HERE] v. Davis, 981 P.2d 990 (Cal. 1999)

In re Gaming Related Cases, 331 F.3d 1094 (9th Cir. 2003)

Johnson v. McIntosh, 21 U.S. 543 (1823)

The Kansas Indians, 72 U.S. 737 (1866)

Lone Wolf v. Hitchcock, 187 U.S. 553 (1903)

Mashantucket Pequot Tribe v. State of Connecticut, 737 F. Supp. 169 (D. Conn. 1990).

Mashantucket Pequot Tribe v. State of Connecticut, 913 F.2d 1024 (2nd Cir. 1990)

McClanahan v. Arizona State Tax Commission, 411 U.S. 164 (1973)

Mitchel v. United States, 34 U.S. 711 (1835)

Montana v. Blackfeet Tribe, 471 U.S. 759 (1985)

Northern Cheyenne Tribe v. Hollowbreast, 425 U.S. 649 (1976)

Oklahoma v. Seneca-Cayuga Tribe, 711 P.2d 77 (Ok. 1985)

Oliphant v. Suquamish Indian Tribe, 435 U.S. 191 (1978)

Oneida Tribe of Indians v. Wisconsin, 518 F. Supp. 712 (W.D.Wis. 1981)

Penobscot Nation v. Stilphen, 461 A.2d 478, 489 (Me. 1983)

People ex rel. Department of Transportation v. Naegele Outdoor Advertising Company, 698 P.2d 150 (Cal. 1985)

Red Lake Chippewa Tribe v. Swimmer, 740 F. Supp. 9 (D.D.C. 1990)

Rice v. Rehner, 463 U.S. 713 (1983)

Rumsey Indian Rancheria of Wintun Indians v. Wilson, 64 F.3d 1250, 1255 (9th Cir. 1994)

Santa Rosa Band of Indians v. Kings County, 532 F.2d 655. (9th Cir. 1975)

Seminole Tribe v. Butterworth, 491 F. Supp. 1015 (S.D. Fla. 1980)

Seminole Tribe v. Butterworth, 658 F.2d 310 (5th Cir. 1981)

Silkwood v. Kerr-McGee Corporation, 464 U.S. 238 (1984)

Talton v. Mayes, 163 U.S. 376 (1896)

United States v. Dion, 476 U.S. 734 (1986)

United States v. Farris, 624 F.2d 890 (9th Cir. 1980)

United States v. Kagama, 118 U.S. 375 (1886)

United States v. Minnesota, 271 U.S. 648 (1926)

United States v. Nice, 241 U.S. 591 (1916)

United States v. Wheeler, 435 U.S. 313 (1978)

United States v. Winans, 198 U.S. 371 (1905)

Washington v. Confederated Tribes of the Colville Indian Reservation, 448 U.S. 911 (1980)

White Mountain Apache Tribe v. Bracker, 448 U.S. 136 (1980)

Winters v. United States, 207 U.S. 564 (1908)

Worcester v. Georgia, 31 U.S. 515 (1832)

CHRONOLOGY

1876   Cabazon Band reservation authorized by Executive Order

1877   Morongo Band reservation authorized by Executive Order

1979   In May, Cabazon Band opens a smoke shop

1980   On June 10, the Supreme Court hands down *Washington v. Confederated Tribes of the Colville Indian Reservation*

1980   On October 15, Cabazon Band opens its card club

1980   On October 18, City of Indio raids and closes down the Cabazon card club

1980   On October 22, the Cabazon Band enters U.S. District Court seeking a temporary restraining order and preliminary injunction against the City of Indio

1980   On November 10, Judge Laughlin E. Waters denies Cabazon's application for temporary restraining order but grants its motion for a preliminary injunction

1981   On May 18, Judge Waters grants City of Indio's motion to dissolve preliminary injunction; Cabazon Band files a motion for stay pending appeal

1981   On May 18, Judge Waters grants motion to stay the dissolution of the injunction pending appeal

1982   On December 14, the Ninth Circuit Court of Appeals reverses Judge Waters and rules on behalf of the Cabazon Band

1983   On February 15, the Riverside County Sheriff's Department raids the Cabazon Band's card club

1983   On February 23, Cabazon Band enters U.S. District Court seeking a preliminary injunction and a temporary restraining order against Riverside County

1983   On February 24, Judge Waters grants the Cabazon Band's request for a temporary restraining order against the County

1983   On May 6, Judge Waters grants the Cabazon Band's request for a preliminary injunction

1983   On May 16, the Morongo Band enters U.S. District Court seeking a preliminary injunction against Riverside County from closing down its soon-to-be-opened bingo parlor

1983   On May 20, Judge Waters grants the Morongo Band's request for a preliminary injunction

1983   On October 31, Judge Waters consolidates the Cabazon and Morongo cases. At that same hearing, the State of California files a motion to intervene in the litigation

1983   On November 21, Judge Waters grants the State of California's motion to intervene in the litigation

1984   On June 26, the parties file cross motions for summary judgment

1984   On December 6, Judge Waters grants the Tribes' motion for summary judgment

1984   On December 19, the State of California and the County of Riverside appeal to the Ninth Circuit

1986   On April 8, the Ninth Circuit unanimously affirms Judge Waters's grant of summary judgment and issues a permanent injunction against the State and County

1986   On April 17, the State of California appeals to the U.S. Supreme Court

1986   On May 19, the Tribes move to dismiss the appeal

1986   On June 9, the Supreme Court notes probable jurisdiction

1986   On August 8, the State and County file their Brief of Appellant

1986   On September 24, the Tribes file their Brief of Appellee

1986   On October 6, the Supreme Court announces that oral argument for *Cabazon* is scheduled for 2:00 p.m. on December 9

1986   On October 20, the State and County file their Closing Brief

1986   On December 9, oral argument before the Supreme Court is held at 2:00 p.m.

1986   On December 17, the Tribes file Motion for Leave to File Post-Argument Brief and the Post-Argument Brief

1986   On December 22, the State and County file Motion for Leave to File Response to Post-Argument Brief and Response to Post-Argument Brief

1987   On February 25, Justice White announces the Supreme Court's decision in *Cabazon*

1987   On May 27, the Cabazon Band files Brief of the Appellant before the Ninth Circuit concerning its 42 U.S.C. § 1983 damages suit against Riverside County

1987   On July 10, the County files its Brief of the Appellee

1987   On August 10, the Cabazon Band files its Reply Brief

1987   On September 29, the Cabazon Band and Riverside County reach a financial settlement

1987   On November 13, Judge Waters approves the financial settlement, ending the protracted litigation

1988   On September 15, IGRA passes the U.S. Senate by a voice vote

1988   On September 27, IGRA passes the U.S. House of Representatives by a vote of 323-84

1988   On October 17, President Ronald Reagan signs IGRA into law

1990   On September 4, the Second Circuit Court of Appeals rules in *Mashantucket Pequot Tribe v. State of Connecticut* that, under IGRA, if a state allows any form of Class III gaming, Indian tribes can engage in all forms of Class III gaming

1994   On November 15, the Ninth Circuit Court of Appeals rules in *Rumsey Indian Rancheria of Wintun Indians v. Wilson* that, under IGRA, if a state allows a form of Class III gaming, Indians tribes can engage in that form of Class III gaming

1996   On March 27, the Supreme Court rules in *Seminole Tribe of Florida v. Florida* that IGRA's language authorizing tribes to sue states that refuse to negotiate in good faith to establish tribal-state compacts is unconstitutional

1998   On November 3, the voters of California approve Proposition 5

1999   On August 23, in *Hotel Employees and Restaurant Employees v. Davis*, the California Supreme Court strikes down Proposition 5

2000   On March 8, the voters of California approve Proposition 1A

2007   On November 14, the Governor of Florida and the Seminole Tribe agree to a twenty-five-year compact

2007   On December 19, the Florida House of Representatives files a petition with the Florida Supreme Court disputing the governor's authority to enter into a compact with the Seminole Tribe without legislative authorization or ratification

2008   On February 5, the voters of California approve Propositions 94-97 allowing four Southern California tribes to have up to 7,500 slot machines each

2008   On July 3, the Florida Supreme Court in *Florida House of Representatives v. Crist* declares the compact Governor Crist negotiated with the Seminole Tribe to be invalid because it contradicted state law

2010   On April 28, Governor Crist signs a bill adopted by the Florida legislature approving a compact between the governor and the Seminole Tribe and authorizing the Tribe to conduct card games previously prohibited by state law

2010　On June 24, the Assistant Secretary for the Department of the
Interior for Indian Affairs approves the 2010 compact between the
Seminole Tribe and Governor Crist

BIBLIOGRAPHICAL ESSAY

Note from the Series Editors: The following bibliographical essay contains the major primary and secondary sources the author consulted for this volume. We have asked all authors in the series to omit formal citations in order to make our volumes more readable, inexpensive, and appealing for students and general readers. In adopting this format, Landmark Law Cases and American Society follows the precedent of a number of highly regarded and widely consulted series.

The indispensable source for anyone interested in any of the topics touched upon in this book is *Cohen's Handbook of Federal Indian Law* (San Francisco: LexisNexis Press, 2005) and its annual updates. It was first published in 1941 by Felix Cohen, who worked in the Solicitor's Office of the Department of the Interior from 1933 to 1947. In that position, Cohen played a key role in formulating and advocating federal policy that sought to strengthen tribal governments and reduce federal domination of Indian tribes. Cohen was one of the drafters of the centerpiece legislation of this era, the 1934 Indian Reorganization Act. In 1939 he became chief of the Indian Law Survey, an effort to compile the federal laws and treaties regarding American Indians. The resulting book, published by the Government Printing Office in 1941 as *The Handbook of Federal Indian Law*, brought together hundreds of years of diverse treaties, statutes, and decisions in one source. Today, Cohen is credited with creating the modern field of federal Indian Law. The University of New Mexico reissued the initial *Handbook* in 1971, and updated versions of the *Handbook* were first published in 1982 and then in 2005. In its current version, it is the definitive guide to this fascinating area of federal law. Used by judges as well as practitioners, it is written by experts and addresses such topics as the history and structure of tribal governments and tribal law; the tribal/federal relationship; the tribal/state relationship; criminal jurisdiction; civil jurisdiction; environmental regulation in Indian country; the Indian Child Welfare Act, federal Indian liquor laws; Indian gaming and taxation; tribal and individual Indian property rights; natural resources; water rights; hunting, fishing, and gathering rights; and economic development. Its authors/editors include Carole Goldberg, Professor of Law at UCLA and Director of its Joint Degree Program in Law and American Indian Studies; Nell Jessup Newton, Dean and Professor of Law at the University of California, Hastings College of the Law; Joseph William Singer, Professor of Law, Harvard Law School; Judith V. Royster, Professor of Law and Co-Director of the Native American Law Center at the University of Tulsa; and John P. LaVelle, Professor of Law at the University of New Mexico.

For those interested in approaching these many subjects at a slightly higher level of generality, *American Indian Law*, 4th ed. (St. Paul, MN: West Publishing, 2004), by William C. Canby, Jr., a Senior Judge on the U.S. Court of Appeals for the Ninth Circuit and a former Professor of Law at Arizona State University, is an excellent choice.

The background information for *California v. Cabazon Band of Mission Indians* comes from several sources. An essential source was Ambrose I. Lane, Sr., *Return of the Buffalo: The Story behind America's Indian Gaming Explosion* (Westport, CT: Gergin & Garvey, 1995). This rambling book includes a series of lengthy and fascinating interviews with the key players of the Cabazon Band who were instrumental in the Tribe's decision to open first a smoke shop, then a card club, and finally a high-stakes bingo parlor. It is excellent at conveying their sense of dire economic necessity as well as their passionate conviction that they were a sovereign people and authorized by that high station to provide for their own economic self-sufficiency and governmental self-determination.

In addition to relying on Lane's book, I interviewed a number of key players in the litigation, including John James, longtime chairman of the Cabazon Band, and Brenda James Soulliere, James's daughter, now a tribal leader in her own right, and as a teenager an employee in both the smoke shop and the card club—she was present when the club was raided first by the City of Indio and later by the County of Riverside. I also had repeated conversations with Mark Nichols, longtime CEO of the Cabazon Band and the son of John Philip Nichols, the Tribe's first general manager and the charismatic force that led the Cabazon Band to the forefront of tribal gaming. I interviewed on two occasions Glenn M. Feldman, the attorney who has represented the Cabazon Band since 1979—he was counsel of record through the entire litigation of *California v. Cabazon Band of Mission Indians*, and he argued the Tribe's case before the U.S. District Court, the Ninth Circuit Court of Appeals, and the U.S. Supreme Court. He opened his extensive files on this lengthy litigation to me—approximately 15,000 pages of court pleadings and motions beginning with his application of October 18, 1980, for a temporary restraining order and a preliminary injunction filed before U.S. District Court Judge Laughlin E. Waters when the City of Indio raided the Cabazons' card club, and ending with Judge Waters's approval of the financial settlement between the Cabazons and Riverside County on November 13, 1988. This was an incredibly rich source of materials and insights into the twists and turns of this high-profile, nationally significant case. I am indebted to him more than I can say.

I also relied heavily on the Joint Appendix that the State of California and the Cabazon and Morongo Bands filed when the U.S. Supreme Court noted probable jurisdiction. Not everyone will have access to the full-record of a Supreme Court case, but anyone interested in learning as many details about a particular case as possible should consult the Joint Appendix for that case.

The Rules of the Supreme Court specify that this document, filed jointly by the parties, should contain the docket entries, pleading, findings, conclusions, judgments, orders, and opinions in the courts below for the case at hand, as well as "any other parts of the record that the parties particularly wish to bring to the Court's attention." This document is typically filed simultaneously with the Petitioner's/Appellant's Opening Brief; it is a rich resource of materials, providing details and context that simply relying on the briefs or the Court's eventual summary of the facts in a case can never provide. The Supreme Court frequently cites Joint Appendixes in its opinions. For anyone interested in engaging in an in-depth case study of a Supreme Court case, the Joint Appendix should be one of the first documents consulted after reading the Supreme Court opinion(s); it should clearly come before a careful examination of the briefs.

For an excellent overview of the legal and constitutional meaning of tribal sovereignty, see Charles Wilkinson, *Indian Tribes as Sovereign Governments: A Sourcebook on Federal-Tribal History, Law, and Policy*, 2nd ed. (Oakland, CA: American Indian Resources Institute, 2004).

The contrast between tribal sovereignty as understood legally and constitutionally by the Congress and the Court and tribal sovereignty as understood culturally by many tribal leaders and members is well articulated in Wallace Coffey and Rebecca Tsosie, "Rethinking the Tribal Sovereignty Doctrine: Cultural Sovereignty and the Collective Future of Indians Nations," 12 *Stanford Law and Policy Review* 191–210 (2001). See also Rebecca Tsosie, "Introduction to Symposium on Cultural Sovereignty," 34 *Arizona State Law Journal* 1–14 (2002).

The discussion of how the United States, initially under the Articles of Confederation and subsequently under the U.S. Constitution, has treated with Indians is based on Charles J. Kappler, *Indian Affairs: Law and Treaties* (7 vols., Washington, D.C.: Government Printing Office, 1904). It contains the full text of virtually every Indian treaty and is as close as we have to a comprehensive text of U.S. laws, treaties, and executive orders regarding Native Americans. Oklahoma State University's Electronic Publishing Center has made this reference work available online at http://digital.library.okstate.edu/kappler/. It is an invaluable source, for like the published edition, it is divided into seven volumes, with volume 2 cataloging treaties from 1778 to 1871, when Congress ended all future treaty making with native nations and replaced them with bilateral agreements between the U.S. government and tribes to 1883. The other six volumes contain laws and executive orders up to 1971. The online version of volume 2 is organized unlike the others. It offers two tables of contents: one lists Indian nations in alphabetical order with links to documents pertaining to each tribe; the other lists the documents in chronological order. The tables of contents for the other volumes follow a different format: they list laws passed during individual sessions of Congress, as well as proclamations, treaties, and agreements.

Another key source concerning treaties between the United States and Indian tribes is Vine Deloria, Jr., and Raymond J. DeMallie, eds., *Documents of American Indian Diplomacy: Treaties, Agreements, and Conventions, 1775–1979* (2 vols., Norman: University of Oklahoma Press, 1999). While it does not include all the treaties that Kappler includes, it includes some treaties Kappler does not, along with railroad agreements, settlement acts, treaties between Indian nations and the Republic of Texas, treaties between Indian nations and the Confederate States, treaties between Indian nations, and intertribal compacts. For a discussion of the Senate's role in negotiating treaties and representing interests of states as states, see Ralph A. Rossum, *Federalism, the Supreme Court, and the Seventeenth Amendment: The Irony of Constitutional Democracy* (Lanham, MD: Lexington Books, 2001).

Readers interested in the subject of Indian treaties more generally should consult Francis Paul Prucha, *American Indian Treaties: The History of a Political Anomaly* (Berkeley and Los Angeles: University of California Press, 1994), and *Documents of Federal Indian Policy*, 3rd ed. (Lincoln: University of Nebraska Press, 2000); Vine Deloria, Jr., and David E. Wilkins, *Tribes, Treaties, and Constitutional Tribulations* (Austin: University of Texas Press, 1999); Monroe E. Price, Robert N. Clinton, and Nell Jessup Newton, *American Indian Law: Cases and Materials*, 4th Rev. Ed. (San Francisco: LexisNexis Press, 2003); and David H. Getches, Charles F. Wilkinson, and Robert A. Williams, Jr., *Cases and Materials on Federal Indian Law* (St. Paul, MN: West, 2004).

A major theme throughout the *Cabazon* litigation (and one much emphasized in this book) is the unique canons of construction that have developed with regard to federal Indian law. They are addressed at some length in Cohen's *Handbook of Federal Indian Law*, pp. 115–132. Several recent law review articles are also helpful in their discussions of these canons and their assessments of their continued applicability. I highly recommend Bryan H. Wildenthal, "Federal Labor Law, Indian Sovereignty, and the Canons of Construction," 86 *Oregon Law Review* 413–531 (2007). Readers, however, should also consult David M. Blurton, "Canons of Construction, Stare Decisis, and Dependent Indian Communities: A Test of Judicial Integrity," 16 *Alaska Law Review* 37–60 (1999); George Jackson III, "*Chickasaw Nation v. United States* and the Potential Demise of the Indian Canon of Construction," 27 *American Indian Law Review* 399–420 (2002/2003); Scott C. Hall, "The Indian Law Canons of Construction v. the *Chevron* Doctrine: Congressional Intent and the Unambiguous Answer to the Ambiguous Problem," 37 *Connecticut Law Review* 495–566 (2004); and David E. Wilkins and K. Tsianina Lomawaima, *Uneven Ground: American Indian Sovereignty and Federal Law* (Norman: University of Oklahoma Press, 2001), pp. 141–142. An important article focusing more specifically on the canons of treaty interpretation is Robert J. Miller, "Speaking with Forked Tones: Indian Treaties, Salmon, and the Endangered Species Act," 70 *Oregon Law Review* 543 (1991).

The Marshall Trilogy also figures prominently in this book. The Trilogy has come under withering fire from a variety of prominent scholars who find Marshall's statements faulty and misguided. *Johnson v. McIntosh* comes under particularly heavy criticism. For example, Wilkins and Lomawaima argue in *Uneven Ground*, p. 54, that "at the heart of the decision was Marshall's distorted, historically inaccurate, and legally fictitious construction of the doctrine of discovery." Wilkins elaborates in *American Indian Sovereignty and the U.S. Supreme Court: The Masking of Justice* (Austin: University of Texas Press, 1997), p. 30: "The Marshall Court raised and then proceeded to answer an entirely different and far more troubling question—especially since the Indian tribes were not parties in the suit—as to whether tribes had a title that could be conveyed to whomever they chose. By generating this question and then answering it negatively, Marshall's court, in the process of this unanimous opinion, both created and re-created a set of legal rationalizations to justify the reduction of Indian rights without allowing any room for listening to the Indian voice." See also Wilkins, "*Johnson v. McIntosh* Revisited: Through the Eyes of *Mitchel v. United States*," 19 *American Indian Law Review* 159–181 (1994); in this article, Wilkins contends that in the 1835 case of *Mitchel v. United States*, the Supreme Court implicitly disavowed the claim that discovery vested absolute ownership of America in the discovering states. Wilkins argues that, while Justice Henry Baldwin never explicitly disclaimed the doctrine, he "noted that 'friendly Indians were protected in the possession of the lands they occupied, and were considered as owning them by a perpetual right of possession in the tribe or nation inhabiting them . . . .' Baldwin continued by declaring what he thought the status of Indian title was: 'it is enough to consider it as a settled principle, that their right of occupancy is considered as sacred as the fee simple of the whites.'"

Marshall's opinions in *Cherokee Nation v. Georgia* and *Worcester v. Georgia* have also been criticized. See Vine Deloria, Jr., *Behind the Trail of Broken Treaties: An Indian Declaration of Independence* (Austin: University of Texas Press, 2000), pp. 113–140; Matthew L. M. Fletcher. "The Iron Cold of the Marshall Trilogy," 82 *North Dakota Law Review* 627–696 (2006); Lindsay G. Robertson, *Conquest by Law: How the Discovery of America Dispossessed Indigenous Peoples of Their Lands* (New York: Oxford University Press, 2005); Jill C. Norgren, *The Cherokee Cases: The Confrontation of Law and Politics* (New York: McGraw-Hill, 1996); and Joseph C. Burke, "The Cherokee Cases: A Study in Law, Politics, and Morality," 21 *Stanford Law Review* 500–531 (1969).

The Marshall Trilogy is given the attention it receives in this book not because these three cases were necessarily decided correctly but because, for better or worse, they provide the constitutional backdrop for the *Cabazon* decision. But for these three cases, federal Indian law would have developed in a different way; Congress's power over the tribes would have been different; so, too, would the power of the states to enforce their sovereign authority in Indian country. As Judge Canby puts it in *American Indian Law*, p. 14, these cases fashioned "legal doctrines that would influence Indian Law for the next century and a half." Even the Trilogy's fiercest critics agree on that point; as Vine Deloria, Jr., and Clifford M. Lytle acknowledge in *The Nations Within: The Past and Future of American Indian Sovereignty* (Austin: University of Texas Press, 1998), p. 17, "A good deal of the subsequent history of conflict between the United States and the Indian tribes has revolved around the question of preserving the right to self-government and the attributes of Indian sovereignty as suggested in Marshall's decisions." Not even the harshest critics of the Marshall Trilogy can dismiss their significance or disagree with Philip P. Frickey, who argues in his "Marshalling Past the Present: Colonialism, Constitutionalism, and Interpretation in Federal Indian Law," 107 *Harvard Law Review* 381–440, 385 (1993): "The interpretive legacy of John Marshall better resonates with the fundamental normative and institutional problems of federal Indian law today than does the current Court's considerably more grudging approach."

The tragic chapter of American history known as the Trail of Tears is very briefly addressed in this book, not because it is not important but because it is a huge topic by itself and not central to my overall argument. Readers interested in the subject must consult Francis Paul Prucha, *The Great Father: The United States and the American Indians* (Lincoln: University of Nebraska Press, 1984), and Ethan Davis, "An Administrative Trail of Tears: Indian Removal," *American Journal of Legal History*, vol. L, no. 1 (2010), pp. 49–100; and *Cohen's Handbook of Federal Indian Law*, pp. 45–54.

The period of the creation of the reservation system is well described in Robert A. Trennert, Jr., *Alternative to Extinction: Federal Indian Policy and the Beginnings of the Reservation System, 1846–1851* (Philadelphia: Temple University Press, 1975), and Bethany R. Berger, " 'Power over this Unfortunate Race': Race, Power, and Indian Law in *United States v, Rogers*," 45 *William and Mary Law Review* 2017–2052 (2004). The Dawes Act and the allotment process are well described in *Cohen's Handbook of Federal Indian Law*, pp. 66–84; Canby, *American Indian Law*, pp. 20–24; Francis P. Prucha, *American Indian Policy in Crisis: Christian Reformers and the Indian 1865–1900* (Norman, University of Oklahoma Press, 1976), and *Americanizing the American Indian: Writings by the "Friends of the Indian"* (Cambridge: Harvard University Press, 1973); Wilcomb Washburn, *The Assault on Indian Tribalism: The General Allotment Act of 1887* (Philadelphia: J. B. Lippincott, 1975); Janet A. McDonnell, *The Dispossession of American Indians: 1887–1934* (Bloomington: Indiana University Press, 1991); and Henry E. Fritz, "An American Dilemma: Administration of the Indian Estate under the Dawes Act and Amendments," 37 *Journal of the Southwest* 123–130 (1995).

The assimilationist era ending with the passage of the Indian Reorganization Act is well told in *Cohen's Handbook of Federal Indian Law*, pp. 84–89; William H. Kelly, ed., *Indian Affairs and the Indian Reorganization Act* (Tucson: University of Arizona Press, 1954); Lawrence C. Kelly, *The Assault on Assimilation: John Collier and the Origin of Indian Policy Reform* (Albuquerque: University of New Mexico Press, 1983); and Vine Deloria, Jr., ed., *The Indian Reorganization Act: Congresses and Bills* (Norman: University of Oklahoma Press, 2002). For information on Native Americans serving in World War II, see Thomas D. Morgan, "Native Americans in World War II," *Army History: The Professional Bulletin of Army History*, no. 35 (Fall 1995), pp. 22–27; and Alison R. Berstein, *American Indians and World War II: Toward a New Era of Indian Affairs* (Norman: University of Oklahoma Press, 1991).

For the definitive discussion of Public Law 280, see Carole Goldberg's *Planting Tail Feathers: Tribal Survival and Public Law 280* (Los Angeles: UCLA American Indian Studies Center, 1996). Robert N. Clinton, in his article, "Enactment of the Indian Gaming Regulatory Act of 1988: The Return of the Buffalo to Indian Country or Another Federal Usurpation of Tribal Sovereignty?" 42 *Arizona State Law Journal* 17–97 (2010), says the following of Goldberg's article, "State Jurisdiction over Reservation Indians," 22 *UCLA Law Review* 535–594 (1975), which is reproduced in *Planting Tail Feathers*: "Relying heavily on (in fact appropriating the entire theory of) a then recently published article by a junior scholar at UCLA Law School, Professor Carole Goldberg, the *Bryan [v. Itasca County]* opinion held that the primary purpose of Public Law 280 was to deal with law enforcement in Indian country. The Court concluded that civil provisions in Public Law 280 had a limited role in providing state forums for the resolution of disputes in Indian country but were never intended to grant any state taxing or regulatory power over Indians in Indian country."

The chapters on the briefing and oral argument before the U.S. Supreme Court include observations for attorneys regarding how to be most effective in arguing before appellate courts. The primary source relied on here is a recent, charming, and eminently readable book: Antonin Scalia and Bryan A. Garner, *Making Your Case: The Art of Persuading Judges* (St. Paul: West Thomson, 2008). Also highly relevant is Otis Christian Jenson, *The Nature of Legal Argument* (Oxford: Blackwell, 1957).

The party and amici briefs and joint appendix submitted to the Supreme Court in the *Cabazon* case are available at both LexisNexis and Westlaw for readers who have access to these powerful online resources. The oral argument in *Cabazon* is available at http://www.oyez.org. This remarkable Web site provides, among many other things, a transcript of the oral arguments of all Supreme Court cases going back to 1955 and of selected cases even before that. The transcript continuously scrolls down the screen as one listens to counsels' arguments before the Court, and the justices' frequent interrogatories.

For a detailed political history of the passage of IGRA, there is simply no better source than Robert N. Clinton's already referenced article, "Enactment of the Indian Gaming Regulatory Act of 1988: The Return of the Buffalo to Indian Country or Another Federal Usurpation of Tribal Sovereignty?" 42 *Arizona State Law Journal* 17–97 (2010). I wish to acknowledge that my discussion of the passage of IGRA relies heavily on this source, and I thank Professor Clinton for making it available for me to use prior to its publication. Clinton recommends, and so do I, Sidney M. Wolf, "Killing the New Buffalo: State Eleventh Amendment Defense to Enforcement of IGRA Indian Gaming Compacts," 47 *Washington University Journal of Urban & Contemporary Law* 51, 74–87 (1995). Students seriously interested in the legislative history concerning the eventual passage of IGRA should read Senate Report 99-493 to accompany H.R. 1920, 99th Congress, available online at http://www.nigc.gov/Portals/0/NIGC%20Uploads/readingroom/Senate%20report%20 99-493.pdf; House Report 99-488 to accompany H.R. 1920, 99th Congress, available online at http://www.nigc.gov/Portals/0/NIGC%20Uploads/read ingroom/House%20Report%2099-488.pdf; Senate Report 100-466 to accompany S. 555, 100th Congress, available online at http://www.nigc.gov/ Portals/0/NIGC%20Uploads/readingroom/Senate%20Rept%20100-466 .pdf; Senate Debate on S. 555, September 15, 1988, available at http://www .nigc.gov/Portals/0/NIGC%20Uploads/readingroom/Senate.Debate.IGRA .1988.pdf; and House of Representatives Debate on S. 555, September 26, 1988 available online at http://www.nigc.gov/Portals/0/NIGC%20Uploads/read ingroom/House.Debate.IGRA.Sept.1988.pdf.

In the text, I mention that many tribal advocates saw *Cabazon* as a major victory recognizing complete tribal authority over gaming on their reservations. Law review articles that take this position include Gregory Elvine-Kreis, "The Effect of the Indian Gaming Regulatory Act on California Native American's Independence," 35 *San Diego Law Review* 179, 193 (1998): "The Supreme Court in *Cabazon* allowed tribes to conduct casino-style gaming as well as bingo"; Guy Levy, "*Western Telcon v. California State Lottery*: Will Native Americans Lose Again?", 19 *Thomas Jefferson Law Review* 361, 373 (1997): "After the *Cabazon* decision, Indians were allowed to operate whatever gambling ventures they chose"; Mark C. Wenzel, "Let the Chips Fall Where They May: The Spokane Indian Tribe's Decision to Proceed with Casino Gambling without a State Compact," 30 *Gonzaga Law Review* 467, 474 (1994–1995): "The *Cabazon* case has been perceived as even more deferential to the Indian tribes because it allows casino-style gambling as well as bingo"; Joseph J. Weissman, "Upping the Ante: Allowing Indian Tribes to Sue State in Federal Court under the Indian Gaming Regulatory Act," 62 *George Washington Law Review* 123, 124 (1993): "The *Cabazon* decision allowed unregulated gambling to flourish on Indian reservations"; T. Barton French, Jr., "The Indian Gaming and Regulatory Act and the Eleventh Amendment: States Assert Sovereign Immunity Defense to Slow the Growth of Indian Gaming," 71 *Washington University Law Quarterly* 735, 741 (1993): "The *Cabazon* decision . . . allowed tribes to conduct casino-style gaming as well as bingo."

In the text, I mention that tribal gaming advocates have also over-generalized the decision, suggesting that the Court had upheld the exclusive power of Indian tribes to regulate reservation gaming. Law review articles that fall under this description include Brian P. McClatchey, "A Whole New Game: Recognizing the Changing Complexion of Indian Gaming by Removing the 'Governor's Veto' for Gaming on 'After-Acquired Lands,'" 37 *University of Michigan Journal of Legal Reform* 1227, 1244 (2004): "Due to the *Bryan/Butterworth/Cabazon* line of cases, tribes had exclusive control over reservation gaming"; Brad Jolly, "The Indian Gaming Regulatory Act: The Unwavering Policy of Termination Continues," 29 *Arizona State Law Journal* 273, 278 (1997): "In the IGRA, Congress stated that 'Indian tribes have the exclusive right to regulate gaming activity on Indian lands' and claimed to codify the Supreme Court's decision in *Cabazon*."

The many provisions of IGRA are well spelled out in *Cohen's Handbook of Federal Indian Law*, pp. 858–888, and in Michael D. Cox, "The Indian Gaming Regulatory Act: An Overview," 7 *St. Thomas Law Review* 769–789 (1995). The implementation of IGRA nationally is perhaps best presented in Steven Andrew Light and Kathryn R. L. Rand, *Indian Gaming and Tribal Sovereignty: The Casino Compromise* (Lawrence: University Press of Kansas, 2005); in their "How Congress Can and Should 'Fix' the Indian Gaming Regulatory Act: Recommendations for Law and Policy Reform," 13 *Virginia Journal of Social Policy and the Law* 396–472 (2006); and in their "The Hand That's Been Dealt: The Indian Gaming Regulatory Act at 20," 57 *Drake Law Review* 413–443 (2009).

For the impact on IGRA of the Supreme Court's decision in *Seminole Tribe of Florida v. Florida*, see Nancy J. Bride, "*Seminole Tribe v. Florida*: The Supreme Court's Botched Surgery of the Indian Gaming Regulatory Act," 24 *Journal of Legislation* 149–163 (1998); Martha Field, "The *Seminole* Case, Federalism, and the Indian Commerce Clause," 29 *Arizona State Law Journal* 3–23 (1997); "The *Seminole* Decision and State Sovereign Immunity," 1996 *Supreme Court Review* 1–64; Alexander Tallchief Skibine, "Gaming on Indian Reservations: Defining the Trustee's Duty in the Wake of *Seminole Tribe v. Florida*," 29 *Arizona State Law Journal* 121–169 (1997); Jerry C. Straus, "Florida's War on Indian Gaming: An Attack on Tribal Sovereignty," 13 *St. Thomas Law Review* 259–268 (2000); and Matthew L. M. Fletcher, "Bringing Balance to Indian Gaming," 44 *Harvard Journal on Legislation* 39–95 (2007). And, of course, with the *Seminole Tribe*'s invalidation of the congressional requirement for states to negotiate in good faith, the importance of various revenue-sharing provisions attractive enough to bring the states to the negotiating table is critical. Two excellent articles on the how the tribes have come to trade revenue for exclusive gaming opportunities are Gatsby Contreras, "Exclusivity Agreements in Tribal-State Compacts: Mutual Benefit Revenue Sharing or Illegal State Taxation," 5 *Journal of Gender, Race, and Justice* 487–511 (2002), and Katie Eidson, "Will States Continue to Provide Exclusivity in Tribal Gaming Compacts or Will Tribes Bust on the Hand of the State in Order to Expand Indian Gaming," 29 *American Indian Law Review* 319–339 (2004–2005).

And finally, for insight into the complicated and caustic compacting experience in Florida, see Allison Sirica, "A Great Gamble: Why Compromise Is the Best Bet to Resolve Florida's Indian Gaming Crisis," 61 *Florida Law Review* 1201–1231 (2009).

for federal Indian law, 49, 51–53,
58, 73, 76–78, 82
general, 49–51
Latin maxims, 50–51
liberal construction, 20–21, 51, 52,
76, 82
qualifications, 52
Carcieri v. Salazar, 52–53
card clubs
of Cabazon Band, 10–11, 12–17,
114–115, 144
in California, 14, 114–115
in Riverside County, 102
casinos
Atlantic City, 155
management companies, 174
Nevada, 155, 158, 172, 174
slot machines, 167, 168–169,
174–175, 179
tribal, 1, 2–4, 6, 163, 167, 174–175
See also Class III gaming; tribal
gaming
CAUG. *See* Coalition against
Unregulated Gambling
Cherokee Nation
removal, 54
treaties, 32, 40, 45
tribal courts, 69
See also *Worcester v. Georgia*
Cherokee Nation v. Georgia, 5, 42,
45–46, 51
*Cheyenne River Sioux Tribe v. South
Dakota*, 170
Chickasaw Nation, 32, 54
Chickasaw Nation v. United States, 52
Chippewa Nation, 31–32, 38–39
Chippewa Tribe of Minnesota, 75.
See also Red Lake Band of
Chippewa Indians
Choctaw Nation, 32, 54
cigarette sales. *See* smoke shops
citizenship of Indians, 62, 65

civil laws
gambling laws as, 79, 82
Public Law 280 provisions, 68,
74–76
state jurisdiction on Indian
reservations, 68–69, 74–82,
130–131, 136
See also criminal/prohibitory
laws, distinction from
civil/regulatory laws
Civil War, 40, 55–56
Clark, Bernard J., 13
Class I gaming, 151–152, 154
Class II gaming, 152, 161
Class III gaming
definition, 152
regulation of, 152, 158–159
slot machines, 167, 168–169,
174–175, 179
state taxes or fees prohibited,
152–153, 166
without compacts, 169
See also compacts, tribal-state
Clinton, Robert N., 8, 150, 153, 161
Clinton administration, 169
Coalition against Unregulated
Gambling (CAUG), 172
Coffey, Wallace, 25–26
Collier, John, 66
colonial period, 26–29, 43–44
*Colville Indian Reservation. See
Washington v. Confederated
Tribes of the Colville Indian
Reservation*
Comanches, 64
Commission on the Review of the
National Policy toward
Gambling, 98
compacts, tribal-state
in California, 168–175
in Connecticut, 163–167
diversity, 6, 181

tribal governments
alternative revenue sources, 133
operations, 22–23, 128–129, 131–132, 135
self-sufficiency, 22, 151
See also tribal sovereignty
Tribal Self-Governance Act of 1994, 73
tribal sovereignty
in colonial period, 26–29, 43–44
compared to state sovereignty, 121–122
constitutional basis, 35–36
cultural, 25–26, 146, 156, 157
definition, 25
dependence on federal government, 5, 31, 49, 53, 60–61, 65, 135–136
federal support, 70–73
gaming compacts and, 181
inherent, 15, 25–26, 73
limits on, 44–45, 48
Marshall Trilogy understanding, 48, 95
traditions, 99
tribal-state compacts. *See* compacts, tribal-state
tribes
amici curiae briefs, 115–116
political advocacy, 1–2, 6, 173
See also reservations
Tsosie, Rebecca, 25–26

Udall, Morris, 146–147, 149, 153, 157
United States v. Dion, 52
United States v. Farris, 21, 138
United States v. Kagama, 60–61
United States v. Minnesota, 13
United States v. Nice, 65
United States v. Paradise, 134
United States v. Wheeler, 25
United States v. Winans, 51–52

Victoria, Francisco de, 26
Virginia
Indian treaties, 27
lands ceded to United States, 31, 42
Vucanovich, Barbara, 158, 160

Walker, John M., 165
Wallace, William J., 100, 109, 142
Walston, Roderick E., 119, 120–126, 132–133, 135, 143, 146
Walt Disney Company, 172
War, Department of, 36, 54
Washington, George, 38–39
Washington, State of, amicus briefs, 17–18, 88–89, 105
Washington v. Confederated Tribes of the Colville Indian Reservation
conflict with *Cabazon Band* case, 85–86, 107–108, 127
differences from *Cabazon Band* case, 91
majority opinion, 9–10, 22, 85–86, 138
Waters, Laughlin E., 12–13, 14, 16, 18, 23, 133, 144, 145
Weicker, Lowell, 167
Welmas, Arthur, 145, 146, 181
Werdegar, Kathryn, 173
Wheeler, United States v., 25
Wheeler-Howard Act. *See* Indian Reorganization Act
White, Byron, 5, 9–10, 124–125, 132, 134–141, 150–151, 161
White, Edward, 64–65
White Mountain Apache Tribe v. Bracker, 21
Wilkins, David, 44
Wilson, James, 29–30, 34
Wilson, Pete, 168, 169, 170–171, 173
Winans, United States v., 51–52
Winter, Ralph K., 165